Common Sense Horse Keeping

It's All About the Horse

Lori E. Tankel

Library of Congress Cataloging-in-Publication Data
Names: Lori E. Tankel, author
Title: Common Sense Horse Keeping: It's All About the Horse/Lori E. Tankel
Publisher: Lilith House Press, Colorado, USA
ISBN 979-8-9858101-7-2 (softcover)
ISBN 979-8-9858101-8-9 (E-book)
Library of Congress Control Number: 2024912171
Subjects: Horses-Health/ Horses-Stable Management

The ideas and suggestions contained in this book are not intended as a substitute for consulting with appropriate and
trained professionals. All matters regarding horse training, horse care, and/or horse management should be sought out from
a veterinarian and/or trained equine professionals. Neither the publisher or the author shall be liable or responsible for any
loss or damage allegedly arising from any information or suggestion in this book.

This book was generated by a human expert on the subject, and the content was edited, fact-checked and proofread by
humans. In no manner or context of this book was Artificial Intelligence utilized.

Cover and interior design: Jane Dixon-Smith/jdsmith-design.com
Editor: Diane Hartman Postrech
Cover photograph: Jennifer M. Toegel (main photo and middle inset photo)
Author photograph: Courtesy of Lori E. Tankel
All other photographs courtesy of Lori E. Tankel, except pages 14, 185
(Jennifer M. Toegel); page 55(a)(Erin Winget Hoyer)

Printed and bound in the United States of America
Lilith House Press,
Colorado, USA

Lilith House Press

Lilithhousepress.org

Table of Contents

Introduction

The women in my family rode…my grandmother, my mother, and a cousin, so I guess one could say it is in my DNA to love horses. I was the one though who took that love of horses and ran, or rather galloped away with it, never once entertaining the thought that I should give up my passion, as everyone else in my family eventually did.

My grandparents lived on a farm outside of Pittsburgh, and for a few years, we had Misty and Foggy, a mother-daughter pair of ponies. The first photo of me sitting on a horse before I could walk was taken on the back of Misty.

Although the ponies were eventually sold, my grandfather allowed a friend to use the pasture in the summer for his broodmares. They were accompanied by a palomino named Little Chief for me to ride. Another neighbor also boarded his horses at my grandparent's farm, giving me plenty of time in the saddle (and just as much bareback time!).

After my parents divorced and we moved to Florida, my grandmother bought me a 13-month-old yearling for the princely sum of $75 and paid for her upkeep. It was insurance to keep me out of trouble and away from boys! We could only afford to pasture board her until I discovered another barn where Star Dazer could have a stall, but I would have to muck her stall. I was only 13 years old, but I rode my bike to the barn, approximately 6 miles away, every day after school to tend to her. I became involved in 4-H, took lessons, and competed in hunters and later jumpers before I discovered eventing.

I was fortunate to grow up in a generation when "barn rats" were the norm. Weekends and many summer days were spent at the barn, from early morning until our ride arrived at dinner time. We were kids who mucked stalls, removed cobwebs, scrubbed buckets, and once we gained the owner's trust, we could groom and tack up the horses….just so we could get a lesson or two every week. Sadly, today's generation doesn't know what it is like to experience that, nor do they know what it is like to disappear all day long with your friends and on horseback. I fondly recall leaving my grandparents' farm in the morning with friends, usually riding bareback, with no helmet, no cell phone, and no care in the world. We might carry something to eat or return briefly for lunch, only to roam the countryside on horseback until it was time for dinner. I grew up riding like this in West Virginia, Ohio, western Pennsylvania, and Florida.

My horses were always boarded at self-care barns, and I didn't want it any other way. I loved mucking stalls, learning about feed and nutrition, how to recognize illnesses, and how to wrap legs. As an adult with young children, when it was necessary for me to go full board due to time constraints and family obligations, I was still at the barn as much as possible, soaking up all the knowledge that I could, choosing to board at facilities that experienced horsemen and horsewomen ran.

Sadly, over the years, I learned that many barn owners don't have a good grasp of basic horse care, whether through my experience as a boarder or employee or by hearing about their reputation through other horse people. Many don't understand equine nutrition or how to medicate a horse. I experienced terrible care, from dirty stalls, horses left out in lightning storms, sick horses left unnoticed and unattended, to other areas that gave me cause for concern. Even in barns where I cared for my horses, the overall experience left much to be desired, as I saw other partial care boarders not understanding basic horse care.

In addition, I realized that many boarders had no clue that they were spending a lot of hard-earned money on mediocre care, but they didn't know any better. Some horse owners just want to ride and not be bothered with learning how to bandage legs for traveling, be able to identify good quality hay from bad hay or learn to identify toxic weeds in their horse's pasture. I learned that one way to avoid costly vet bills is to take the best care possible of my horse. It's a cheap insurance policy.

My daughters both inherited my love of horses. They became involved in the United States Pony Club, one of the best youth organizations for horse-crazy kids. The kids have to learn horsemanship. It is part of the curriculum; it's not just about riding. As a volunteer, I expanded my knowledge and became passionate about the horse management portion. I volunteered as a horse management judge at rallies and regularly held clinics and meetings to teach the kids about properly caring for their horses.

Over the many years (decades, if you want to know!) I have been involved with horses in many capacities: owner; competitor in hunters, jumpers, dressage, and eventing; trainer of many horses, including a wild-eyed six-month-old PMU foal, who became one of my best eventers; instructor of kids and adults alike; co-founder of a non-profit horse rescue; and as a pony club volunteer and official. I have been a vet tech, barn manager, and barn owner. All of these experiences have taught me how to best care for horses. My mantra has always been that "*It is all about the horse*" and everything I do involves learning how to keep giving the best care possible to my horses. The information we are given is constantly changing, thanks to research, technology, the internet, and social media. What I fed my horses in the 1970s is vastly different than what I feed now, just as therapies are better. We now have a better understanding of horse diseases, injuries, and what happens to the horse's structural bones when we push them too fast and too early. Research is showing that the mental state of the horse is just as important as their physical well-being. Horsemen and horsewomen need to be willing to accept new data and new research if they are going to do right by their horses, whether it involves improving their riding skills or taking a nutrition course. A rider does just that: they ride. A horseman or horsewoman, however, does more than just ride. They manage, doctor, muck stalls, analyze feed and hay, groom, and so much more.

While there is a level of stress of owning a barn that I had not experienced before as a boarder, there is also peace and satisfaction that comes from being able to run a barn your way and know that the horses under your care will never have to worry about missing a meal, being turned out in a lightning storm, injuring themselves on a broken fence board or eating a bad flake of hay. There is no better feeling than looking out of your window and seeing your horse grazing contently in your pasture, which you have gone to great lengths to maintain and keep free of weeds.

I am continually striving to expand my knowledge of horses and their care. I hope this book will encourage horse people, whether they have been around horses their whole lives or are just starting the journey, also to adopt the mantra "*It is all about the horse.*"

Chapter 1
So You Want to Keep Your Horses at Home, or You Want to Board Horses!

You've decided to open a horse boarding facility or perhaps you bought a farm so you can keep your horse at home. Congratulations! But before you make that decision, are you sure you want to do this?

If you answer yes to any of the following questions, you may want to re-think your decision:

> *1. Do you think it is fun and glamorous?*
>
> *2. Do you think you can make lots of money?*
>
> *3. Do you think it is easy?*

Running a horse farm or a boarding facility is not glamorous; it is hard work, and you may not make much money *if* you do it correctly. In other words, you must avoid cutting corners and ensure that the horse's well-being comes first. To do so means feeding a good quality hay and grain, bedding stalls deeply, and hiring well-qualified and knowledgeable employees.

Traditionally, the boarding business has notoriously been a lousy business model because barn owners feel the need to justify the cost of the board bill. Barn owners may think they will only be able to attract boarders if they don't charge a lot of money, their current boarders will leave if rates are increased, or they cannot set a fair board due to their location. But at the end of the day, nobody should subsidize someone else's hobby. As a barn owner, you are entitled to cover your expenses, not just hay and feed, but whatever it costs for employees, insurance, taxes, farm equipment, and even your time! Barn owners should never operate at a loss and they should be able to make money from their hard work.

If you provide excellent service, the horses are well cared for in a drama-free barn, you provide good-quality hay and grain, and you have nice riding areas, then you will have no problem attracting and retaining boarders! Most horse owners would rather pay extra to know that their investment is well cared for rather than worry about its care and have to shell out more money for vet bills due to sickness or injuries caused by inadequate care.

Teaching, training, attending horse shows, breeding, and selling are all ways to boost your earnings, and if you have your farm as a home base, offering any of these services will supplement your income.

If you're a horse owner ready to make that giant leap and move your horse to your home, remember that while there is no better feeling than looking out your window and seeing your horse grazing in your pasture, there are drawbacks. In a boarding barn, there is something to be said about the companionship of others with the same goals and interests as you. Unless you plan on offering boarding, it can get lonely! The same goes for your horse. Will he have companionship, whether it be from another horse or donkey? Horses are herd animals, and most prefer the company of other horses. Other drawbacks include hiring someone to care for your farm when you travel, being financially responsible for damages and maintenance costs, and having to fork over the money for equipment such as wheelbarrows, tractors, and manure spreaders. If you plan on offering boarding, your need for equipment will increase. More horses means more wear and tear on your property, and you will lose your privacy if your home is located close to the barn. These are all things that barn owners must consider, whether keeping only their horses or providing board for others.

When I finally convinced my husband to sell our home in the suburbs and move to a farm in the country, his catch- phrase soon became, "Did you know how much work this was?" or "Did you know how much money it was going to cost?" While I do most of the physical work, he pays for the new fencing, farm equipment, and Shoo-Fly system. Even though I had managed barns and had leased a facility for many years with boarders, I was unprepared for how lonely it would be to have my farm. My daughters are no longer living at home to ride with or help with chores, and we moved into a neighborhood with no horsey neighbors. I desperately missed the social life of my old barn! My young Thoroughbred has two donkeys and two goats for companionship. Still, the drawback to being an only horse was that seeing new horses could send him into a complete meltdown when we began to leave the property. I think he believes he is a donkey! Traveling to visit our kids means having a reliable farm sitter. There is a level of stress associated with leaving the care of your horse to someone else, not to mention the added expense for a farm sitter.

The purpose of this book is to provide the basic and essential knowledge one needs for caring for horses, regardless of whether you run a large boarding stable, keep horses of your own at home, or whether you're a boarder who is new to the horse world and you want to be sure you're able to pick the boarding barn that is right for you and your horse.

The horse boarding business will not get anyone wealthy, and it can be frustrating and challenging work, however, it can also be a fulfilling career if you remember that you are doing this because you love horses. What's not to love about having a career where you get to be outdoors, where every day is different, and where you are surrounded by horses?

Chapter 2
Knowledge, Love and a Tad Crazy

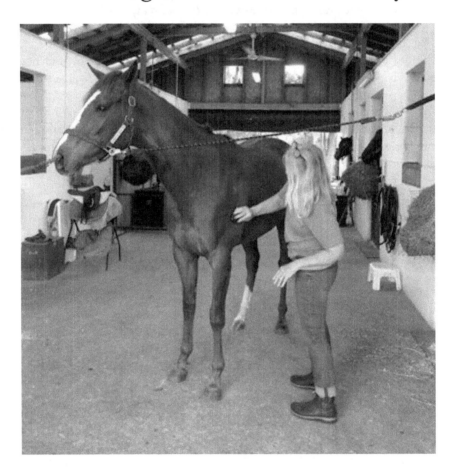

Running a barn means more than hanging a sign at the front gate and calling yourself a business. Unfortunately, many in the horse world do just that while lacking the basic skills required to properly care for horses. And with no standards or rules to follow when it comes to boarding, training, or teaching (in the United States), anyone can call themselves a professional, even with little to no experience, which is what many people do.

There is so much more to running or owning a barn than being able to say that you have been riding for five, ten, or even twenty years. Unfortunately, many so-called professionals don't know the basics of being a horseman and, therefore, cannot teach their students the fundamentals of horsemanship. Old-school pros were trained to be true horsemen and were instructed on how to care for their horses in any situation. That is rarely the case anymore.

> *I am such a fan of the United States Pony Club (despite its name, it is not limited to just ponies!) This organization teaches more than just riding. Horsemanship is a significant component, with members tested on their horsemanship skills at rallies and ratings. The USPC now allows adults to join, and the Old People's Riding Club is another option for adult riders to learn horse management skills.*

Owning or managing a barn means identifying a sick horse and knowing how to manage pastures, identifying toxic plants, understanding proper nutrition, having a disaster plan, and knowing barn safety. Good horsemanship means properly bandaging a leg, knowing the difference between shipping and standing bandages, and knowing when to use them. You should be able to manage the never-ending supply of manure and know how to muck a stall and repair broken boards twenty-four hours a day, seven days a week, 365 days a year in all kinds of weather, regardless of how you feel in the morning when you wake up.

> *My mother-in-law recently asked me who takes care of the animals and does the farm work if I am sick. I replied, "I do." She asked, "But who cares for them if you are really sick?" I replied again, "I do." Then she asked, "But what about if you are hurt?" And I replied once more, "I do."*

Having a love…a genuine love of horses, and being a tad crazy will help you succeed at running a barn. Even if you have employees, you will always be on call, especially when there is a colicing horse on Christmas morning or the water pipe breaks because a horse has kicked and broken it and it is 35 degrees outside. There is a never-ending list of chores, from repairing broken fence boards, mowing lots of acreage, chasing down loose horses, fixing broken stall doors, scrubbing water buckets, and, of course, mucking those stalls. All those stalls, day after day, month after month, year after year. Are you still interested? Keep reading!

Besides being able to recognize a colicing horse, you need to know the difference between good quality hay and grain and that which is moldy. You should understand and implement a schedule for vaccinations and deworming, devise disaster plans, and deal with the disposal of dead horses. Are you hiring employees? Are you sure your new employee can legally work in the country? Are you hiring an instructor? Are you providing insurance or requiring the instructor to provide their own? And more importantly, are you able to deal with people? You need to be able to deal with barn drama and politics. You will encounter novices who think they know more than you do; others will place unreasonable demands upon you.

These are scenarios that should be considered before you decide to operate a boarding barn.

If you are a horse owner, the information in the following chapters will enable you to make wise decisions to ensure your horse is well cared for and that you are getting the best care for your dollar, whether you're considering boarding your horse or keeping your horse at home.

Boarding barns have broad discretion regarding the level of care they provide for your horse. Unless stated in a contract, how they operate, whether it be how much hay is fed, if turn-out is provided, how often they muck stalls, and the general overall care of your horse is not regulated by any law. Therefore, it is in your best interest, as an owner and as the person who is paying good money for someone to care for your horse, to know the difference between that which is acceptable and that which is not acceptable. Suppose your horse is suffering sores from inadequate stall cleaning, is losing weight because of poor-quality feed, or is constantly injuring itself due to poorly maintained fencing. In that case, you have two options: 1) negotiate with the barn owner or manager to rectify the situation, or 2) move your horse.

Some basic horsemanship skills every barn owner/manager and every horse owner should know how to do:

- Be able to identify sick horses

- Know basic feed nutrition

- Be able to identify types of hay and know when hay is moldy or unsafe to feed

- Knowledge of feeding rules

- Be able to medicate horses

- Know how to correctly bandage legs

- Knowledge of basic first aid

- Know horses' TPR (Temperature, Pulse, and Respiration) and how to take them

- Be able to identify common toxic plants in your region

- Be able to handle and lead horses safely

- Know how to muck stalls properly

- Ability to perform daily horse care

- Knowledge of current rules for deworming horses and how to administer dewormers

- Know and understand basic horse behavior

- Understand equine welfare

The barn manager and the boarder should enter into a boarding contract having done their homework on each other, just as if one was renting a house. Budgets, as well as needs and expectations, should be considered when comparing them to other boarding barns. If something doesn't feel right to the boarder, they should follow their instinct and not enter a boarding relationship with that particular stable. Potential boarders should seek reviews on social media and from other equestrians they know. Inferior barns will develop a reputation very quickly, and in today's world of social media, news travels fast. Talk to current boarders and employees as well to get a feel for what kind of environment the barn is and whether it is a good fit for your horse.

Conversely, barn managers should ask for and check out boarders' references. Ask for their boarding history. Like bad barns, bad boarders are also known in the community, and it is better to save yourself the drama by allowing a well-known problem boarder to move into your stable. Just as lousy boarding barns can be found on social media, there are Facebook groups whose sole purpose is to warn barn owners of troublesome boarders.

What Boarders Should Look for in a Boarding Barn (And What Barn Owners Should Be Providing):

- The barn should be safe, with no sharp objects in the stalls

- Pastures should have safe and secure fencing

- The barn and pasture should be high and dry- constant standing water will mean mosquitoes and poor-quality hooves

- The barn should have good ventilation

- There should be good natural light in the barn

- There should be no exposed wires. Lights and wires should not be able to be accessed by horses

- The barn aisle should be clean. There should be no signs of rats or insect infestations

- The feed room should be clean and tidy

- What about the tack room? It should be clean and have adequate storage for tack and equipment

- The barn should have a proactive fire safety plan in effect. There should be no inappropriate fans in use, no excessive number of extension cords, no exposed wiring, and the barn should be free of cobwebs

- There should be fire extinguishers easily within reach and alarm systems should be used

- The barn should have a disaster plan in effect

- The barn should practice fire and disaster plans and the boarders should be aware of the plans and required to participate in drills

- Horses should be in good weight and health and they should appear happy

- Stalls should be clean, well-bedded, and free of urine smells

- Water buckets and troughs should be clean, with fresh water, and free of algae and scum

- Hay and grain are of good quality and stored correctly to deter vermin and prevent spoilage

- Pastures should be free of weeds

- While they should not be church-quiet, barns should convey a sense of peace. It should not be chaotic; there should not be any yelling or running

- Biosecurity measures should be in place if horses are frequently coming and going, such as to horse shows or if a sales barn

- The riding areas should have good footing

- The barn should have designated areas for grooming and tacking as well as a wash stall to bathe your horse. There should also be an area for the vet and farrier to use as needed

- You should know who will be handling your horse when you are not present

- Boarders and employees should be happy and engaged, and horses should be relaxed

Advice from Barn Owners to New Barn Owners:

- You will always be mucking stalls. Accept that fact!

- Your mental and physical health comes first

- You need to have business and marketing skills. It would help if you were a good bookkeeper

- Set limitations with yourself

- Find your niche

- Understand you will be dealing with people- all kinds of people. They may be crazy or angry

- Understand your income will not be consistent

- Pay yourself. You are not doing this to lose money

- Be able and willing to teach anything and everything horse-related. You will have horse owners who know absolutely nothing

- Don't let anyone take advantage of you

- This is not a 9-5 job. There is no overtime pay or vacation days!

- Expect emergencies to happen at the worst time!

- Reputations can make or break you

- You will not make everyone happy 100% of the time

- The care you give the horses will speak volumes

- You will need good verbal and written communication skills and the ability to relate to educated and wealthy people alike

- Never think you know everything there is to know about horses. Read books, take lessons, watch videos

- Know how to remove a shoe

- Set boundaries with your boarders

- Don't burn any bridges. The horse community is tiny

- Remove toxic boarders from your life. They aren't worth it

- Barn owners should work with other barn owners in their area to determine a reasonable boarding fee

- Hire only qualified staff

Chapter 3
Different Types of Boarding Options and Services

If you operate a boarding facility, you must decide what services you will offer. Boarding typically falls into two categories: partial and full boarding.

Partial or rough/dry boarding means that the horse's owner is responsible for most, if not all, of the work. The horse owner typically pays a fee for renting the stall or a pasture. The horse owner is responsible for providing their hay and grain, feeding their horse, and mucking the stall. However, there are varying degrees of this type of board. Rough or dry board typically implies that a person is renting out a stall or an entire barn, with the expectation that the owner of the barn will not be doing any of the work or providing any hay, feed or shavings. Rough board works well for a trainer who is looking to establish a home base and needs a group of stalls to rent.

Partial boarding involves both the horse owner and the barn owner coming to an agreement as to what level of care is provided by each. Some barn owners will, at the very least, distribute the horse's feed for the horse owner, thus ensuring that all horses are fed at the same time. It can be stressful for a horse when his neighbor in the next stall is fed, and he is not. These situations can lead to the horse developing bad habits, such as kicking the wall, pacing, and weaving, among other bad habits.

Other barns may include mucking stalls in addition to dropping feed. This ensures that the barn is cleaned at the same time of day and to the barn owner's standards. What is not included in partial boarding is grain, hay, and bedding. That is left up to the horse owner, and from the horse owner's point of view, it is a way to give them more control and say over what their horses eat. Partial boarding is an economical way of keeping costs down for the horse owner, especially when the horse owner is not looking for lessons or training or does not need a full-service facility.

For the barn owner, partial boarding is an excellent way to earn extra income without the labor and expense involved in full boarding. For the small farm owner with an additional stall or two, it is a great way to have the companionship that may be missing from boarding and to have someone available to help cover barn chores when you want to get away.

The most significant disadvantage to the barn owner is that you may end up with a horse owner who does not understand that partial boarding means they are required to be at the barn daily. Stalls should be cleaned, at a minimum, once a day. If the horse owner does not keep enough feed on hand and doesn't clean their stall daily, then the barn owner will find themselves in the position of having to take care of the horse. Whether or not you are being paid as a barn owner, the horse's welfare is ultimately your responsibility. If the horse owner decides not to feed or care for their horse, you must absorb the cost and labor until the situation is resolved.

For this reason, many barn owners may stipulate in their boarding agreement that stalls must be cleaned by a specific time of day. If, for any reason, the horse owner fails to provide enough feed or does not clean their stall, the barn owner can charge a predetermined fee to cover those services.

We know that life happens. There are legitimate reasons that a horse owner may not be able to show up. But if you have a chronic owner who neglects his duties, then it may be time to have a heart-to-heart discussion with them. They must either agree to go on full board or move their horse.

If you offer a partial boarding arrangement, you need to be sure you have the space to accommodate all the feed, hay, and shavings from all the different boarders.

The horse owner is responsible for anything beyond the basic care of the horse, such as medicating, bandaging, and holding for the vet or farrier. The owner of the horse also provides hay and grain. It is up to the barn owner to decide what other options may be included and whether or not to charge extra for the following:

- Mucking stalls

- Dropping AM and/or PM feed

- Turning horses out/bringing in

- Removing and/or applying blankets

- Providing shavings

- Filling water buckets

The other option is full boarding, which typically falls into two categories: basic full board and deluxe full board.

In both situations, the barn owner is responsible for providing feed and hay, mucking stalls, turning the horse out, and bringing him back in. This responsibility should also include other aspects of basic horse care, such as hosing off sweaty horses before returning them to their stall and basic medicating and blanketing in the winter.

Deluxe board is usually offered in show barns. Lessons, training, and even grooming may be included in the price. It is not uncommon for show barns to provide a deluxe boarding package and require riding lessons as part of the package. Some barns will even tack the horses up and have them ready for their rider.

There are other differences between basic and deluxe boarding. While most barn owners feel that blanketing, medicating, applying fly spray and fly masks, and administering dewormers are part of doing business, others will charge an extra fee.

While some fees may seem ludicrous, keep in mind that running a boarding barn is a business. A barn owner cannot be expected to stand and hold 20 horses for the farrier, especially when it lasts from 20 minutes to several hours per horse. That is just not reasonable and barn owners should be compensated if required.

Whether you offer regular or deluxe full boarding, you need a plan. What services are covered? What is considered a la carte? If you are charging for extra services, what fees do you plan to charge?

Full Boarding Considerations:

Stall fee

Included in stall fee:

- Mucking stalls

- Providing good quality hay and feed

- Feeding a minimum of twice daily

- Cleaning and filling water buckets

- Turning out and bringing in

- Rinsing off hot horses

Services Provided, Whether Included or Charged Extra:

- Blanketing
- Holding for vet or farrier
- Administering medications
- Applying fly masks, boots, flysheets, etc
- Lessons
- Training
- Grooming
- Bathing
- Clipping
- Trailering
- Trailer parking
- Private turn-out
- Extra bedding
- Soaking hay or grain
- Sheath cleaning
- Laundering of pads and blankets
- Tacking up

Mucking stalls, turning out, providing clean and fresh water, and feeding are all part of boarding, and anyone who thinks they should charge extra for these services should consider a different career. In addition, these services should be done daily, 365 days a year, on holidays, when you are sick and in bad weather. There should never be any question as to performing any routine chores. These are all part of running a barn. Blanketing, applying fly spray, turn-out boots, and fly masks are also part of running a boarding barn, but some feel they should charge extra for these services. It is understandable that in large boarding facilities, applying boots to every horse before turn-out and putting on and removing blankets for every horse can be very time-consuming. Employees must be paid to assist with these chores, however, most horse owners prefer these tasks to be included *in* their board bill rather than be nickeled and dimed to death. Your best bet is to determine the entire cost of doing business, including the time required for these extra services, and come up with your boarding rate.

Trailer parking is also becoming a debated service. Many barns may not have the room to accommodate trailer parking. Multiple trailers take up valuable space, and if parked on the grass, they need to be moved often to mow the grass. In other cases, boarders will park an old trailer and let it sit and rust, leaving an eyesore for the barn owner to look at daily.

It is not uncommon for barns to charge a trailer parking fee, ranging from $25 to $100 per month, depending upon the size of the trailer. Be careful though when charging these fees; some insurance companies will hold the barn owner liable for any damages to the trailer should they occur. Regardless of whether you choose to charge for trailer parking or not, having a boarder sign sign a waiver releasing the barn owner of any damages to a trailer is a good idea.

Horse owners should be mindful when parking their trailers at their boarding barn. Be considerate of the management and move your trailer often so the grass doesn't die and can be mowed. Remove old, dilapidated trailers rather than letting them be an eyesore for the owner to look at. Be a good boarder!

A sampling of extra charges throughout the U.S. and the going rates as of 2024:

- Blanketing: $30-50 per month or charged by the day, typically $1-2 per occurrence

- Grooming: $25 and up

- Clipping: $25 and up for trims; $100 and up for full-body clipping

- Holding for farrier/vet: $10-20

- Administering dewormers: $5-10 (plus the cost of medicine, or owner provides.)

- Medicating: $5-25 and up. More extensive medicating, especially treating eyes and medicating around the clock, will incur higher fees

I boarded at a farm that charged $300 for full board, which in 2004 was considered average for the time. It was a no-frills barn with no riding ring. The fee included feed, mucking, and turnout. However, I soon discovered that the shavings the barn supplied barely covered the stall mats. My yearling would come in after being turned out all night and, exhausted, would lie down for a good nap after breakfast. Since there were not enough shavings to soak all the urine, he would lie in puddles of pee. I had to pay extra for enough shavings to bed the stalls deeply. Then, when the weather turned cold, I discovered that I would be charged $30 per month per horse for blanketing. I had never heard of a barn charging a blanketing fee, and the owner did not tell me this when I moved my horses there months earlier. This boarding experience shows why providing horse owners with all charges upfront is a good idea. In the long run, I would have been happier being charged a flat rate of $400 or $450 rather than finding out that I had to pay extra for services that I felt should have been included. Because the barn owner sprung these fees on us without notice, the barn lost six boarders within a month.

Other Options to Consider:

Turn-Out: Will you be offering group or individual turn-out? How many hours per day? Horses should be out as much as possible. It keeps them healthier and happier, and the stall stays cleaner and more manageable. What are your plans when the weather does not cooperate, especially in storms?

Parking: Where will your boarders park their vehicles? Would you have adequate space to accommodate all the cars if everyone showed up simultaneously? Vehicles should never be parked in front of the barn or anywhere that would block access by emergency vehicles, so plan the parking area carefully.

Trailer Parking: And what about those horse trailers? Do you have enough room to park trailers of all sizes? At most barns, it is not uncommon for a boarder to have a trailer and require a place to park it.

Restrooms: Does your barn have a separate restroom? Or will you let boarders into your home? Small, private farms may be okay with allowing boarders into their homes, or when nature calls, many a horseperson has found an empty stall. But if you have more than two or three boarders, you need a restroom in the barn, or you need to rent a port-a-potty.

Tack Room: Where will boarders put their stuff? Will you have a tack room with lockers or allow boarders to bring their trunks? Regardless of where trunks are located, a tack room is necessary for hanging bridles and storing saddles. The tack room should be kept clean, tidy, rodent-proof, and locked at night.

Security: Horse owners want to know that their horses are safe from thieves, particularly in areas where stealing horses is common. The state of Florida, in particular, has seen more than its fair share of horses being stolen for meat, with some horses even being butchered on site of the farm. Will your gates be locked at night? Are there security cameras? Are there other measures in place to keep horses safe?

What Type of Boarder Are You Hoping to Attract? Most barns categorize themselves by one or two riding disciplines and have a trainer or instructor available. Other barns will be general boarding barns with all disciplines welcome, with several instructors or trainers available or allowing outside professionals. Others prefer to attract retired horses or trail riders for less wear and tear on their property. Will your facilities be adequate for what you are offering? If you want to attract eventers, you should have a dressage arena, even if it's just an area marked off by cones, a jump field, and, ideally, some cross-country jumps. A stable geared towards dressage should have a formal dressage arena and barrel racers will need barrels to practice on. Reining horses have different footing requirements than hunter riders, so you must ensure you can accommodate whatever discipline you are boarding.

What about Freelance Trainers and Instructors? Are you planning to hire an instructor or trainer and require boarders to use them, or are boarders allowed to bring in their own trainer? What about outside riders? Many barns will allow outside horses to come onto the property, either for lessons or to school, while charging a nominal fee, anywhere from $10 to $50, depending upon their activity. Open schooling is especially common where barns have cross country courses or an indoor arena.

Setting Your Boarding Fee: Before hanging up that **Open for Business** sign, do your homework and figure out what you plan on charging for the board. You should have a well-thought-out business plan, just as if you were opening a coffee shop, clothing boutique, or a tack store. You are operating a business, and while you probably won't get rich from boarding horses, your goal is to make money, not to lose money. It can't be said enough: No barn owner should be subsidizing anyone else's hobby!

Once you decide who you want to attract for boarders and what services and amenities to offer, ask around and see what other barns in the area charge for roughly the same services. How does your barn compare with horse care and amenities? For most areas, boarding fees typically stay within the same range, and fees will significantly vary from region to region. Amenities, trainers, and reputation will also determine how much a barn can charge.

Next, determine what your monthly expenses are most likely to average. Include not just hay and grain, but bedding, insurance, employee wages, repairs, property taxes, water and utilities, and farm equipment expenses. Take into account the hours you will be working, because no barn owner should be working for free!

Consider the fluctuating price increases, especially for hay and grain. In winter, you will pay more for feed, and in addition, you will be blanketing horses. By adding an extra $30 per month to your boarding fee to cover the time and labor involved in blanketing during cooler weather, that same fee can then be used to cover the time and labor involved in dumping and refilling buckets during the heat of summer.

And the Boring Stuff: Legal Documents, Insurance, and Rules: You will need to decide on whether or not you want to post barn rules and what type of insurance you will need. Will you incorporate your business as an LLC? How will you handle the hiring of employees? Will you require a boarding contract? A good boarding contract should spell everything out in detail. A contract protects both the farm owner and the boarder. Chapter 14 will cover these topics more thoroughly.

As a potential boarder, here are some questions to ask:

- What is included in the boarding fee? Do you require a deposit?
- What additional charges are there?
- When is the board due, and is there a grace period? Is there a late fee?
- How can I pay my board bill? With a check or through an app?
- Are outside trainers allowed?
- What are the barn hours?
- What kind of hay and grain is provided?
- How much hay is provided every day?
- What will the feed schedule be for my horse? Can I request a special diet?

- How are supplements fed? Is there a fee for providing them?

- How often are stalls mucked? How are the stalls bedded?

- How often are water buckets and troughs dumped and cleaned?

- Are horses turned out individually or in groups?

- How will my horse be introduced to their turn-out if with other horses?

- What will the plan be if my horse doesn't get along with his new herd mates?

- What is the turn-out contingency plan in the event of bad weather?

- Where can I store my tack and equipment?

- Is there a restroom?

- Where am I permitted to ride?

- Will there be any times that the riding area is off-limits?

- Do lessons take priority for arena time? Or can the ring be shared?

- What are the barn rules?

- What is the policy on dogs, children, and visitors?

- Who will be handling my horse?

- Can I park my trailer on site? Is there a fee?

- Where am I allowed to ride offsite? Are there trails nearby?

- Are the employees experienced? How long have they been employed?

- What is the longevity of boarders?

- Is there a fire and disaster plan? Are there drills?

- How do you handle emergencies in case my horse is hurt?

- Is there a charge to hold my horse for the vet or farrier?

- Can I use my vet and farrier, or must I use the barns?

- In the event of the death of my horse, what is the barn protocol for handling the body?

- Who is responsible for damage caused by horses?

- Is there a boarding contract?

- Am I required to provide insurance for my horse?

- How many days' notice must be given prior to leaving?

When shopping for a new barn, consider a boarding barn's location, travel time, amenities, and budget.

The new horse owner would benefit by boarding in a barn where the staff is knowledgeable and helpful and lessons are available. Even if keeping your horse at home is an option, if you are new to the horse world, it will be beneficial for you and your horse to be under a professional's guidance and supervision until you feel qualified to bring your horse home.

Good boarding barns will offer plenty of turn-outs, with adequate-sized paddocks and pastures, excellent and safe fencing, and weed-free grazing areas. Ideally, barns should have more areas for turning out than they have horses so that pastures can be rotated often. Horses are physically and mentally better off with more time spent outdoors, socializing with other horses, grazing and just being a horse. Barn managers will need to decide what type of turn-out they plan on offering, including:

- Individual, small grouping (1-3 horses), or large herd turn-out?

- Will the groupings be by sex or be mixed herds?

- Will there be a quarantine paddock for new or ill horses?

- Can you accommodate mares and foals, weanlings, or stallions?

- Will you provide nighttime turn-out?

- Can you provide for senior horses?

- What will your turn-out plans be in case of inclement weather?

- How long will horses be turned out for?

Horse owners should know what turn-out situations their horse does best in, whether it is private turn-out or in a group setting. Barn managers and the horse owner should be flexible when determining what turn-out works best for each horse and work together to figure that out. New surroundings as well as herd dynamics can affect how a horse reacts in turn-out. New horses should be introduced slowly to group settings and carefully watched initially to ensure no injuries are incurred as a result of fighting. Horse owners should also realize that some horses may need more time to settle into a new setting, whereas others may walk into the barn from day one and act as if they have been there their entire life. Just like us, everyone is different. The mental well-being of horses should always be taken into consideration, especially when a horse is expected to leave behind friends, whether of the four legged or two legged kind, and thrust into new surroundings.

Depending on your climate, some farms may have lush pastures with all the grass a horse could ask for, and other farms may be lacking in good pasture and find it hard to maintain. When there is little to no forage, whether due to the season, climate, or bad management practices, alternative choices should be offered, by way of hay blocks or hay rolls. Horses should have the ability to graze as often as they want. Pastures and paddocks should be maintained to exclude weeds and have safe footing. Pastures and paddocks that are maintained and manicured will have less chance of toxic weeds taking hold.

Horses should be turned out as much as possible, weather permitting and care should be taken that horses are not turned out in lightning storms. Just by their sheer size, horses risk being struck by lightning, whether by a direct hit, ground current, side flash, or contact strike. Some areas are more prone to lightning strikes, including the Southeast, especially Florida- considered the world's lighting capital; the Gulf states; the Mississippi and Ohio River Valleys; the Front Range of the Rocky Mountains; and some mountainous regions of the Desert Southwest.

Horses stalled for prolonged periods are at a higher risk of developing ulcers and taking up boredom-fighting vices, such as cribbing and weaving. Horses with long turn-out periods and access to fresh water and good quality hay are also at less risk of developing a multitude of physical problems, including sand impaction, because the combination of movement, water, and good hay will aid in flushing out the sand from their system. In addition, their mental state will be better off, the longer they are permitted to behave as horses are meant to be.

Most barns post barn hours, and it is not unheard of for a barn to close for a day, usually on Mondays. I thought I would have a problem boarding at such a barn, but after being reassured that I could come out if needed, I appreciated having that one day to get other things done and not worry about getting to the barn. Mondays became my house cleaning and running-errands day, and I knew the barn owners would have a day to rest up for the rest of the week. However, being closed does not mean that stalls are not mucked or the horses aren't turned out though! Chores still must be completed, but the stable management can slow it down a bit and not have to worry about boarders intruding on their privacy for a day!

Amenities

Boarding barns can vary from the very basic in terms of what amenities to offer, with nothing more than a stall and turn-out, to the very extravagant, with indoor arenas, mirrors, luxurious lounges, and water treadmills for the horses. While the cost of the board will increase with the amenities, that does not necessarily mean that the level of care will also increase. Be careful "not to judge a book by its cover."

Most amenities are included in the board, while some barns charge extra for the more extravagant, such as treadmills and thermoplates. However, be careful not to have a whole list of add-on fees. Boarders would rather know what to budget for every month than have a lot of extras added on that they should have accounted for. Services should not be confused with amenities.

Amenities include:

- Restrooms
- Covered or indoor arena
- Dressage arena
- Mirrors
- Jumps
- Cross country course
- Barrels or poles
- Lounge
- On-site trainer
- Heated and/or air-conditioned tack room
- Trailering to events
- Access to trails
- Round pen
- Automatic fly spray system
- Therapeutic equipment, such as water treadmills and therapies
- Private turn-out
- Rubber mats in stalls
- Outdoor shelters/run-in sheds

Chapter 4
Barn Cleanliness and First Impressions

This chapter is not an instruction manual on how to muck a stall! Every person has their own method, and if you ask a dozen people how they muck stalls, you will get a dozen different answers! Or better yet, go to YouTube if you need a tutorial, and there are hundreds, if not thousands, of videos showing one how to properly (and probably improperly) clean a stall.

Everyone has their method, and there is no right or wrong way as long as the stall is cleaned correctly with wet spots (urine) and manure removed. Some prefer a deeply bedded stall of pine shavings with banked walls. Others prefer to use straw, while others prefer to use pellets for bedding. And if using stall mats, keep in mind that they still need some type of bedding on top of the mats. Stalls should have enough bedding to soak up urine and prevent hock sores.

Dirty stalls, especially those with strong urine odors, can pose a respiration issue for horses. Cobwebs can also be a fire hazard if enough dust and cobwebs cover electrical outlets. Dirty aisles and barnyards invite pests and rodents, and unnecessary items littering the aisle can pose hazards to horses and humans alike.

The importance of cleaning stalls, buckets, and troughs, sweeping barn aisles, picking up items, and raking the front of the barn is not just about first impressions for a potential boarder. It's about safety. Some chores should be done daily without fail, such as mucking and cleaning buckets, while other tasks can be done weekly or monthly, such as removing cobwebs. Shrubbery that is near a barn should be maintained regularly, for they are potential fuel for a fire, just as cobwebs and dust are. Tack rooms should be swept, and tack and supplies should be kept in trunks or lockers. Scattered feed on the ground in the feed room should be swept up daily to prevent rodent or pest infestation, and the hay room should also be kept in good order.

From a potential boarder's point of view, a clean barn signifies that the owner or manager cares about how their barn looks and will most likely care about the rest of horse management as well.

I once toured a barn with the intention of looking for a new boarding barn closer to my home. I was commuting nearly an hour each way and wanted to decrease the time I was driving so I could increase the time that I was riding. The barn manager was a young girl who had foregone going to college to instead realize her dream of running a barn. Her grandfather set her up with the funds to do so, and at first glance, she seemed to be thriving. The barn was immaculate, and I was impressed with her barn management skills. The barn was clean, the pastures mowed and grassy, and the horses appeared happy. A few months later, I decided to move my two horses to her barn.

In hindsight, I should have paid the barn another visit. Instead, I moved my horses without a second visit. I was dismayed at what I found when I got there. Paddocks that had once been lush with grass were now sandy and full of weeds, and those weeds had taken hold everywhere around the barn. A flatbed trailer containing manure was parked beside the barn by the entrance, waiting to be dumped. The trailer sat there until it was full of manure, inviting every fly to the barn until it was dumped, usually after 4 -5 days. The once pristine tack room was now full of trash, and garbage was everywhere from the owner's dogs constantly getting into the garbage cans. She had also acquired a goat, which roamed freely, meaning there was goat poop everywhere, including on top of boarders' trunks. The barn was a total disaster. Because I was going to work off my board,

I decided to stay and give it a try, but I spent so much time cleaning up after the dogs and the goat that I finally gave up. The young manager had obviously lost interest when she realized that running a barn was much more work than she'd bargained for. She eventually lost many boarders and closed the barn less than a year later.

Many will agree that while mucking a stall is work, it is mindless work and a great place to solve the world's problems! It is peaceful, and you are exercising your body as well. Stalls should be cleaned daily, and good barns will perform a light cleaning several times throughout the day. If manure is picked up at bedtime, it usually makes the stall easier to clean in the morning, especially if the horse is particularly messy in his stall. Sick horses on stall rest should never be standing in dirty stalls. Their stalls should be cleaned throughout the day, which is why a barn owner may choose to charge extra for horses requiring stall rest. Likewise, if the weather is not conducive to a horse going out for the day, his stall should also be picked throughout the day.

There are a variety of tools and equipment that can be used to make mucking easier. Long gone are the days of using a pitchfork. The invention of manure forks made stall cleaning much simpler. The question remains as to what method is best for removing the manure from stalls and what should be done with your manure? Do you use a muck bucket, a wheelbarrow, or a spreader? People trying to improve the cleaning process have invented and devised an array of gadgets- however, whether or not they save time is debatable. Some of these devices include:

- Power wheelbarrow

- Central vac/ manure suction system

- Conveyor belt

- Vibrating tables that separate the manure from the shavings

In addition, barns that previously served as dairy barns may have wood slats in the floors, which allow manure and urine to fall to the bottom level to be collected.

The most common methods of removing the dirty bedding from stalls include:

- Slinging manure into the spreader, whether it's pulled up to the stall door or stationed in the barn aisle. The closer it's parked near the stall being cleaned, the easier it is to fling manure into it and there is less mess on the ground

- Using a muck bucket in the stall to transfer to a spreader in the barn aisle

- Using a muck bucket, which is then transported by a side-by-side, tractor, or carried to either a Dumpster or compost pile

- Using a wheelbarrow or yard cart

- Dumping manure, urine, and dirty shavings into the center aisle and using a tractor to push the pile out of the barn so it can be scooped and dumped in a Dumpster or into a spreader. Some farms will spread a tarp on the ground first and drag the tarp out with the tractor

I met a woman who lived on a large cattle ranch where her husband was a ranch foreman. She told me she didn't put shavings in her stalls; there was just a sand base, and she never cleaned them. As I stood there with my mouth open, she told me she didn't need to clean them because every morning, her flock of chickens came through and cleaned the barn for her, and the urine drained through the sand. I was skeptical— until I had chickens myself and saw that they liked pecking, scratching, and dispersing manure. I always found them congregating around the barn when I allowed them to free range. They didn't do enough work for me not to clean my stalls, but they certainly helped maintain the paddocks! Who knew?

Oh, Manure…Now What?

You have collected the manure. Now what to do with all that manure?

Barn owners have gotten very creative with how to clean stalls and remove and dispose of the manure. Once the dirty bedding has been removed, it must be disposed of. Not all of these methods are user-friendly though, and many are physically demanding, and can be a source of injuries that lead to employees quitting, such as lifting heavy muck buckets, pushing wheelbarrows through mud or deep sand, or having to push a wheelbarrow up a steep narrow ramp into a manure spreader or Dumpster.

After a new manager took over at a barn where I had previously boarded, they had the bright idea to push the wheelbarrow full of manure out the back side of the barn, which sloped to a river, where they proceeded to dump the manure, without covering it. The horses were turned out on this health hazard, and eventually, the manure caught fire. Thankfully, the fire was extinguished before it spread to the barn but the barn owners not only had to attend to the manure but they were also cited for dumping near a river.

The backbreaking and potentially dangerous methods barn owners and managers create for their employees when dumping manure should not be tolerated. Barn owners must do better by their employees and create better working conditions, starting with ways to better handle manure.

I worked at a high-end boarding barn where the monthly fee began at $1500 per month. The owners had a rather enormous Dumpster to which barn workers could walk the wheelbarrow and dump the contents. While it was easy enough on the employees, the issue was that the Dumpster was parked right next to one wing of the barn. Every horse on that side of the barn had a view of the smelly Dumpster, not to mention the irritation of the flies that were attracted to the Dumpster. Because it was so large, that recepticle was emptied just once a month.

Manure spreaders make spreading manure easy and fast. They come in an array of sizes and costs. Compact spreaders, such as the Newer Spreader, are smaller and affordable, making it feasible for the small hobby farm to utilize a spreader without the cost or maintenance of a bigger spreader. Disposing manure via spreaders will be the most suitable for the environment, if done properly, and will be the least labor-intensive method.

With manure spreaders, you are done with your manure daily! The manure is spread directly onto pastures. Rotating fields and keeping animals off the pastures is the best method when spreading, to prevent parasite infestations and possibly spreading diseases. In addition, medications and dewormers may be dispersed along with the fresh manure, so animals should be kept off the grass for several weeks, although many horses will instinctually avoid the areas independently. It is best to spread when the temperatures are high so the manure has a chance to dry quickly, aiding in the killing of parasites. Manure should be applied thinly to reduce flies and to ensure an even application of nutrients to the pasture. Manure should never be spread near water or where the land slopes toward a waterway. Avoid applying on wet areas, because this will result in the soil becoming over-compacted, resulting in poor grass growth. The goal of spreading is to retain the good nutrients for the soil to absorb and for the parasites and any other unwanted elements to dry out and become harmless. The downside to spreading is that it may not be legal in your area, depending on drainage, the location of drinking water, and the watershed. Neighbors may also complain of the odor from freshly spread manure.

The best use of manure is to compost the manure before spreading. There are pros and cons to composting first before spreading, as to just spreading the manure while fresh. One benefit of composting your manure is that the nutrient release is slower, which benefits plants. Weed seed germination rates will be lower than if you just spread the fresh manure. The bedding and hay collected from mucking the stalls will also compost along with the manure rather than being spread across your pastures. Compost will create less mud if you are in an area prone to such, and probably the biggest argument for composting is that parasites and fly larvae will be killed off. However, to compost, you will need some system in place, and it is more labor intensive because you will need to turn the compost every few weeks. If you have a tractor, this should not be an issue. But if you don't, you will be shoveling the compost from one pile to another and then into a wheelbarrow or spreader when it is ready to be spread. Ideally, the compost system should be covered so the nutrients aren't lost from runoff, and if it is not covered, you should install a drainage system. Composting also takes several months. There are many resources and articles that can help you build a self-regulating manure composter. Universities like the University of Massachusetts are excellent resources for finding diagrams and information for constructing a compost system. Grants may be available through your soil and water conservation office, or you can contact your extension office or state agriculture department for more resources. The manure compost pile should be located where the area is not at risk of contaminating water. It should not be near the barn or other structures; it should be out of sight but easily accessible.

Another option is to contact local gardeners. They will be happy to come and haul away your manure, especially if you have composted it. One method to make the manure easy for gardeners is to place it in empty feed bags, where it will start composting. This provides an easy way for the manure to be transported.

And One More Thing…..Let's Talk Bedding!

Just as there are different ways to muck a stall, there are other ways to bed the stall and other methods to use.

Options include:

- Pine/wood shavings
- Pelleted shavings
- Hemp shavings
- Straw
- Sawdust

- Shredded paper
- Peat moss
- Sand
- Husks or shells

They all have pros and cons; some types may be more common in one area while not familiar elsewhere. Other factors to consider include price, availability and ease of storage.

Cedar or black walnut should never be used for bedding due to toxicity. Cedar shavings contain a significant oil content within the wood, which can irritate horses' lungs. Black walnut is extremely toxic and will cause a horse to founder. Even small amounts of black walnut can cause a horse to become ill.

Your bedding storage must be considered when deciding what product to use. Straw comes baled, just like hay. Shavings can be delivered in bulk, which will require an area to store the pile where it is protected from rain (if a building is not available, tarps will suffice), or they can be purchased in bags, which will also require a dry storage area. Ideally, shavings should be stored in a separate building, away from the barn, as they are combustible.

> *I am a big fan of having decent mats in the stall and topping it with good-quality pine shavings. I prefer a deeply bedded stall, and I am old school in that I like to "bank" the sides with extra shavings, which help prevent a horse from getting cast. As you clean your stall, you can draw down new shavings rather than having to open new bags or load a new wheelbarrow full every day.*

The main goal of mucking your stalls should be to provide a clean environment for your horses and boarders. Clean stalls reduce flies and rodents. Stalls should be mucked daily, and you will find that your good barns will pick stalls throughout the day. If you are scouting for a barn, be aware of horses standing in manure with strong urine odors and no concern for where or how the manure is disposed of. How a barn manages its stall cleaning will significantly indicate how it manages the rest of the barn. Likewise, the rest of the barn should be neat and tidy, providing a safe environment for your horse.

Chapter 5
Feeding and Nutrition

In his book-"Horseowner and Stableman's Companion," written in 1869, author George Armatage describes the feeding of horses as…"*When properly understood, they indicate the principles of an economical system of feeding animals with a view towards the preservation of health and vigour under continued laborious exertion, as well as preventing an undue rate of mortality resulting from it, and at a low rate of cost.*" He continues to write that food should be nutritious, contain elements of a mixed character, be of proportionate bulk, should be readily available, and lastly, that the digestive organs must be in a state of healthy action.

Armatage further states that the secret to avoiding health issues is *prevention*. He advises that this is achieved through cleanliness, ventilation, care, and attention to the quality, quantity, and regularity of feeding and a due proportion of work.

Nothing has changed much in theory in more than 100 years. This should be the goal of every horse person!

Managing a barn requires some basic knowledge of feed and hay, including knowing the different grains available, identifying quality hay, knowing what types of hay and grain work for each horse, and knowing how to store them properly, especially the hay. By providing good quality feed, we can prevent many health issues.

Horses are designed to be grazing animals, moving constantly and eating small amounts frequently. Their digestive system is designed to handle small amounts of roughage and plants, a little at a time, grazing 15- 20 hours a day. The stomach can only hold 2- 4 gallons of feed at a time and works best when it is 2/3 full. Too much feed can result in colic, so it is best to feed small amounts of grain often. The digestion process takes from 36 to 72 hours to pass food through the digestive tract. If the stomach is empty, it begins to secrete acid, which can lead to ulcers.

Feeding Grain

There are a good number of feeds on the market today. The science of feeding horses has come a long way since 1869, when Armatage writes of feeding turnips, potatoes, peas, beans, Indian corn, denominated corn, as well as linseed. One thing that hasn't changed is the principle that providing quality feed will go a long distance in keeping one's horse healthy… "*Carefully carried out, these principles will have an enormous saving, and I have no hesitation in stating that among the numbers of animals employed in Glasgow and other large towns of Great Britain, it may be raised to thousands of pounds annually, and in addition, a corresponding sum by the avoidance of disease. The farmer need not grudge his horse corn, since it can be shown that he can be fed at less cost than many now incur on inferior hay, straw, and provender generally, and derive greater aptitude for work,*" and he continues further that "*All food should be of the best quality and kind.*" Armatage relates the story of a celebrated mare named Old Sal, who ran in a coach line between London, York, and Leeds, 14 miles out and 14 miles in, six days a week. The mare was never sick or lame, and when she retired in her twenties, she was "*as fresh as paint!*" Another mare, "Maggie Lauder" pulled a fly-boat between Glascow (sic) and Edinbro' (sic), twice a day, for a total of 32 miles per day, 6 days a week. When she retired, never having a sick day, she was sold at the age of 29 years old!

According to the Horse Feed Global Market Report of 2023, the global horse feed industry grew from $7.58 billion in 2022 to $8.14 billion in 2023, with an expected growth of more than $11 billion by 2028. The American Horse Council Foundation states that the horse population in the United States is more than 9 million as of 2021, which will continue to propel the growth of the horse feed market. Feed companies employ equine nutritionists and spend countless hours and untold dollars in research to improve the quality of feed for our horses so we may get the best results from our investments. Major feed companies are concentrating on developing new and innovative products, including microbiome optimization supplements, veterinary diets for certain diseases, immunomodulatory nutrition, and improving digestibility and palatability.

It is both convenient and economical to feed a commercial or concentrated feed. Concentrates are high in digestible energy and are usually mixed with a variety of additives or supplements. The energy source comes from either starch, fat, and/or digestible fibers. Typically sold in 50-pound bags, feed manufacturers tailor their products to meet the different lifestyles of horses. There are feeds designed for the pleasure horse, competitive horse (further categorized as light/moderate or strenuous), broodmares, young horses, senior horses, and horses with metabolic disorders.

Digestible fibers are essential to a horse's diet, so commercial mixes contain some roughage. These can be made by adding beet pulp, oats, barley, wheat, rice, soybeans, or even sunflower seeds.

Sweet feeds are pelleted feed to which molasses has been added for either binding reasons or to add flavoring. Keep in mind that feeding sweet feed will raise blood sugar levels in horses after eating, and just as in children who misbehave after consuming large quantities of candy, so can horses. If this occurs, the horse may be better off being fed a straight pellet diet. Care should be taken when feeding sweet feed in hot climates. It will spoil much quicker; therefore, large amounts of feed should not be ordered all at once. Some horsemen believe feeding sweet feed will attract more flies in the summer, so they will only feed it in the winter. A good compromise is a textured feed, which is relatively new to the feed market. It will contain a mix of grains, such as oats and corn, to the pellets, but the binding may be an oil rather than molasses, so the feed is not as high in protein or as likely to spoil in warm climates, yet it is very palatable.

There was a time when horsemen were mainly concerned about protein levels. A 12- 14% protein was considered high and fed only to active horses. Pleasure horses were fed an 8- 10% protein. It was a common misconception that high protein made a horse hot.

Today, other ingredients are considered just as important as the protein content and can factor into what makes a horse hot or lethargic. Knowing the content of fats, starch, fibers, and calories is just as important. Again, it all comes down to what level of activity your horse is doing. Easy keepers who get minimal exercise will require fewer calories, less protein, less fat, and have a lower starch requirement than a horse competing several times a month and in moderate to strenuous exercise. In addition, horses that have laminitis, are insulin resistant, are under a year old, more than 20 years old, or are breeding will all have different nutritional requirements. Some will even factor the breed of a horse into the feeding program. Thoroughbreds will have different feed requirements than draft horses or ponies. Draft horses and certain other breeds are prone to EPSM (Equine Polysaccharide Storage Myopathy. Also referred to as PSSM) and should not be fed sweet feed. EPSM diets are high in fat and low in starch and sugar.

Types of grains and feeds:

- Oats are high in fiber and low in energy. They can be fed whole, rolled, or crimped. Oats are the safest grain to feed.

- Barley is higher in energy than oats and lower in fiber. It is considered less safe than oats because it is easier to overfeed. Feed them rolled or flaked to remove the outer husk.

- Corn is the highest in energy and lowest in fiber. It is also the most concentrated food, so care should be taken when feeding it. One quart of corn equals two quarts of oats.

- Bran is the ground-up hulls of wheat. It is usually mixed with other grains or fed as a mash. Bran should not be fed in large quantities because it contains large amounts of phosphorus, which can upset the calcium-phosphorus balance, leading to bone issues.

- Sweet Feed consists of mixed grain and pellets with molasses added. It is difficult to store in hot and humid conditions, spoils easily, and attracts flies.

- Pellets are dried grains that are ground up and pressed into pellets. They can be single-ingredient pellets, such as alfalfa meal or mixed grain pellets, or supplements and complete feed containing grain and hay.

- Textured Feed is a mixed grain pellet with the addition of oil. Textured feeds are considered to be very palatable and ideal for picky eaters.

- Beet Pulp is a by-product of processed sugar beets. It is suitable for horses with heaves or allergies. It is shredded and must be thoroughly soaked to avoid choking. It is more digestible than hay.

Just as there are different types of feed, the quality of feed varies as well.

Many barns will try to cut costs, beginning in the feed room. In the long run, however, you are not saving money, because the horse's performance level may suffer, and you will likely end up with costly vet bills due to feeding poor quality feed and hay. Feeding an "All Stock" feed, which is designed for all kinds of farm animals, is a poor choice to feed your horse, because horses, pigs, cows, and goats all have different nutritional requirements.

A good-quality 50 pound bag of feed will cost between $20 and $30. Usually, the better the quality, the less you will have to feed. Good-quality feeds do not contain unnecessary fillers and additives. It is possible to feed as much as 50% less of a good-quality grain than a product containing fillers such as rice hulls.

Guidelines for Feeding

Ponies, idle horses, mature horses, and horses on stall rest do best on a diet consisting of 80- 100% roughage (good hay and pasture).

When and why do you begin to add in concentrates?

Horses in moderate to strenuous exercise or kept on poor-quality pastures will need to have their diet supplemented with grain. These horses all need to have their diet supplemented with enough nutrients to meet their maintenance requirements, plus take into account their workload, replenish vitamins and minerals lost to exercise and repair and maintain stress to tissues and joints. As the workload increases, so do their protein and calcium requirements.

Senior Horses may not digest and process their feed as well as other horses. Many times, the loss of teeth will hamper their chewing process. Therefore, it is essential to provide a diet that is soft and palatable, high in fat and calories, and contains highly digestible fibers. Many brands on the market today also include added herbs, vitamins, and minerals to address metabolic disorders, poor teeth, and digestive upset, all common in older horses. With advances in senior feeds, there is no excuse to have a skinny old horse.

Young horses and broodmares have different nutritional requirements from other horses in terms of growth and development, lactation, and calcium and phosphorous requirements. Because young horses are vulnerable to deficiency diseases and nutritional imbalances, the calcium/phosphorous ratio is critical, because an imbalance can cause skeletal and joint issues. Foals should be fed grain as soon as they will eat it by sharing it with their dam. As the foal grows and relies less on its mother's milk, its need for good hay and grain will increase. Weanlings should be fed protein levels of 14%. Too-fast growth can result in developmental orthopedic disease (DOD), especially if the foal is stalled with limited turn-out. Protein requirements taper off by the time they are yearlings, dropping to about 12% and then 10% as two-year-olds.

There are many excellent books that discuss feed nutrition in detail; every barn owner or manager should have at least one for reference. In addition, most reputable feed companies have reps who should be more than willing to answer your feed questions. Your veterinarian is also an excellent source for devising a nutritional plan for your horse.

Questions to ask when deciding the daily ration of a horse:

- Does the horse need to lose or gain weight, or is his current weight fine? What is his body score, which will aid in making this decision? Is the horse in a heavy work schedule, getting fit, or being let down for the winter?

- What is his breed and body type? Tall, ribby, and lean horses, such as off-the-track Thoroughbreds, will require more feed than a compact, chunky Quarter Horse.

- What is his temperament? A nervous or high-strung horse will burn off calories much faster than a horse that is laid back or lazy.

- What is his feeding behavior? If fed in a pasture setting, horses that consume their feed fast and then run off the timid horse must be separated. Picky eaters or slow eaters need to be given ample time to finish their meals.

- How is his health? Horses that are seniors, ill, or on stall rest for an injury need to have their diets adjusted. Laminitic horses, those suffering from Insulin Resistance, or those with other metabolic disorders will also have different requirements.

- Is the horse stabled more than 12 hours a day? How much nutrition is he getting from pasture?

- Is the horse being fed according to his daily exercise? A horse that goes from moderate to strenuous exercise daily will need his grain ration cut back on days he does not exercise. Feed extra hay to make up for the reduced grain ration.

- What is the weather? Horses in colder climates need extra calories to help keep warm, especially if they are not getting blanketed. Provide extra calories by feeding more hay.

When I was a teenager, I took the barn owner's word for what was best for my horse to eat. He fed a nationally recognized brand of pellet, but it was at the low end for price and, as I came to find out later, of lower quality. My horse, a Thoroughbred, received six pounds of feed, twice a day. He was in good weight. However, when I left that barn and went the partial boarding route, the feed store owner convinced me to try the same brand of higher quality. I spent about $3 more per 50 pound bag, but within a month, I had reduced the amount of grain that my horse was eating by 50%, to 3 lbs., twice daily! So even though the grain cost me a little bit more, I was saving money! In addition, my horse looked better. His coat took on a deeper shine, and he developed dapples. Overall, he looked much better after I switched feeds!

Feeding the equine is a lot like feeding yourself. A human who eats nothing but junk food such as fast food, candy, and soda will need to eat more often as the sugar high wears off. They may become lethargic, fat, and out of shape. The person who takes care of his body, feeding it salads, vegetables, fruit, and foods high in protein while limiting their sugar intake, will be more energetic and healthy. Horses are no different. It is unfair and unreasonable to expect a horse to be at its peak performance when being fed an inferior diet.

Once you have identified which brand of feed to feed, it is a good idea to speak with a company rep to determine which feeds will suit the horses in your barn. You must understand that not all horses are the same and will have different nutritional requirements. It isn't reasonable nor practical to expect to supply just one type of feed to a barn full of horses. Your boarding business will consist of several different types of horses. A hard-to-keep-weight-on Thoroughbred will require a different kind of feed than the 17-hand warmblood in the stall next to him. The broodmare across the aisle will have a very high protein requirement compared to the 15-hand Quarter Horse in the stall next to her that shows in the hunter division or that 12-hand Welsh pony stalled on the other side of her.

Select a feed company with a good reputation for producing quality feed. Be careful of feed companies that also produce cattle and poultry feed in the same plant, because cross-contamination has occurred with an ingredient known as Monesin, which has been found to be toxic to horses. Monesin, a feed additive to promote growth in other livestock, has been accidentally added to horse feed. One high-profile case occurred at a farm in Davie, Florida, in 2014, when 22 horses were unknowingly fed

Monesin-containing feed. Some horses had to be euthanized within days of consuming the toxin, and the remaining horses would eventually succumb to the poison and not survive.

There are a few feed manufacturers that do offer a "complete" feed to avoid having to feed a wide variety, but it is best to feed that only if all your boarders are very similar in breed, activity level, and age. Many barns will stick to one brand, but good barns will offer a variety of those brands, and a great barn will be open to hearing what a boarder or vet feels their horse needs, and if it is a legitimate concern, they will provide that feed.

> *While barn shopping for my draft cross, I ran into a situation that ended practically before it even started. Tucker had severe allergies, EPSM, and a host of other issues, and I inquired at a particular barn as to what they fed. I was told it was X brand and that all horses got that feed. I mentioned that my horse needed a specific feed due to his EPSM and allergies, and the reply was that their feed would be just fine and that there was no need to feed anything else. Needless to say, that ended our conversation right there. Don't be afraid to leave or not pursue a boarding situation if it's not a good fit for your horse!*

Feeding Grain Rules

1. When changing diets, do so slowly. Introduce a new grain in a small amount and gradually transition over 7- 14 days, gradually increasing the new feed while decreasing the old

2. Feed small amounts of grain often. Two to three meals a day is ideal. Horses have small stomachs and should not be fed more than 5- 6 pounds of grain per feeding. "Little and often."

3. Feed regularly, with as much as 30- 60 minutes of leeway. A flexible schedule allows for horses traveling to shows, an employee who is late, or in the event of inclement weather to not stress if the feed is not fed at the exact time each day

4. Horses should not be ridden immediately following a meal. The general rule is to wait 45 minutes to an hour after feeding, as exercise can affect digestion

5. Food should be weighed because nutritional recommendations are given in pounds. One pound of corn will not be the same scoop as one pound of oats or pellets, so while it is ok to resort to scoops at feed time, the food must be weighed first to know how many scoops (or half scoops) should be fed to the horse. Food scales or even fishing scales work well

6. Provide clean, fresh water at all times

7. Provide a salt block

8. Feed no more than 1% of a horse's body weight in grain daily

9. Feed only good quality grain, which is free of dust and mold

10. Give feed buckets a quick glance before dumping new feed in the bucket, particularly in the morning. Check for bugs or rodents that may be helping themselves to leftover feed. In addition, some horses have been known to poop in their feed buckets, or shavings may have been kicked into the bucket when lying down at night

11. Leftover feed may indicate a problem. Does the horse need to have his teeth checked? Is the feed fresh, or is it moldy? Horses with ulcers or under stress may leave feed. Therefore, it is important to know each horse and its eating habits

12. Feed buckets and tubs should be cleaned regularly, as should water buckets and troughs

13. Feed according to workload and condition

14. Is the horse consuming enough water? As you check the feed buckets, you should also check the water levels. Again, get to know each horse's drinking habits. Too much water consumption may indicate a problem or simply be the result of a hot day. Not having enough water consumption is always a concern, especially after a workout, in cold weather, or on a hot day. If you use automatic waterers, install the kind with meters to monitor each horse's intake

15. Are manure balls normal? Get to know each horse's potty habits. Constant soft piles may indicate that the horse is getting too rich a diet, and dry fecal balls may indicate insufficient water consumption

To survive, horses require six different types of essential nutrients, which can be provided by the environment or feed.

Water comprises 50% of a horse's body weight and is the only nutrient that does not need to be broken down or changed by the body before use. It is essential to every cell, carries nutrients to all parts of the body, helps eliminate waste, and regulates the body's temperature. Horses need 8- 15 gallons of water daily, and it should always be clean and cool. Water is the most important nutrient, because without it, horses cannot live very long.

Most of the fuel a horse gets for energy comes from **carbohydrates**, which can be found in hay, grains, and grass. They are the cheapest and most abundant source of energy. Carbs will help regulate a horse's body temperature, aid in keeping him warm in the winter, and are the source of energy needed during hard work. Excess energy is stored as fat. Carbs are derived from plants, which create starch during photosynthesis. As the horse eats the grass, hay, or plants, the carbs are broken down into starches and sugars for energy and cellulose, which provides fiber. The cellulose comes from the stems of plants and is necessary to keep food moving along the digestive tract. Horses with metabolic disorders should be fed a diet lower in carbs, so look for a feed that meets those needs.

Proteins are comprised of amino acids, which break down plant protein into animal protein and are essential to every cell. They are vital for the growth, maintenance, and repair of tissues. Lysine and methionine are two of the most essential amino acids; without them, the remaining 22 amino acids cannot be utilized by horses. Proteins are expressed as percentages, and the horse's workload, breed, and use will dictate the protein requirements within a 24-hour period. Care should be taken not to feed more protein than needed, because the excess protein can cause liver and kidney damage. Horses will drink more and as a result, urinate and sweat more, which can lead to dehydration. Horses with a deficiency of protein will have a rough coat, suffer weight loss, decreased milk production, stunted growth, and poor performance.

Fat: Fatty acids or lipids, such as linoleic acid and a-linolenic acid, and Omega-3 and Omega-6 fatty acids are needed to carry vitamins through the bloodstream, maintain cell membrane integrity, and play essential roles in immunity and inflammation. They affect the quality of hair and coat and the growth rate of young horses. Fats produce 2½- 3 times as much energy as carbohydrates, providing an emergency energy source. Most horses require small amounts of fat. However, older horses may be given extra fat as their metabolism slows. In addition, for horses who need less starch in their diet, such as horses with EPSM (Equine Polysaccharide Storage Myopathy), feeding oil can replace the calories lost when reducing the starch content. Providing extra fat will increase the energy density of the diet, allowing for a reduction of concentrates required to meet the horse's energy needs. Don't overfeed fat, as obesity can result. Corn oil and wheat germ oil are good sources of fat rather than feeding grain, which may spoil in hot climates.

Vitamins are required in small amounts to regulate certain chemical reactions in the horse's body. They can be water-soluble or fat-soluble. Fat-soluble vitamins, such as A, D, E, and K, are stored in the liver and body fat, while the water-soluble vitamins C, thiamine, riboflavin, B12, B6, niacin, biotin, pantothenic acid, choline, folacin and aminobenzoic acid, are produced in the intestine from natural plant sources and cannot be stored in the body. Horses get most of their vitamins from good-quality hay, grass, sunlight, and supplements.

Minerals are inorganic (whereas vitamins are organic) and are not produced by living things. They are also necessary in small amounts in a horse's diet. Their purpose is to build and maintain bones and to act as a trigger for specific body functions, such as fluid balance in cells, nerve conduction and muscle contraction. They are necessary for the metabolism of every cell in the body. The six major minerals include salt, calcium, phosphorous, potassium, iodine, and other trace minerals.

Horses lose salt through sweating and, therefore, need to have it offered free choice, either in a salt block or top-dressed on their feed. It is beneficial to give extra salt top-dressed when horses need encouragement to drink more water, such as in the winter.

Calcium and phosphorous are essential for sound bones and are closely associated with magnesium and Vitamin D. Without Vitamin D, a horse cannot absorb calcium. Ninety-nine percent of calcium and 80% of phosphorus is found in the bones. Mature horses need twice as much calcium as phosphorous in their diet while growing horses need equal parts. The minerals should be in balance, or they will not be utilized properly. Hay and grass are high in calcium, but low in phosphorous, and grains are high in phosphorous but low in calcium. This is why providing the correct diet is crucial for different life stages of your horse's growth!

Potassium is needed to maintain the pH and fluid levels in cells. Horses lose potassium through sweating, so electrolytes should be given in hot weather.

Iodine regulates thyroid activity and is only needed in small amounts. It is usually found in the soil, but if the soil is deficient, you can add iodized salt to your horse's diet.

Additional trace minerals will be found in the horse's regular diet, and unless you suspect your horse is deficient in a particular mineral, there is no need to add more.

Nutrient	Source	Reason
Water	Supplied in buckets or troughs or streams: 10- 15 gallons minimum per day	To sustain life. Essential to every cell.
Carbohy-drates	Grass, hay, grain	Starches and sugars necessary for energy; cellulose (plant fiber) for digestion
Proteins	Oats, corn, alfalf	Growth, maintenance of body, repair. The building blocks of cells
Fatty Acids, Lipids	Corn oil, wheat germ oil	Produces extra energy when carbs are not enough. Aids in digestion
Vitamins	Hay, grain, sun, supplements	Body functions
Minerals	Hay, grain, salt, supplements	Build and maintain tissue and bones. Acts as triggers for body functions.

Hay and Roughage

It is essential that the majority of a horse's diet consists of fiber, which provides the complex carbohydrates that are necessary for a healthy horse. Horses are grazing animals, and in order to keep the horse's digestive system functioning correctly, as well as reduce the chance of developing vices such as cribbing and to prevent health issues such as ulcers and colic, it is important that horses be fed a minimum of 2- 3% of their body weight in roughage daily. Because the protein and energy requirements will vary from horse to horse, determining the suitable type and amount of hay is very important depending on age, workload, and health. Horses should consume enough forage to obtain the necessary nutrients and to ensure the fiber maintains normal gastrointestinal function. The fiber concentration should contain 30-45% of acid detergent fiber (ADF) and 45- 65% of neutral detergent fiber (NDF) in order to provide for normal gastrointestinal function.

To calculate the amount of hay you should be feeding each horse per day, assume that if you have a 1,000-pound healthy horse consuming 2.5% of body weight each day with a primary hay diet and no pasture access or grain concentration in the ration, then 1,000 lbs. x 0.025 = 25 pounds of hay EACH DAY! That is roughly 9,125 pounds each year!

Therefore, you should plan on roughly 183 bales per horse per year if you are feeding small, square bales that weigh roughly 50 pounds each. In addition:

- Add a minimum of 10% more to account for waste during feeding and storage

- Plan on at least an additional month's worth of hay to account for acclimation and weather issues

- Subtract days on good pasture grass

- Horse body weight, activity level, health, and total diet will impact hay needs.

CALCULATING HAY NEEDS

Assumptions

- 1,000 lb. adult horse, healthy
- Consumes 2.5% of body weight daily
- Primarily hay diet

Calculations

- 1,000 lbs. x 0.025 = 25lbs. daily
- 25 lbs. x 365 days = 9,125 lbs yearly

Bales Needed

- Small square bales
@ 50 lbs = 183 bales per horse per year
- Round bales
@ 900 lbs = 10 bales per horse per year

The types of hay available will vary depending on the area in which you live. There are two categories of hay: Legume and Grass Hay.

Legume hays include alfalfa, clover, and perennial peanut. Legumes produce seeds in a pod and have more protein and calcium than grass hays.

The most common legume hay is alfalfa. Typically, alfalfa is higher in nutrients than other hays and is the preferred choice of hay for broodmares, young horses, and horses in strenuous exercise. It usually contains 30% or more protein, making it an excellent and economical source of protein. It also has more digestible energy and fewer non-structural carbohydrates (sugars and starches). Because of its high protein content, many horse owners will mix it with a grass hay to balance the fiber and protein content. Alfalfa is also high in calcium and low in phosphorous, so another benefit of mixing with grass hay is that it will balance the calcium-phosphorous ratio. Alfalfa hay is a good choice for underweight horses since it is nutrient-dense. It is also suitable for horses prone to ulcers, because the extra calcium acts as a buffer against stomach acid.

Horses with muscle disorders, such as EPSM (Equine Polysaccharide Storage Myopathy, also referred to as PSSM), can also benefit from alfalfa due to the lower amount of NSCs (non-structural carbohydrates). There is mixed response for feeding alfalfa to horses with metabolic disorders, such as IR (Insulin Resistance) due to the protein levels. Because alfalfa is lower in sugar and some grass hays are too high in sugar, feeding a combination of the two can help reduce sugar intake levels. Vets should always be consulted when creating a diet plan for such horses. Care should also be used when feeding it to weanlings and yearlings to ensure they are not growing too fast, putting them at risk for the Development of Orthopedic Disease (DOD).

Alfalfa hay can also be sold as chopped or bagged, which proves convenient for horsemen in areas where alfalfa is challenging to get or where storage is limited. Chopped alfalfa can be mixed with grains. Alfalfa cubes are another option. They provide the same nutritional content but are less bulky and easily stored. It is necessary to soak the cubes, as dry cubes can pose a choking hazard. Soaked cubes also provide an excellent source of roughage for senior horses that lack teeth and cannot digest grass or hay properly, and it is a perfect way to provide more water intake. Offering a soaked mash at lunch will ensure water intake and provide an additional feeding. It is not uncommon for alfalfa to be mixed with grass hays when baled, such as an alfalfa/timothy or an alfalfa/orchard mix. These types of hays are beneficial for horses who need the lower sugar that alfalfa provides but not the additional calories.

Bales of alfalfa should be examined for blister beetles. These flying insects are typically found in alfalfa hay harvested in the west and usually in hay baled in late summer. First cuttings and sometimes the second cuttings will usually not contain the beetles, as they typically don't emerge until June. These insects contain the toxin cantharidin, which can kill a horse if eaten. The blister beetles feed on alfalfa blossoms and can be killed by the haying equipment, thus ending up in the bale.

There used to be many myths regarding feeding alfalfa: it made horses too hot, it was high in NSCs, it weakened hoof walls, and it caused kidney damage. These have all been proven again and again not to be true. The biggest problem from feeding alfalfa arises when feeding it to horses who are not in an exercise program and they develop obesity. It should also be avoided when the temperatures are high, as the protein metabolism creates more heat. This extra heat can impair the ability of the horse to dissipate heat, leading to heat stress, increased urination, and dehydration.

Grass hays contain less protein and energy than legumes but have more fiber. The protein averages between 8- 15%. It is less nutrient-dense than legumes, so your horse needs to consume more of it to feel full. Grass hays are an excellent choice for horses who are not expending much energy, retired horses, and easy keepers. Because it is less nutrient-dense, it can satisfy your horse's appetite and provide the necessary roughage without the excess protein and calories. Most of the nutritional needs of the adult horse can be met by feeding a good quality of grass hay.

Common grass hays include timothy, orchard, smooth bromegrass, Kentucky bluegrass, coastal Bermuda, and tifton. Grasses are harvested either in the warm climates, such as coastal or tifton (grown in southern states where winter temperatures are milder), or cool season grasses (including timothy or orchard) found in northern areas where summer temperatures are cooler.

Timothy is the most common grass hay grown in northern climates. It has an average nutritional protein content (7- 10%), is easily grown, and tends to remain dust- and mold-free. Look for hay cut in early to mid-bloom for the highest nutrition and palatability, and consider combining it with a legume to increase its nutritional value.

Orchard grass is also produced in many areas and is of good quality and average protein (9%). In the Midwestern states, bluegrass is another excellent source of roughage. Early-cut bluegrass can be as high as alfalfa in protein but is usually not harvested until it is mature, leaving a much lower protein level of about 8%.

Determining what type of hay to feed will depend a lot on where you live, the activity level of your horse, and its age and health. Good quality hay may cost more, but it will provide better results in the long run. In addition, horses are less likely to waste good hay. Inferior hay will not meet sufficient energy levels for an active or breeding horse and can cause illness, which can result in colic.

The barn owner/manager must be able to identify good hay. A good barn owner should have an established relationship with their feed store and be able to convey their needs to avoid wasting money. Good feed stores will have an established relationship with a hay supplier, which will provide quality and consistent hay, year round.

Many factors determine what makes agood quality hay. Drought, flooding, mineral deficiency in soil, and infertile soil will affect the quality. Hay should be cut before the plant matures and goes to seed. Before cutting, the moisture content of hay is generally about 25- 28%. With proper drying, this number will be reduced so that baled hay should have a moisture content of 12- 16%. Too much moisture, over 18%, will result in moldy hay, while hay with moisture over 25% is at risk of spontaneous combustion. Spontaneous combustion results from a build-up of mold and bacteria, due to the high moisture content. When hay is stacked, the heat increases, which can result in the hay bursting into flames. Hay with insufficient moisture will result in brittle stems, less nutritional values and will not be palatable. Properly harvested and cured hay retains most of its nutritional value, but cutting or baling in inclement weather or failure to properly dry hay will result in moldy hay. Hay should be free of trash, weeds, animal carcasses, and foreign objects. Dead animals can cause botulism, which can be fatal to horses.

Good quality hay will be low in moisture content and should be green in color. It should smell sweet, like the smell of a freshly mowed lawn. It will be free of dust, mold, dirt, and rocks. The stems should be fine, and there should be a high proportion of leaf to stems. Stems that are coarse, woody, and have more stems than leaves, are of poor quality, as is hay that is brown or yellow in color. If it is black or gray, that is an indication of mold. Hay should be cut before it reaches maturity, before the seed heads mature for grass hays, and legumes should be cut early in bloom.

Factors Affecting Quality of Hay:

- Type of hay

- Soil and growing conditions: Poor soil or drought will affect the quality

- Stage: Hay should be cut before the plants mature. Once hay reaches maturity, the hay becomes stemmy and coarse and has less nutritional value. It is also less palatable, so hay is wasted due to horses not eating it

- Harvesting: Hay that is properly cured will retain its nutritional value. Weather and improper handling can affect the quality

- Moisture Level: Baled hay should have a moisture content of 12- 16%. Hay that contains too much moisture will develop mold

- Storage: Heat, humidity, and sunlight can reduce the nutritional values

One should understand how hay cut and baled affects its quality. Depending on weather conditions, most farmers will cut hay two, three, and even four times a year. These are referred to as cuttings.

First-cut hay is harvested in late spring or early summer, having grown over winter and spring. The plant will be mature and, therefore, will have thicker stems and stalks, resulting in a higher fiber content. It will be much coarser than the second-cut hay. It will also contain more seed heads, especially in grass hays. Some horses will find this hay less palatable as it can be too tough or coarse. First-cut hay tends to be lower in protein and energy, so it is ideal for easy keepers. The high fiber content will provide the necessary roughage for a horse's diet.

Second-cut hay is harvested in late summer. It has had a shorter growing cycle and is cut before the seed head forms, so that the plants will be leafier, greener, and softer than the first cutting. It has a higher crude protein content but lower fiber and will be more palatable and nutritious. It usually just contains the leaves, with few stalks or flowers present. Horses with higher nutritional needs, such as broodmares, horses needing to gain weight, and competition horses, will benefit from second-cut hay.

Where climates are conducive to a longer growing season, harvesting hay a third and even a fourth time is possible. This hay will be even softer and leafier due to being cut when the growing season is slowing down. This means a higher leaf-to-stem ratio, which means higher protein levels and overall energy, making this cutting the richest cutting. Care should be used in feeding this hay to horses with metabolic disorders because it is too rich and caloric dense. Competition horses, as well as older horses, will benefit significantly from this hay.

Regions, growing conditions, the type of hay, and even the farm where it is harvested will affect the quality of cuttings, so it is possible for second-cut hay from a farmer in a different area to be less nutritious than first-cut hay from somewhere else.

Performing a hay analysis will give you a good understanding of the hay you are feeding. If you are concerned about the hay you purchase, have issues with a horse maintaining weight, or have a horse with a metabolic disorder, a hay analysis will help you determine if you are providing the right hay. The results of a hay analysis will provide you with insight into the levels of protein, minerals, fiber, starch, and sugar levels. Several labs will test your hay; fees average around $20- 30 per test. Your hay source can provide you with a good reference.

Reading a Hay Analysis

Deciphering a hay analysis can be daunting with all its abbreviations, but it can be easy to understand once you understand what to look for. There are six main items to look for in a hay analysis:

- Moisture Content

- Crude Protein (CP)

- Digestibility indices (ADF and NDF)

- Digestibility energy

- Calcium and Phosphorus

- Non-structured carbohydrates (NSCs)

The analysis will be broken into two columns, "As Sampled" and "Dry Matter." "As Sampled" will report the nutrients in their natural state, including water. "Dry Matter" is the result of the nutrients with the water removed. Using the Dry Matter column to figure out your results is best. As already mentioned, moisture content should be around 12- 16%. Hay under 10% will be brittle and dry, whereas hay over 16% can be moldy. Hay over 25% is at imminent risk of spontaneous combustion.

In addition to the moisture content of the hay sample, the analysis will measure the crude protein. The CP can range from 8- 14% for grass hays, 14- 17% in mixed hays, and 15- 20% in legume hays. Most adult horses require around 10- 12% of crude protein. Young horses, lactating broodmares, and horses in strenuous exercise will require a higher CP value. Legumes will have a higher CP than grass hays, and the plant's maturity will also affect the CP. This reading is also an indicator of amino acids in the hay.

Carbohydrates fall into two categories: structural carbohydrates (fibers) and non-structural carbohydrates (sugars, starch, fructans, etc.) The ADF and NDF will provide insight into how much fiber is in the hay. The more mature the plant, the higher the fiber it will contain.

- The Acid Detergent Fiber (ADF) content will be analyzed. ADF measures how digestible the nutrients in the hay are. ADF is comprised of cellulose, lignin, and other components that are poorly digested. The lower the value, the more digestible the nutrients, with ideal values between 30- 45%. Look for values under 45%, while anything above 45% will be of poor nutritional value and not palatable

- The Neutral Detergent Fiber (NDF) is a measure of insoluble fiber. Ideal ranges are between 45- 65%. NDF levels over 65% are not palatable. The higher the number, the less hay your horse will eat

For easy-keeper horses, ADF and NDF numbers should be on the higher end of the range, while growing horses, broodmares, and horses in hard work should have ADF and NDF values at the lower end of the range.

Relative Feed Value (RFV) should be 100, but this value is seldom used and is primarily for cattle nutrition.

Horse Digestible Energy (DE) should show values from 0.76- 1.1 Mcal per pound. Most horses need roughly 20 Mcal of DE daily, but the ideal number will vary depending on your horse's energy needs. Digestible energy is the amount of energy the horse digests and uses. This value is used to balance the energy requirements of your horse's diet.

Calcium (Ca) and Phosphorous (PP): Adult horses should have a Ca to P ratio between 3:1 and 1:1. The mineral content will vary between hay types.

Fat or Crude Fat measures the fat content. It is an energy-dense nutrient, roughly 2.25 times the energy found in carbohydrates. Hay and grasses will be low in fat.

The analysis will measure the different types of non-structural carbohydrates (NCS), including starch, water-soluble carbohydrates (WSC), and ethanol-soluble carbohydrates (ESC). ESC measures simple sugars, such as monosaccharides and disaccharides, while WSC measures simple sugars and fructans. Hay greater than 10- 12% NCS of dry matter is unsafe for horses with metabolic disorders and should be soaked before feeding. Starches will also be a low number. They are a good energy source, but care should be taken when feeding horses with EPSM, limiting the total daily calories from starch to no more than 15%. There is no ideal NSC number for all horses, and the analysis may not include NSC, but you can estimate it by adding the WSC and Starch together.

Remember that horses' nutrient requirements will vary as they age and their training increases. Health, activity level, age, and body condition are all factors that determine the nutrient requirements. A 4-year-old in training will require higher CP and DE values and lower ADF and NDF values, while a 15-year-old trail horse will require lower CP and DE values but higher ADF and NDF values. A horse with laminitis will require an NSC of less than 10- 12%, while a horse in perfect health and weight can have a higher NSC.

A hay analysis will provide useful information in determining the proper forage for your horse and providing a balanced diet. Hay should be selected based on your horse's needs.

Term	Definition	Typical Value
DM	Dry matter: water is removed	~85%
Moisture	Amount of water in hay	11- 16%
CP	Crude Protein in hay	8-20%
ADF	Acid Detergent Fiber (cellulose + lignin): a measure of fiber	30- 45%. Above 45% is of little nutritional value
PDF	Neutral Detergent Fiber (hemicellulose + cellulose): a measure of fiber	40- 65%. The higher the number, the less the horse will eat.
NSC	Non-Structural Carbohydrates: a measure of simple sugars and starch.	5- 25+%.
WSC	Water Soluble Carbohydrates: measures simple sugars and fructans	
ESC	Ethanol Soluble Carbohydrates: measures simple sugars	
C and P	Calcium and Phosphorous	Ratio between 3:1 and 1:1 for adult horses
DE	Digestible Energy: the amount of energy digested and used by horse	0.75- 1.0 Mcal/lb.

Most Common Types of Hay:

Grass Hay

Timothy

Brome

Orchard grass

Ryegrass

Prairie hay

Coastal Bermuda

Kentucky Bluegrass

Tifton

Legume Hay

Alfalfa

Clover

Lucerne

Perennial Peanut

Common Hay Myths

- Feeding alfalfa makes horses hyper

- Alfalfa is high in NSC's

- Alfalfa creates weak hoof walls

- Feeding alfalfa will cause kidney disease

- Horses can consume enough hay to satisfy their daily nutritional needs

Hay	Category	Nutrition Values	Notes
Timothy	Grass Hay	8- 10% It has low protein, high fiber, and high energy content.	Prefers cool, wet springs for growing. Requires water to grow.
Orchard	Grass Hay	10- 12% Higher in calories than Timothy. It contains the same balanced levels of calcium and phosphorous as Timothy.	Easy to grow, drought tolerant. Highly palatable and digestible. Soft for older horses to chew.
Coastal Bermuda	Grass Hay	5- 8% protein High in fiber	Horses must consume water if they eat coastal hay, as it loses moisture in the intestines, which can lead to impaction.
Kentucky Bluegrass	Grass Hay	10- 12%	It is not a good choice for hay, as its palatability declines as it matures. It is best for pasture grazing. It does not tolerate hot and dry conditions.
Brome	Grass Hay	8- 10% Low sugars	It is highly digestible with a good balance of minerals. Very palatable. Soft hay, suitable for senior horses
Alfalfa	Legume Hay	15- 20% protein. High in calories, fiber, and minerals. Low in sugar 3x calcium	Suitable for hard keepers, broodmares, and horses with ulcers. It can cause enteroliths. Feed in moderation.
Clover	Legume Hay	13- 16%	It is easily affected by a mold that causes slobbers.
Perennial Peanut	Legume Hay	14- 20% protein Higher in sugars and NSCs	Palatable and highly digestible.

Other Roughages

Another option for feeding fiber is to feed straight beet pulp, which is a by-product of the processing of sugar beets. It must be soaked before feeding, because it comes as dry pellets or shreds and presents a choking hazard to horses if fed dry. When feeding beet pulp, weigh the feed when dry, as it expands considerably once wet! Beet pulp is an excellent alternative for horses that suffer from heaves or allergies or are missing teeth. It makes a good mash and is an excellent source to promote water intake in summer and winter.

Other roughage alternatives include hay cubes and hay chaff. Chaff is dried forage and cut into small pieces. It is commonly bagged and is typically fed to senior horses who are missing teeth and may have difficulty chewing traditional hay. It may also be more readily available in places where hay is not, however, it is less nutritional and weighs less than cubes or regular hay. In addition, chaff may contain additives and sweeteners, such as molasses.

Hay cubes are made from coarsely chopped hay that is compressed into small hard squares or cubes and can include stems, leaves and seed heads. They are typically derived from alfalfa, Timothy, or both. Hay cubes must be soaked because is fed dry, they can present a choking hazard. They are an excellent source of nutrition for the senior horse, and because they are fed wet, they are an excellent source for water intake. Many barns will feed a mush of hay cubes for lunch: using cold water in the summer, and using warm water in the winter. This will aid in keeping horses hydrated, and if they are used to eating it daily, it can be fed with warm water in colder weather, when it is just as critical for horses to stay hydrated. Like chaff, hay cubes come bagged and, therefore, can be a good source of fiber when hay is hard to come by.

> In Florida, it is not uncommon in the winter to have 40, 50, and even 60-degree temperature drops in a 24-hour period. After having a Thoroughbred mare that was very sensitive to such temperature fluctuations, I learned the benefits of feeding a warm mash, because it warms the horse up from the inside, while a blanket will keep them warm on the outside. I provide a soaked hay cube mash every day of the year. I soak the cubes in the summer with cold water; I use warm water in winter. I may also add a small amount of flax seed and treats to make eating more inviting. It is an excellent source of keeping your horses hydrated as well.

Equines have a delicate digestive system because they are monogastric. Unlike ruminants, who have multi-chambered digestive systems that allow for the detoxification of toxins, horses' single stomachs make them more sensitive to toxins, which enter their gut and then their bloodstream.

Horses are also more sensitive to diet changes, sugars in forage, fiber content, and molds. Humans have caused most of these issues in the modern horse by feeding just one type of hay or limiting grazing to just one kind of grass, resulting in a gut that cannot tolerate a variety of feeds. Cushing's, Insulin Resistance (IR), and other metabolic disorders are at an all-time high (and feeding those sweet, sugary treats doesn't help!), with horses of all breeds and ages now being affected by what used to be considered an old horse problem.

By offering your horse a variety of hays and grasses, you will help create a stronger gut that will hopefully be able to better process small amounts of toxins. In contrast, a horse fed strictly one type of forage will be more likely to suffer side effects of a small amount of toxins. Horses should be able to graze a variety of grasses in their pastures, such as Bermuda and Bahia, and their hay menu should consist of a variety, such as Orchard, Alfalfa, and Timothy. Doing so will prevent any issues if you have difficulty getting any particular hay from your feed store or if the quality could be better.

Most boarding barns will offer horses 1-2 flakes of hay at predetermined times of day, usually breakfast, lunch, dinner, and maybe at bedtime. Barn managers are reluctant to offer more hay, despite it being healthier for the horse, due to costs. However, my personal experience is that once a horse knows he has a hay bag containing hay all the time, he will not devour it all at once. When a horse is given his breakfast hay, usually 8-12 hours after his last meal, his body has gone into starvation mode, and he will greedily gulp down his hay as if it is his last meal. By stuffing a hay bag full in the morning, there is a good chance you won't have to refill it until afternoon or even dinner time, because they will casually graze on it rather than eat it all at once. I have come to realize that I go through no more hay by making it constantly available and free choice than when I gave them each two flakes of hay at meal times. Making hay readily available at all times is a healthier option for horses so they are allowed to graze as nature intended them to.

WATER

Water is the most vital nutrient of all the nutrients a horse requires. While a horse can live for weeks without food, a horse will begin to suffer from the side effects of no water within 24 hours and will die within 4- 5 days.

Horses typically consume between 8 and 15 gallons of water a day. Water is what keeps all living creatures functioning. It is critical for digestion and thermoregulation as well as for supporting organs. Without water, a horse's organs will shut down, and death can occur. In other words, providing good, clean, and fresh water should be just as important as providing good quality hay and feed, yet somehow, it is sometimes overlooked. Barn managers will fret over what type of feed and hay to offer but do not think to check the water temperature or clean out the trough or buckets regularly.

Horses should always have access to clean and cool water. They prefer a temperature between 60- 68 degrees, even during cold weather. Water that is colder than that, especially in the winter, will decrease their intake.

It is imperative that the buckets be clean of algae and scum. Water should be available free-choice at all times and it should never be withheld. It does no good to the horse if the water is hot, frozen, or dirty.

If the water is not palatable to the horse, the results will be a decreased feed intake, inability to perform, dehydration, impaction colic, and death.

There can be factors that influence the amount of water consumed. Fresh pasture grass contains between 60- 80% of moisture and can be a source of water requirements while grazing. However, consuming hay and grain, which are very low in moisture content, will cause a horse to drink more water. In addition, adding sodium to grain or a diet high in protein will also increase the water intake. It is common to hear one complain about the additional urine in a stall due to a horse being fed an alfalfa hay diet.

Additionally, warmer temperatures will increase the volume intake, whereas colder temperatures will decrease their consumption. Adding a teaspoon of salt to their meals will increase water consumption in the winter.

Lactating broodmares will require more water, as much as 80% more per day, and performance horses should be allowed to drink as much water as they want while competing.

There are other factors which may affect the intake of water. Many horses are picky about the smell and taste of water. It is not uncommon for horses to not want to drink while away from home at a horse show or in a new barn. Horse owners can add Gatorade to their horse's water at home to get them used to the taste and continue this at horse shows. Some people will bring enough water from home to ensure the horse keeps drinking. In addition, providing soaked hay cubes will also help with water intake. Just make sure that the horse is already used to eating soaked cubes.

Horses should never be ridden for long periods, especially when the temperatures are high, without providing frequent water breaks. Heat exhaustion and dehydration will occur, both of which can cause death.

Water buckets, just like feed buckets, should be dumped daily and cleaned. Big barns with center aisles have a big problem doing this, because they want to avoid lugging buckets down the aisle way. This can be remedied by dumping the buckets out the back window or dumping the water into the wheelbarrow, manure spreader, or any other vessel easily maneuvered outside. Line up empty feed buckets outside the barn and then dump the buckets of water into the feed buckets for them to soak. Writing the horse's names on their buckets or putting numbers that correlate to stalls will ensure that the buckets are returned to the appropriate horse, or smaller barns can use different colored buckets for each stall. There are many creative ways to dump and clean buckets; the bottom line is that there is no excuse to have dirty buckets. Keeping a sponge or scrub brush handy will help guarantee that buckets are scrubbed regularly. In hotter climates, care should be taken that water is replenished often. A good manager will stick a finger in water buckets often! It is better to fill buckets halfway and dump them as needed throughout the day, and this is a good reason for providing two water buckets in every stall. If a barn manager is unwilling to dump and refill water numerous times throughout the day when the weather is hot, they should rethink why they are in the boarding business. For outdoors, it is better to use smaller troughs or even muck buckets to reduce wasting water, particularly in areas with water restrictions. Large troughs tend to be ignored and become hot and slimy because they are too much work to dump and refill. Running water for 10- 20 minutes to "clean" the trough is just a waste of water and the algae will form again by the end of the day. Place troughs in the shade; if that is not possible, be diligent in checking their temperature throughout the day.

Barn managers should ask themselves if they want to drink the same water that they expect their horses to drink. If the answer is no, the horse will most likely not drink it either.

Just as water needs tending to in hot weather, it is just as important to look after it in colder weather. Horses will not drink freezing water, so care must be taken to prevent ice accumulation on the buckets or troughs. Dumping troughs in snow is not as logical as dumping them during the summer, so it is best to provide smaller amounts of water again and constantly check the temperatures, adding warm water as needed.

By not providing free choice water to horses at all times, that is clean, fresh, and cool, the manager is risking the horse's health, whether from dehydration, organ failure, colic, or death. There is simply no excuse for slimy and hot water or water that is icy cold. It is nothing short of laziness. As a horse owner, inspecting water quality in a potential barn will indicate the quality of care. Inspect not only whether or not troughs are clean or full of scum but stick your finger in the water to determine the temperature.

Supplements

Feeding supplements to a horse is a hotly debated subject. Some feel that horses obtain all the minerals and vitamins they need in their feed, hay, and pasture grass, while there are those on the other side of the fence who feel that they should be giving their horse every supplement on the planet. They believe that if feeding one supplement is good, then feeding 5 or 6 will be even better. And then there are those in between, who will take into account the workload of their horse, the nutritional value of their grass and feed and hay, the age of the horse, and any health issues, and from there, make a rational decision.

Whether or not you feed supplements, one must agree that it does no good if it is not fed correctly or if it is never fed at all. Boarding barns should ensure supplements are fed to their boarder's horses, whether they agree or not. Horse owners should inspect their supplements to make sure that they are being fed. If providing more than one supplement, it is best to utilize a system such as SmartPak or create your own system, where the person making up feed does not have to scoop multiple supplements into feed buckets but instead adds supplements from just one source. This will help guarantee that your horse is receiving his supplements.

When choosing supplements, it is best to consult with your veterinarian. It can be easy to overdose on some minerals, such as Selenium or vitamins, and if feeding herbs, care should used when feeding to broodmares or when combining certain herbs with other supplements.

Salt and Electrolytes

Salt (sodium chloride) is an essential mineral for horses. Salt aids in the function of nerves and muscles and encourages horses to drink, preventing them from becoming dehydrated.

The average horse at rest on a cool day requires about 10 grams of sodium and 40 grams of chloride. Feeding 30 grams of salt daily, roughly two tablespoons, will meet the horse's maintenance requirements. Supplementing horses with salt is essential, since grain, hay, and grass contain very little sodium chloride.

As horses work harder and the temperatures increase, salt requirements will increase. Salt should be administered in accordance with sweat production. Feeding salt will replace that which is lost from sweating. Horses should be fed salt year-round, even in winter, to encourage horses to drink and stay hydrated.

Horses will benefit from having access to a salt lick; however, offering salt as a top dressing on their grain will ensure they are getting their daily requirement. Himalayan salt blocks also provide potassium, iron, and magnesium.

Feed regular, iodized table salt. The additional iodine will be helpful unless you feed any supplement containing kelp, which is already high in iodine.

Electrolytes, including potassium, calcium, and magnesium, will replace the minerals lost through sweating. These macro-minerals are essential to normal nerve and muscle function. It is vital to replenish these lost minerals, or your horse will be left with a nutritional imbalance.

Some horses may require both salt and electrolytes to meet their needs. Electrolytes contain salt but not enough to meet the daily sodium requirements.

Chapter 6
The Feed Room

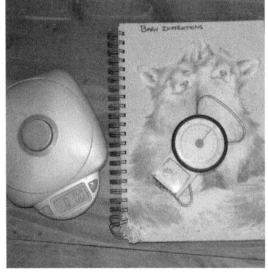

Storing Grain

It is crucial to have a dry and cool location to store your grain. Feed rooms should be enclosed, climate-controlled rooms with no access by loose horses, rodents, or other creatures. Grains should be stored in airtight containers, such as trash cans or bins designed especially for feed. Many barns order their feed in bulk, which is more economical but requires planning, shopping for price comparison, and ample storage. You will need to calculate how much feed you will require, by determining the amount of grain you use per week per horse and then project the total amounts required for the period of time you are ordering for, whether you order bi-weekly or monthly. Be sure to take horses coming and going into consideration. Unopened bags should be stored on pallets, up off the direct ground, and only order enough feed so that you avoid spoiling. Sweet feeds are especially prone to spoilage in hot, humid climates, so don't order more bags than you can safely use in a week.

Upon opening each bag, you should inspect the contents before you empty it into the feed container. Does it smell good? Are there any bugs in it? Is it free of mold? Occasionally, a bag may have come in contact with water at the feed store, and you only know that the feed is bad once you open it. Nothing is more aggravating than pouring a bag of moldy feed on top of fresh feed, so checking it before pouring on top of feed will save you a lot of aggravation. If you open a bag of defective feed, set it off to the side and notify your feed store for a refund. Usually, they will want to see the bag, so wait to throw the feed away until you have asked.

Feed rooms should be kept clean and free of bugs and rodents. A feed room should not be a place to be afraid to venture into! If there are rodents, they will chew open the feed bags. Roaches will leave droppings in the feed. It is critical to prevent infestations for health reasons (for both humans and horses). Employ a barn cat or a terrier to remove the rodents or welcome the rat snake into your barn, for they will keep rodent populations under control. Poison should never be used due to the harm it will cause an unsuspecting owl, hawk, or cat that eats the carcass of a dead rodent. There are several good rat traps on the market as well.

A well-kept feed room will require good lighting, a workspace, and a storage room. Since feed should be fed by weight, not volume, a kitchen scale should be available, and a fish scale can be used to weigh flakes of hay. Scoops for measuring out the feed are essential as well. Supplements will need a place to be stored, whether on shelves or in a cabinet, and they should be labeled by each horse's name with instructions. Feed instructions should be posted and kept current. A dry-erase board or chalkboard is handy for a feed chart. Feed instructions should also be written down in a BARN BOOK. Label the feed chart with the horses' names, stall locations, types and quantities of grain and hay they get, and supplements. If feed can be stored in individual feed buckets without the risk of bugs or rodents invading, many barns will make up the next meal, stacking them in order of feeding. Doing so eliminates hungry horses from banging on their stalls and making a commotion as you try to hurry and prepare multiple buckets of feed. Other barns may utilize feed carts on wheels, which streamline the feeding process in large barns. Feed bags can be emptied directly into the compartments, and the cart is wheeled along the barn aisle, scooping feed up in front of each stall and depositing it in the awaiting horse's feed bucket. This type of feeding setup works well in barns with many horses, where there will be little feed left over. Any leftover feed should be stored in the feed room and covered to avoid attracting flies.

Hay Storage

Hay should also be stored in a cool, dry environment, ideally in an area separate from the main barn. Unfortunately, many farms do not have the space for a separate hay barn and have to store the hay either in the feed room along with the grain or in an empty stall.

Just like grain, hay needs to be stored up off the floor on pallets to encourage air circulation and to prevent hay from coming in contact with water. The storage area should be well-ventilated and provide easy access to the hay truck for delivery. Use the old hay first before starting on a new bale of hay. There are two reasons for this. First, most obviously, is the desire to use the older hay before it can spoil. Second and more important, hay is combustible, which is why it is preferable to store the hay away from horses. Freshly baled hay can be warm down inside the bales, but if the temperature reaches 120 degrees, there is a risk for spontaneous combustion. Therefore, never store fresh, green hay next to older, dryer hay.

Barns in dry and cool climates have the luxury of ordering enough hay to last a season, especially when snow is a problem and enough hay is ordered to last throughout the winter. An experienced barn manager can calculate the number of bales required to last them through the winter. In hot and humid climates, storing large quantities of hay is not possible, because the hay will go moldy before it is all used up unless the storage area is climate-controlled.

For your hay storage area, hay hooks and gloves will help to move the bales around easily. Scissors or wire cutters are necessary to open the bales. Utilizing a wheelbarrow or some type of cart to move the hay down the aisle for dispersal is essential in large barns. In addition, a fish scale within easy reach allows for the hay to be weighed. To weigh the hay, tie a few flakes with hay string and attach them to the scale's hook.

Feed and hay are some of the most significant barn expenses, so how can you save money?

If you live in the north, where humidity is relatively low, or you have an air-conditioned hay room, it is possible to purchase large quantities of hay at a discounted rate, either directly from the grower or from your hay supplier. Search local social media pages for persons who have returned from a hay-buying trip and are offering to sell off some of their bounty at a discounted rate. You may be able to go in with a group of friends to purchase a trailer load of hay, or if you are traveling out of state and have room in your truck or trailer, purchase hay if it is cheaper than what you would typically pay in your area. If you have your hay delivered, the more hay you can purchase can reduce the number of deliveries to your farm and save you in delivery fees. Just be careful not to order more hay than you can use up before it becomes dry or moldy.

Some feed stores will offer bulk discounts on bags of feed. This is beneficial if you have enough horses to go through the bags fast enough, but keep in mind that bags of grain should not be sitting longer than 5 or 6 weeks. Feed stored in air conditioning will also last longer, especially if it is textured or a sweet feed.

Feeding cheap or inferior quality hay is just an expensive vet bill waiting to happen. Horses will waste the hay if it is not palatable, and if it is moldy or contains toxic weeds such as foxtail, they can become sick. Cheap feed will cost you more, because you will have to feed twice as much as a decent feed and your horse will not perform at its best. Skimping on quality hay and grain is not where expenses should be cut.

Prospective boarders should:

- Ask to see the hay and feed rooms. Are they well stocked, or are there just one or two bags of feed or bales of hay? If there are just a few bags or bales, they could be waiting for delivery, but it can also be a red flag. Look at the quality of the hay

- Ask who the hay supplier is. Is it a reputable dealer?

- Look to see if the feed is stored correctly. Is the feed room clean and tidy? Are there signs of roaches and rat droppings?

- Inspect the grain and hay for freshness and quality

- Ask about the type of grain being fed. If there is only one feed brand, ask why they feed just one type. Good barns should offer a variety of grains based on each horse's individual needs

- Ask about feeding supplements. Many barns require supplements to be bagged and labeled if they are not in a SmartPak. Do they charge extra for feeding supplements?

- Try to schedule a visit after feeding time. Look at the quality and quantity of hay being fed. Are they given a small flake or generous portions?

- Ask how often the horses are fed and at what time. It is a red flag if a horse goes for many hours without feed. Great barns feed three meals daily and never let their horses go more than 6 hours between feedings

- Is there hay in front of the horses at all times while stalled? Great barns will also ensure that horses have enough hay to last throughout the night

- Look at the water buckets and troughs. Are they filled with clean and cool water? Dirty buckets and slimy troughs are a red flag

- Can you request a different type of grain or hay?

- A locked hay or feed room the manager doesn't want to show you is cause for concern

    When one of my daughters took her horse to college with her, the barn owner at one barn where she boarded her horse kept the feed pre-packaged and in baggies. Her reason was that her mother fed sometimes, and it was easier for her to dump the baggies. On our first visit, the feed room contained good-quality feed. However, after about a month, our Thoroughbred began to lose weight. My daughter commented several times that she had found him eating cheap coastal hay, not the good quality hay we were paying for. She did what most of us would: went into the feed room and gave him the correct hay. Then, she discovered that the grain our horse was supposed to eat was nowhere in the feed room. There was a very high-end feed, which the barn owner fed to her horses, and then just bags of All Stock, the cheapest grain you can feed your horse. Despite horses having vastly different nutritional needs than goats or cows, there are some who will feed this to horses. When asked about the grain and hay, the barn owner made excuses, and soon after, the feed room was kept locked. Needless to say, our horse came back home.

As a prospective boarder, ask as many questions about feed as possible. A good feeding program will help keep your horse healthy and the vet away. Take the time to study the basics of feed and nutrition and be informed about feeding your horse.

A very high-end barn claimed to feed only good quality hay. However, an employee spilled the beans to me that there was a secret hay room where the cheap coastal hay was kept. After the boarders left for the evening, the good hay was scooped out of their stalls (she timed the feedings so that they would start haying as the last of the boarders were finishing up and leaving at the designated cut-off time for barn hours) and was replaced with the cheaper quality hay. Eventually, this employee, who had a long list of horror stories in her short time there, left, and she informed boarders of what was happening. This same barn would not allow more than ½ of a wheelbarrow load of manure and urine to be removed from each stall daily. On the first day working there, she was chastised for removing a full wheelbarrow load from a stall and instructed to dump half of it back into the stall.

Chapter 7
The Horses Health

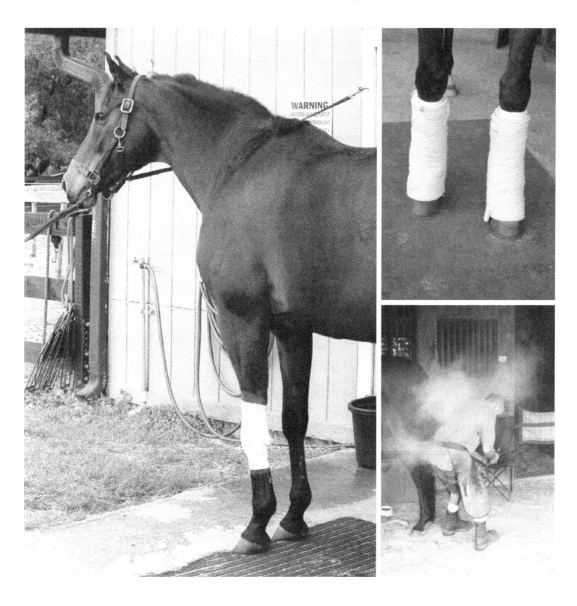

Part of running a barn is being able to identify when a horse is in crisis, whether from ingesting a toxic weed or having an episode of Colic, foundering, or tying up.

Remember that each horse is different and may react to pain in different manners, so it is good to know each horse thoroughly. Get to know their normal behavior and the parameters of their vital signs. All horses should have their vitals taken soon after arriving, and their normal vitals should be recorded in their health records. If they are suspected of being sick, comparing their current vitals with their normal numbers will help determine if there is a problem.

All barn and horse owners should be on good terms with a veterinarian. Vets should be used for routine visits, such as vaccines, not just for emergencies. Having a professional relationship with your vet will mean that when you do have an emergency, your vet will respond as soon as possible because you are considered an established patient. Horses should be ready for your vet, not turned out in the pasture or in a lesson. There should be a good working area for your vet to treat your horse, with good lighting, and it should be safe. Communicate to your vet any safety concerns you might have with any particular horse, such as a fear of men or needles. Is the owner capable of holding their horse for the vet, or will you or one of your employees be needed for the task? Who will transport the horse if there is an emergency and it needs to be trailered to a vet clinic? And suppose a horse needs long-term vet care. In that case, the barn owner, horse owner, and vet must communicate thoroughly on what precise treatment the horse needs and be able to come up with a plan for treating the horse, including medicating, stall rest, hand walking, and rehabbing. If rehabbing or medicating is something that you or its owner are not capable or comfortable doing, then the horse owner should consider sending the horse to a rehab facility. If the horse is to stay, what fees will the barn owner charge to cover time and labor for medicating, providing lay-up and rehabbing the horse?

If a horse owner refuses to contact a veterinarian to treat their sick or injured horse, the barn owner needs to double down and explain to the owner why the horse needs to see a vet. This is a good reason to include a vet care clause in your boarding contract. Having such a boarder in your barn is a liability, and your reputation can be stained as a result.

Owners are responsible for ensuring that their horses are in good health and treated as necessary for routine vaccines and when they are lame, sick, or injured.

My daughter's Thoroughbred mare was extremely stoic. She was having a bad colic episode but exhibited none of the signs that one would typically attribute to Colic. She stood with her head in the far corner and she would occasionally paw the ground, but not violently. After observing her for a few minutes, I knew she was in distress and called our vet. On the other hand, my Thoroughbred gelding is quite the baby and will be hollering his head off if he doesn't feel good. After having some baby teeth extracted and the pain meds wore off, one would have thought he was about to die from all the noise he was making at us.

Know the signs of good health:

- A healthy appetite and normal water intake

- Will be bright and alert. The eyes should be clear, and the ears should be constantly listening for sounds

- Their coat will be shiny and smooth

- Nostrils are free of any discharge

- They should move without any lameness. There should be no swelling in their joints or limbs

- Hooves should be balanced, well-shaped, and in good condition, showing evident care from a farrier

- Teeth should show signs of good dental work, and gums will be pink and moist. There should be no discharge from the nostrils

- Manure should be moist but not messy with cow patties or diarrhea, and urine should be pale in color and clear

A good barn manager and a good horse owner will know the vital signs in general. A great barn manager and a great horse owner will know each individual horse's resting vital signs!

- Normal Temperature: 99.5º F - 101.5º F

- Pulse: 30- 40 beats per minute

- Respiration: 8- 15 breaths per minute

- Dehydration: less than 1-second pinch test

- CRT (Capillary Refill Time): 1- 2 seconds of pressing gums

- Mucous Membranes: moist, pale pink

In addition, one should know how to take vitals! Quick read thermometers are best for taking temperatures. The thermometer should be lubricated and is inserted into the rectum. Thermometers should always be held to prevent them from being sucked into the rectum and many times, they will contain a string, which is clipped to the tail with a clothes pin, in case such an accident happens.

The pulse is taken by listening to the horse's heart rate with a stethoscope, placed behind the left elbow in the girth area. You can listen for 15 seconds and multiply the beats by 4 to get the beats per minute. A rapid pulse can indicate pain or cardiovascular issues and requires a call to your vet. It should be noted that the horse's heart has two sounds, such as a dub-dub sound, and should not be counted as separate heartbeats!

To obtain the respiration rate, watch and count how many times the flanks rise and fall. Just like taking the pulse, observe for 15 seconds and multiply by 4 to get your results. An increased respiration indicates pain or illness.

The gums should be wet and pink. Pale gums are a sign of blood loss. If they are tacky to the touch, it could indicate dehydration and dark red or purple indicate shock and is very serious. Press the gums to perform a capillary refill time. The length of time for the gums to refill to normal color indicates the CRT, which should be about 2 seconds.

To check for dehydration, pinch a fold of skin along the neck. If the horse is hydrated, the skin will immediately release. The longer it takes to return to its shape is an indication of dehydration.

Anytime a horse is not acting normally, the owner should be notified. Emergencies require a call to the vet immediately. Due to a shortage of equine vets, the barn manager or owner must know what constitutes an emergency. Some situations will need immediate vet care, such as colic or choke. Other times, while a call to the vet is necessary, the vet may wait a day or two before scheduling an appointment. Emergencies include:

- Colic: keep in mind that Colic is NOT a disease in itself but rather a symptom that something is not right. It can be gas, a reaction to eating a toxic plant, overeating grain, or a twisted intestine

- Eye injuries

- Deep cuts, profuse or uncontrollable bleeding

- Severe lameness

- Unable to move

- Labored breathing

- High temperature

- Choking

- Collapse

- Snake bite

- Impact accident

- Shock

- Puncture wound to hoof

- Fractures

- Tendon injuries

- Foreign objects protruding from the body (do not remove!)

- Mares in active labor for more than 20 minutes without progress

- Burns or smoke inhalation

- Multiple horses are sick at the same time

- Profuse diarrhea

- Suddenly aggressive or unusual behavior

- Neurologic signs

- An open wound at a joint

- A wound exuding clear, sticky fluid

It is up to the barn manager to be able to identify the signs of each condition so that the horse is not left suffering and in pain. Eye injuries can quickly deteriorate and become a significant problem requiring medications around the clock or, worse, enucleation (removal of the eye), so it is vital to begin treatment immediately. Colic cases can escalate from mild to very serious in a short amount of time, and medical attention should never be put off.

> *I boarded at a barn where the owner required each owner to provide a vial of Banamine in case of Colic. I was very dismayed to find out a week after the fact that my horse had coliced and the barn manager had given my horse an injection. I was never notified nor gave permission and was very upset that I had come out the day after and ridden my horse on a long trail ride. I would never have ridden him if I had known he had coliced the day before. Not only that, but the vet was never notified. Barn owners and managers should always contact the owner before making decisions regarding a sick horse!*

Horses that stop eating, are lame, have skin irritations, diarrhea, difficulty chewing, loss of weight, or a sudden change in attitude require vet attention. While these may not be considered emergencies requiring immediate attention, a vet should be notified. Again, knowing each horse will help determine what needs immediate vet care or what can be put off until regular vet hours resume.

It is vital for the mental and physical health of the horse that they be allowed to act like a horse! Their turnout time should be longer than their time spent in a stall- the longer the turnout, the less likely they are to develop ulcers or vices, such as weaving or cribbing, and are less likely to injure themselves.

Horses are herd animals, and as such, they prefer the company of other horses, or if that is not feasible, donkeys, mules, and even goats can provide companionship to a horse. Sadly, some horse owners believe that a horse should be kept stalled to prevent injuries, and when they are allowed turnout, it is in a small turnout area. Thankfully, more and more horse owners are dispelling this myth and allowing their horses, even those of Olympic caliber, to be horses. Horses will be less likely to run around and injure themselves if they regularly get plenty of quality turnout time, and they will be less stressed and be happier. Barn managers and horse owners will always take into account the emotional well-being of their horse.

First Aid Kits

Barns should have a first aid kit, and barn managers should know the basics of first aid, including how to clean a wound, wrap a leg, give medicines by mouth and injection, and change bandages. There should also be a first aid kit in the horse trailer.

A first aid kit should contain, at the minimum:

- Thermometer

- Scissors (regular and bandage)

- Assortment of bandages

- Assortment of sterile, non-stick gauze dressings

- Self-adhesive bandages such as Vet Wrap

- Poultice

- Syringes and needles of assorted sizes

- Banamine paste and/or injectable

- Bute powder

- Stethoscope

- Antibiotic spray or wound dressing

- Antiseptic ointment

- Antiseptic cleansing liquid, such as Betadine

- Triple antibiotic eye ointment

- Linament

- Adhesive tape

- Pressure pads (sanitary napkins work well)

- Sterile saline solution for cleaning wounds (if none is available, 1 teaspoon of table salt added to 1 pint of boiled and cooled water is an adequate alternative)

- Rubbing alcohol

- Four leg bandages and quilted leg wraps

- Diapers for hoof abscesses

- Tools for removing horse shoes

- KY jelly

- Duct tape

- Knife

- Sponges

- Towels

- Latex gloves

- Twitch

- Headlamp or flashlight

- Human first aid kit

A good first aid kit will also be stocked with certain medications your vet has prescribed. While most barn managers should be well versed in administering drugs such as Bute (Phenylbutazone) or Banamine, they should only administer a drug to a boarder's horse after first speaking with a vet and getting consent from the owner. Though rare, reactions can and do occur. Be sure to check expiration dates and make sure you have complete instructions for using the drug.

Avoid the following circumstances when dealing with illness or injuries:

- Do not administer Bute before discussing the issue with your vet, as it can mask vital signs. Most vets will ask you to wait until after they have examined the horse, or if that is not possible, take the horse's vitals *before* administering.

- Bute and Banamine can be dangerous when administered in the muscle.

- Do not wait when dealing with colic. It can become fatal very quickly.

- Wounds that involve joints, tendon sheaths, the chest, or the abdomen should also be treated immediately.

- Sick foals and donkeys can go downhill very quickly, so never put off a call to the vet if you suspect them of being sick.

  I arrived at our boarding barn, and one of our horses was in the barn, frantically pacing in her stall while all the other horses were out. When I inquired what the reason was, I was informed that the barn manager had given an injection to a horse in the adjacent paddock to my mare, and the horse had a reaction and dropped dead, which resulted in my horse panicking at the sight of her deceased neighbor. This exemplifies why certain drugs should only be administered by a vet, and all horse owners should consent before treatment.

Common prescribed drugs include:

- Tranquilizers such as Acepromazine, Dormosedan, and Rompun.

- Pain-relieving drugs such as Banamine (Flunixan Meglumine)

- NSAIDS such as Phenylbutazone/"Bute"

- Corticosteroids such as Dexamethazone

- Antibiotics

Items in your first aid kit should be labeled, well organized, and in an accessible location. In an emergency, it does no good if you have to search for your kit. Keep a Vet Book with your kit in case your clear thinking gives rise to panic. You can even copy and paste vital information from a book onto your kit or cabinet door, such as vitals, emergency numbers, and other first aid notes.

Health Care Records

As a barn or horse owner, keeping health care records on every horse will make your life easier. You need to include immunizations, the date of Coggins tests, deworming and fecal counts, dentals, and any other visits the vet has made for each horse. You should also include each horse's base vitals.

If you are running a barn, you must decide how to mandate horse care. Many barns will stipulate in a contract the minimum vet and farrier care that an owner is to provide, and failing to provide such care will automatically default to the barn owner/manager at the cost of the horse owner. Even if you want to avoid having a boarding contract, it will save you a headache if you have conveyed to the horse owner what is expected of them regarding horse care. Nobody wants to see a sick horse or one that has gone months between trims because the owner doesn't know any better. Barn owners should require proof of updated vaccines and a recent negative Coggins test before any horse moves into the barn. This will protect the horses already there against any illness the new horse may have. It is also not uncommon for a barn owner/manager to ask who the current vet is for a potential new boarder and to contact the vet to ensure they have a good relationship with the horse in question. Whether or not you require a boarder to use your vet or their own is up to the barn manager or owner to decide. It is not uncommon for a barn to require a particular vet and to require all horses to be vaccinated when everyone else is due. Doing so ensures that the vet has a working relationship with every horse in the barn and that all horses are on the same vaccination schedule.

Horse owners should also have a good relationship with their veterinarian, even if your barn manager is the one scheduling routine appointments. Don't abuse your relationship by calling at all hours for non-emergencies. Right before the holidays or vacation is not the time to start a new feed, change their schedule, or vaccinate. By having a good relationship with your vet, your vet will be readily available for emergencies. Keep a health record book so you are aware of what is due and when and if you are boarding your horse, you will be able to provide a health history to your barn manager.

Horses should be vaccinated for a variety of diseases. The most common immunizations include vaccines for Encephalomyelitis, including Eastern, Western, and Venezuelan types (EEE, WEE, and VEE), Equine Herpesvirus (EHV), Influenza, Strangles, Tetanus, Rabies, and depending on what part of the country you live in, West Nile Virus and Potomac Horse Fever. Horses are required by law to be tested for Equine Infectious Anemia (EIA), which is referred to as a Coggins Test. Negative Coggins tests are required by all boarding facilities, horse shows, and any place horses are gathered.

Vaccine	Symptoms	Frequency of Vax	Notes
Equine En-cephalomyelitis: Eastern (EEE), Western (WEE) and Venezuelan (VEE) High fever over 103° F	High fever over 103° F Dullness Lack of appetite Walking in circles Pressing head into the wall Blindness Staggering Seizures	1-2 times a year, boosters may be necessary due to location and incidents of outbreaks	Mosquito-borne illness. It causes inflammation of the brain. Most common in the southeastern U.S. High mortality rate. Highly contagious.
Equine Herpes-virus (EHV). Also known as Rhinopneumo-nitis EHV1 is respiratory but can become neurological (EHM); EHV4 is respiratory and is associated with sporadic abortions	High fever above 106° F Nasal discharge, which becomes thick Coughing Depression Enlargement of lymph nodes under the jaw Abortion in mares	Vaccinate every 6 months: competing horses may need to be vaccinated every 3 months.	Horses that travel and compete should be vaccinated. EHM type is usually fatal and highly infectious. Symptoms begin within 1-6 days of exposure. Spread by horse-to-horse contact through nasal secretions and through contact with contaminated clothing, equipment, etc. Strict quarantine measures must be taken. None of the EHV vaccines prevent EHM.
Influenza	High fever Coughing Lethargic Loss of appetite Lymph nodes enlarged under the jaw Nasal discharge	Twice a year. Horses cannot compete without having been vaccinated within 6 months.	Treat with NSAIDS, isolation, and supportive care. Contagious.

Potomac Horse Fever (PHF)	High fever Depression Loss of appetite Diarrhea	Annual. Horses traveling to areas with outbreaks should be vaccinated.	A bacterial infection from eating dead mayflies and other insects. More common in northern states. Not contagious
Rabies	Ataxia Weakness Aggression Self-mutilation Sensitivity to touch Circling Fever	Annual	Rapidly progressive neurological disease caused by a virus. 100% fatal and highly contagious to humans.
Strangles	Fever Nasal discharge Abscess of lymph nodes Difficulty swallowing Difficulty breathing Cough Loss of appetite	Yearly. Competing horses may require boosters.	Respiratory infection caused by bacteria. Highly contagious.
Tetanus	Sporadic tremors The third eyelid does not retract Convulsions Difficulty walking Stiffness: "saw horse stance"	Two dose series 4-6 weeks apart, and then annually	Caused by bacteria in the soil. Usually fatal.
West Nile Virus	Weakness Stumbling Tremors Lack of awareness	Annual. May need boosters if outbreak occurs.	Mosquito borne virus. It is more common in the southern parts of the U.S. Can be fatal

Your veterinarian will know best which diseases are at risk for your location and when to vaccinate or booster accordingly. Unfortunately, most vaccines today are bundled into 3- 5, or even 7-way vaccines. It is not uncommon for horses to react to vaccines. Finding anything less than a 3-way is more challenging, so you may prefer to schedule vaccines over several weeks to minimize reactions. In addition, giving Bute may help lessen any discomfort caused by the vaccines.

DeWorming and Parasites

Horses, ponies, donkeys, and mules all get internal parasites. Unfortunately, the overuse of wormers, particularly daily dewormers, has meant that there is an increase in parasite resistance, and it is getting harder to treat for parasites as a result. Until recently, barns would deworm on a rotation schedule, alternating between a benzimidazole, a pyrantel, and an ivermectin every two months. The new way of thinking is for your vet to perform a fecal count of a manure sample from each horse and deworm accordingly. Known as a targeted deworming strategy, this method will aid in combating the parasite resistance to dewormers. It is negligent to go to the tack or feed store and buy a tube of dewormer, or worse, a daily dewormer, without knowing precisely what you are deworming for.

Horses not dewormed regularly will look unhealthy. They will exhibit a dry coat, loss of weight, and listlessness. Worms damage the blood vessels, heart, intestines, and lungs. A high number of colic cases are related to parasite damage, especially by large strongyles. Internal parasites can also result in anemia, lethargy, diarrhea, and even death.

The object of parasite control is not to eliminate the parasites entirely but to maintain the parasite burden at a low level. This helps the horse to maintain a partial immunity to overwhelming infection. The ultimate goal of deworming is to minimize the risk of parasitic infestation, control parasite egg shedding, maintain effective drug control, and avoid further resistance to dewormers. By utilizing fecal egg count tests, you can determine precisely how infested each horse is. By testing horses in a large boarding facility, you will have an indication of the parasite levels within the groups of horses if they are pastured together.

The life cycle of parasites is relatively simple. Eggs can lie dormant for years in a pasture until favorable environmental conditions exist, and then eggs hatch into the first stage (L1) as larvae. These grow and molt into the second stage (L2) and progress to the third stage (L3). Even if ingested, horses cannot be infected at the egg, L1, and L2 stages. Infestation occurs when L3 is ingested, burrowing into the gut wall's mucosal lining and molting into stage 4 (L4). If the larvae are not ingested within a couple of days, they will die. To prevent death, they will migrate up blades of grass where they will most likely be eaten. In wet conditions, this is more favorable, whereas in dry conditions, they will most likely die before being able to migrate in the grass. Once ingested, L4 will finish its development in the gut as well as in the liver, heart, lungs, arteries, and intestines, depending on the type of larvae. The larvae will return to the gut, become adults, and lay eggs, passing through the horse and out to the pasture to repeat the cycle.

A fecal egg count will establish the number of parasite eggs present in each gram of manure (EPG). EPG values of 200-500 would indicate treatment for the parasites presenting, while an EPG value of 100-300 is considered normal, and no treatment should be required, or it may not be needed as often as horses with higher EPG values. Testing will also provide insight into whether or not a horse or a herd is developing resistance, in which case your veterinarian will discuss the next step for treatment.

The most common parasites infecting horses are ascarids, strongyles, tapeworms, and bots. Different wormers treat different parasites, which is why the best method to manage internal parasites is via fecal egg count.

Other worms affecting horses include:

- Large redworm

- Small redworm

- Roundworm

- Pinworm

- Threadworm

- Lungworm

Performing fecal egg counts is relatively simple: all that is needed is fresh manure gathered in a plastic baggie. The manure ball should be collected about three months after the most recent deworming, as this will indicate the shedding rate of parasites. Horses with low EPG numbers need to be dewormed no more than twice a year, usually at the beginning of the grazing season and after the last frost, such as during April, and again at the end of the grazing season, in the fall, before the first frost. Moderate "shedders" will probably benefit from a 3rd treatment during the main seasons of pasture transmission (spring through autumn in the North and autumn through spring in the South), and all high shedders should be treated intensively throughout the main seasons of transmission (3-4 times per year.) The goal is to prevent high shedders from contaminating the environment: therefore, manure must be removed from pastures and not spread over them.

Foals are the exception to using egg counting, and they should receive 3- 4 deworming treatments by the time they turn one. Treat at two months with fenbendazole or oxibendazole and repeat at 4- 5 months. A fecal count should be done at this time to track the occurrence of ascarids versus strongyles. Treat at five months with ivermectin, and before the horse turns one, treat with ivermectin plus praziquantel. Yearlings should be treated for strongyles three times with ivermectin followed by a course with moxidectin plus praziquantel. Egg counts should be done as a yearling to check for the presence of ascarids and should be treated with fenbendazole or oxibendazole if needed. Always consult your vet before deworming any foal.

Typical Adult Horse DeWorming Schedule

Low Shedder (<200 EPG of manure)

- Spring (March- April): ivermectin or moxidectin

- Fall((Sept.- Oct): ivermectin w/ praziquantel or moxidectin w/ praziquantel

Moderate Shedder (200- 500 EPG

- Spring (March- April): ivermectin or moxidectin

- Late summer(July): ivermectin

- Fall (Sept.- Oct): ivermectin w/ praziquantel or moxidectin w/ praziquantel

High Shedder (>500 EPG)

- Spring (March- April): ivermectin

- Early summer(June): ivermectin

- Early fall (Sept): ivermectin w/ praziquantel

- Late fall (Nov): moxidectin

In the end, a fecal count is far cheaper than buying random tubes of dewormer every eight weeks and hoping it works. There are labs that you can mail your sample to for an analysis; however, most vets perform the test. It costs about $20- 25 per test.

While parasites are present in all soil, there are ways to help prevent over-infestation of parasites. These include:

- Avoid keeping too many horses on small acreage

- Avoid overgrazing

- Rotate pastures

- Pick up manure from paddocks and pastures regularly

- If you spread manure in your fields, keep horses off those fields for several weeks

- Do not spread manure if you have high shedders

- Keep hay, feed, and water from becoming contaminated with manure

- Horse parasites do not infest sheep or cattle, so grazing these animals and rotating pastures with them will destroy their life cycle

- Drag or harrow pastures to break up the droppings. Sunlight will kill the eggs, especially in extreme heat. If the weather is not hot enough, remove horses from that pasture for the rest of the growing season, so the parasites are exposed long enough to the elements in order to die.

- Compost manure before spreading on pastures. Both ascarid and small strongyle eggs are eliminated through composting

- Treat for tapeworms once a year with a praziquantel classification

- Treat for encysted small strongyles in the fall or near the end of the grazing season before going into winter. Use a moxidectin

- Rotate fields with broodmares and foals to reduce the buildup of ascarid eggs, which will infect new foals in the spring. Foals should never be turned out on fields where known high shedders have been grazing

- Do not feed directly on the ground

- Mow pastures regularly and keep the height between 4-8 inches tall. Mow again at the end of the grazing season to reduce the chances of parasites surviving the winter. Parasites can survive in fecal balls, insulated from the cold

- Foal manure should never be spread in pastures

Dewormer Classifications

Drug Class	Parasites Targeted
Benzimidazoles (fenbendazole, oxibendazole)	Large strongyles, small strongyles (not encysted), ascarids, and pinworms
Macrocyclic lactones (ivermectin/moxidectin)	Large strongyles, small strongyles (including encysted- moxidectin only) ascarids, bots, and pinworms
Pyrimidines (pyrantel)	Large and small strongyles, ascarids, tapeworms (must double dose) and pinworms

Anthelmintics work by targeting specific internal parasites and preventing them from obtaining nutrients. The parasites starve to death and are expelled from the horse's body.

As a barn owner/manager, it is imperative that all horses be tested regularly and treated accordingly. Preventative measures should be taken to reduce infestation. Horse owners should be wary of any barn that requires a daily dewormer, as these do not work and are a waste of money. Good barns and horse owners will take the necessary steps to stop over-treating horses which contribute to parasite resistance through unnecessary deworming.

Injuries

We have all seen the cartoon of a horse wrapped in bubble wrap. As horse owners, we have all felt like wrapping our horses in bubble wrap at one time or another, because it seems it's just a matter of time before they injure themselves. We've all probably seen a horse hurt itself in an almost sterile condition. In contrast, other horses can navigate the most run-down of barns, with broken boards, protruding nails, barbed wire, and other dangerous conditions, and never suffer a tiny scratch. Some will even argue that the risk of injury increases with the horse's value!

I have seen a horse suffer a deep cut to an artery, who was turned out by herself, and with the blood trail beginning in the middle of a field, nowhere near a fence or any potential offender. I have also seen more cases than I can count where a horse suffered an eye injury in a stall, and it was impossible to locate a cause. One horse I owned managed to rip open his eye in the time it took me to carry my tack to the tack room and walk back to his stall, and I never could find the culprit. Good staff will inspect every horse multiple times a day- first thing in the morning, when they come in from turnout, at meals, after rides, and at the bedtime check. I have seen horses who stood bleeding in their stalls because management did not look them over when leading them back into their stall from turnout. The owner showed up hours later and wanted to know why their horse was standing in a stall with dried blood on them. A horse coming in from outside should be inspected all over, and a great manager will look at each horse every time they pass by them, even if just a cursory glance, to judge their attitude and general well-being. Horses can injure themselves in padded stalls and, in an instance. This is just the nature of domestic horses and why horses should be checked often!

Some horses constantly have some sort of injury, and it is the barn manager's duty to know how to handle such emergencies. Bleeding that won't stop requires a vet ASAP, as do lacerations with exposed bone, muscle, or tendons.

Injuries can be categorized as either open or closed wounds. Closed wounds include bruises, contusions, sprains, tendon strains, muscle tears, and fractures. Open wounds include abrasions, punctures, incised, lacerations, tears, and fractures. Treatment should be started immediately, because prolonging treatment can result in infection, the granulation of tissue, referred to as proud flesh, and a longer recovery period.

Knowing how to handle situations before the vet arrives can vary from one injury to another. Superficial wounds will require different care than a cut to an artery. If a vet is needed, clean the wound with a sterile saline solution or plain water, but do not apply antiseptic or ointment to the wound. Cover the wound, if possible, with a bandage or gauze and stall the horse until the vet arrives. Do not give a horse any medication or sedatives until the vet arrives. For serious wounds, apply direct pressure directly on the wound. In case of leg injuries, bandage with a quilted leg wrap, but it is best not to remove any blood-soaked bandages until the vet arrives, because doing so can restart the bleeding. Minor wounds should be hosed off and cleaned with a sterile saline solution and an antibacterial soap such as Betadine, using gauze pads. Apply an antibiotic cream or powder, and if possible, cover with non-stick gauze. For leg wounds, apply a stable wrap.

The size of the wound, depth, location and extent will determine whether or not a wound requires sutures. Generally, the smaller the cut, the less likely it will need stitches, unless the injury is near the eye. Deep puncture wounds will usually not be sutured, as they can trap bacteria and result in abscesses. If the wound is over a joint, such as the hip or hock, movement will likely open the sutures, so these types of wounds are usually not stitched. It can also be difficult to suture a wound that is surrounded by jagged tissue, bruising or missing skin.

Peroxide, Vaseline, alcohol, or strong antiseptics should never be used on wounds, as they can damage tissue. Providone Iodine should only be used around the wound and not in the wound itself due because it can cause tissue necrosis and impair healing. Chlorhexidine can also cause tissue necrosis.

Barn managers should be well versed in how to clean wounds, medicate, and how to properly bandage the horse in case the horse owner does not know how to.

As a horse owner, knowing the basics of first aid for your horse will save you money in the long run if you can perform the basics, such as wound cleansing, medicating, and bandaging. Ask potential boarding barns what kind of first aid kit they have and if they are prepared for treating injuries. Sadly, some barn managers have no idea how to bandage a leg, let alone cleanse an injury. This should be basic horse care 101 and it should be a red flag if there is no first aid kit available. Most injuries require cold hosing, bandaging, poulticing, or heat. Knowing when and how to use each therapy is essential to being a good barn manager.

> There are several excellent vet books on the market, many of which are geared toward the average horseman and have easy-to-understand terms. My favorite is The Complete Equine Veterinary Manual by Tony and Marcy Pavord. In my first aid cabinet is a copy of Dr. Kellon's Guide to First Aid for Horses, a small ring-bound book compact enough to fit into any first aid kit.

Hoof Care

The horse owner is responsible for having their horse on a regular farrier schedule. Depending on the environment and each horse, this can fluctuate between 5- 6 and even 8 weeks. All horses should be trimmed and, if necessary, shod. Not providing regular farrier work will lead to a lame horse. Do not confuse a domesticated horse with a horse that lives in the wild. Their environment and constant moving do an excellent job of maintaining their hooves. Just like horses not being treated by vets, barn owners will need to speak up when they see that one of their boarders is not having regular farrier work done, which can also be put into a boarding contract.

Farriers should be given the same consideration as any other professional. Their time is crucial, and they should not be kept waiting. Horses should be clean and ready for them. Farriers should not be expected to fetch a horse or wait while a rider finishes a lesson. Horses should not be wet from a bath either. Just as vets need a safe area to work in, so do farriers. They need a level surface, preferably a concrete slab. Horses should be taught to stand quietly for a farrier and ideally, there should be a handler to hold the horse for the farrier, especially for a horse who does not stand quietly.

A good horse owner will be able to identify good farrier work. There are many different schools of thought on hoof care, and different disciplines and breeds will require a different type of trim and shoeing.

While many barns may require boarders to use one particular vet, enforcing a one-farrier policy regarding farriers may be more challenging, especially if your barn has more than one discipline. A farrier familiar with shoeing a roping horse may not have had the correct training to shoe a jumper or dressage horse and may end up causing the horse to be lame.

Barn managers and horse owners alike should be versed in good farrier work and able to pull a shoe in an emergency. It is not uncommon for a horse to come in from the pasture with a shoe partially torn off. Your farrier may be on the other side of the county and unable to come pull the shoe for hours if not days. Having the necessary tools on hand will allow you to pull the shoe. Ask your farrier to show you how and invest in the proper tools.

Dental Care

Floating, or occlusal equilibration as many refer to it now, is the process of filing a horse's teeth, which are constantly growing. Sharp points will need to be removed, as well as smoothing enamel points, correcting any dental issues, and balancing the dental arcades. It is also a necessary procedure to ensure good health. Using abrasive discs, the procedure can be done manually, with a rasp, or with power tools. There is much debate about which method is better, and this is a conversation to have with your vet. Because sedatives are usually required, only a veterinarian should perform a dental, especially since floating can irreversibly change a horse's mouth and teeth. In some states, it is illegal for anyone to perform dentals unless they are a veterinarian.

Just as humans get two sets of teeth in their lives, so do horses. The baby teeth are temporary and begin to be replaced by adult teeth around 2-1/2 years of age. By age 5, they should have all of their adult teeth. An adult gelding or stallion will have 40 permanent teeth, while mares have between 36 and 40.

The teeth of a horse are constantly growing, which is why one can estimate the age of a horse by their teeth. Because teeth grow longer as horses age and certain teeth and grooves appear at different ages, knowing how to age teeth can be a valuable skill once a person learns what to look for.

A mouth left unattended can be subjected to sharp edges and hooks, causing sores that will become painful. Other issues include wolf teeth causing discomfort caused by a bit, long or sharp canine teeth interfering with the bit, broken teeth, abnormal bite planes, teeth that are excessively worn or abnormally long, infected teeth or gums, a misalignment, and retained caps. These are all issues that can cause pain and result in changes in behavior. Many attitude problems in horses are rooted in pain from teeth, so it is important to have regular dental care. Most adult horses need to have their teeth done just annually- however, most vets will inspect a horse's mouth regularly to look for potential issues. Senior and young horses may need dental work more than once a year.

A horse that is dropping its grain, losing weight, grinding teeth, or being resistant to bitting or general fussiness while riding may have a problem that is related to its teeth and should be addressed by your vet before his next annual dental. Undigested hay or grain in their manure, head tilting, bit chewing, bucking, a foul odor from the mouth or nostrils, blood coming from the mouth, or swelling of the jaw or mouth are also reasons to have your horse's mouth looked at by your vet.

Sand Purge

Horses consuming sand is a big concern for barn owners and managers, particularly in the South. It is virtually impossible for a horse not to consume sand or dirt, especially horses fed off the ground. Too much sand consumption can result in colic, lack of appetite, and overall poor health. It is estimated that as many as 30% of colic cases are a result from sand in the gut. Not only sand but also ingesting silt and gravel can cause issues.

There are methods one can take to reduce the intake of sand. Horses should not be fed hay or grain directly on the ground. If horses must be fed on the ground, put their hay and feed in tubs and on mats. Horses turned out on sandy pastures with limited grass should be offered hay to eat. In addition, mats should be placed under tubs if feeding grain where it can be dropped onto sand to prevent ingestion of sand.

Testing for sand is relatively easy. Gather a few manure balls from a fresh pile in a plastic bag, add water halfway, and shake the mixture. Allow the bag to sit for a few hours and observe the amount of sand that has settled in the bottom. Horses with substantial sand on the bottom are at risk of sand colic. Small amounts of sand are common and no cause for concern.

Prevention is the best method for sand accumulation, and as the barn manager, you need to decide which method is best for the horses in your care. Many barns will require some sort of sand purge, whether Psyllium, given over a period of days or weeks, a digestive supplement, or chia seeds. Research by the University of Florida has shown that providing good quality hay, fresh water, and movement to keep the gut working properly is the best prevention. Horses fed good quality hay at 2.5% of body weight uniformly produced the largest sand output, compared to hay fed at 1.5% of body weight and hay fed at 1.5% body weight plus Psyllium. Fiber-rich forages will help move the sand through the digestive tract; water will prevent impaction and encourage the movement of the sediment, and plenty of turnouts to encourage movement will help promote a healthy gut. The study by U of F showed there is no advantage to feeding psyllium, bran, or mineral oil over feeding hay to remove sand from the digestive tract. Their take is that hay is primarily responsible for moving sand through the gut, and the higher the hay intake, the faster the sand is moved through the digestive system.

Vices

As a barn manager, you will most likely encounter horses that exhibit different vices. These include cribbing and/or wind-sucking, weaving, pacing and pawing.

There is much debate about the causes of these vices, although most will agree that limited turnout time, boredom, and isolation are most likely to be the causes. While some believe that cribbing and wind-sucking are hereditary, others believe that horses learn vices from watching other horses exhibit the behavior. However, that appears to be more of a myth than truth. Other vices, such as kicking or circling in the stall before mealtime, can result from inadvertent reinforcement by barn managers or employees. Attempting to physically prevent the horse from such behavior does not remove the motivation for the behavior and rarely works. It may cause more distress because the horse has lost its coping mechanism.

Cribbing involves a horse grabbing a fixed object with its teeth. Usually, the stall door or fence post, while arching its neck, pulling backward while making a grunting noise. Windsucking is similar; however, the horse doesn't grab onto an object with its teeth.

Cribbing may increase stomach acidity, decrease saliva production, and increase the risk of ulcers. Attempts to reduce cribbing include reducing stall time, increasing the amount of hay given while reducing the amount of grain, and feeding smaller meals more often. Some owners have success with cribbing collars, but studies show they may increase stress hormones.

Weaving is when a horse stands still but shifts his weight from side to side, much like a parent holding an infant. More turnout time, allowing the horse to see other horses, and even putting a non-breakable mirror in their stall are methods proven to help.

Pawing, pacing and kicking in the stall can be related to feed time. The impatient horse that is fed last may resort to such tactics. Feeding these horses first should eliminate any issues.

Most vices can be attributed to management, whether of the horse or the barn. While vices may not ever be eliminated, they may be greatly reduced by increasing turnout time, turning horses out with others rather than in solitary turnout, providing a forage-based diet, and feeding smaller meals more frequently. Engaging horses in boredom busting activities can also help reduce the likelihood of vices. Positive reinforcement training should always be used over force or abuse. Negative reinforcement will not discourage vices and may make them worse.

Vices are uncommon in wild horses: it is a domestic horse issue that man created. Some horses may be unable to handle the constraints humans place on them and deal with them by developing vices, much as a human relies on smoking, drinking, or chewing their fingernails.

Alternative/Complementary Therapies

Horses who suffered some injuries and health issues, which were once considered career and even life-ending, are now being given second chances, thanks to the development of new alternative therapies. Even a fractured leg is no longer a death sentence for a horse. In addition, alternative therapies can boost the overall performance of sport horses.

Most alternative therapies should be performed by a vet or a licensed professional. Today, some veterinarians only specialize in holistic practices, while more traditional vets may rely on professionals such as chiropractors to enhance their practice.

Acupuncture was developed by the Chinese more than 3,000 years ago. It uses thin needles placed along specific points of the body to achieve beneficial results. The Chinese believed that currents of energy (chi or qi) flow through the body along meridians. If there is blockage along these paths, the energy is disrupted, and the body doesn't function properly. Acupuncture stimulates the nervous system, releasing endorphins, easing pain, improving circulation, and relaxing muscle spasms. Acupuncture has been used to address allergies, neurological disorders, gastrointestinal issues, and respiratory illnesses. Only professionals should perform acupuncture

Chiropractic treatment is used to address orthopedic problems. Horses exerting themselves through riding or rough play, poorly fitting saddles, growth spurts, and injuries can benefit from chiropractic sessions. Chiropractic should address pain, stiffness, weakness, and neurological issues. Many chiropractors will incorporate other therapies, including laser, massage, heat, and PEMF (Pulsed Electromagnetic Fields.) Only licensed chiropractors should be used, and in some states, only vets can perform chiropractic services.

Laser therapy is becoming very popular for wound healing and soft tissue injuries. It stimulates the production of collagen and increases blood flow, which aids in the healing process. In addition, laser therapy reduces swelling and inflammation, stimulates the circulatory and lymphatic systems, and removes cellular waste. It should never be used in conjunction with steroids, because its use produces natural cortisone production.

Massage can be beneficial, whether you are giving your horse a light massage or hiring a professional to provide a deep tissue massage to address body soreness. It benefits horses with soft tissue adhesions or pain in the thoracic and lumbar regions.

Ortho-Bionomy is a gentle bodywork that may appear similar to chiropractic but is very different. Ortho-Bionomy works with the proprioceptive aspects of the nervous system to let the body self-correct itself. The practitioner determines through feel where the tension and stress lies in the horse and assists the horse in releasing tightness. Bones are not manipulated in the way that chiropractic work manipulates.

Other treatments are also gaining in popularity. Water treadmills, Thera-plates, BEMER (Bio-Electro-Magnetic-Energy-Regulation), stem cell therapy, shock wave therapy, and kinesiology taping are all methods that are gaining traction in the equestrian world with proven results. As a horse owner, it is beneficial to be aware of the treatments available to enable your horse to perform at his very best.

The Sick Horse

Unfortunately, at some point or another, you will have to deal with a sick horse, whether it is temporary or terminal. As a manager, plans should be in place for dealing with such horses. If they are contagious, is there a quarantine stall available? How will you handle a horse owner who refuses treatment for a sick horse, preferring to ignore the illness or treat it themselves with no success?

This is where having a good boarding contract is useful. Barn owners should not tolerate a sick horse not receiving medical treatment, nor is it fair for the other boarders to witness. A barn's reputation can be put at risk by allowing an ill horse and subjecting them to a visit from Animal Control or the local sheriff if the animal is suffering and someone reports the horse.

Who will be responsible when a horse is sick or injured and requires rehabbing? If the horse requires round the clock care, such as with an eye injury, who will treat the eye? If the barn manager is capable of treating a horse that needs rehabbing, a fee schedule should be in place. Having the owner move the horse to a rehab facility is not an uncommon request, especially when neither has the necessary skills nor the time to rehab the horse.

Horse owners and managers alike should be able to identify a sick horse. Knowing each horse's routine will indicate if the horse is sick. Horses like to sunbathe, but it's good to make a mental note whenever one is lying down more often than normal or for extended periods. Is the horse having difficulties in getting up? Is the horse breathing hard and fast at rest? Is it sweating while at rest? Is the horse weak and unsteady on his feet? Make a note of anything that appears unusual for a particular horse. Sometimes, there is a simple explanation, but other times, it could indicate that something is wrong with the horse and a call to the vet should be made.

Horses are prone to many ailments, and a good horse owner will be well-versed in the diseases and health issues that can affect their horse. Barn owners should be able to identify the signs of common ailments and contact the owner immediately. These include:

- Abscesses
- Azoturia
- Choking
- Colic
- Heaves
- Lameness
- Laminitis
- Rain rot
- Scratches
- Ulcers

Signs of a sick horse:

- Loss of appetite
- Increased respiration
- Fever
- Increased pulse
- Blood in urine/difficulty urinating
- Diarrhea
- Dull eyes
- Nasal discharge
- Swellings
- Change in behavior
- Reluctance to move
- Dull coat
- Weight loss

The vet should be contacted once a horse is suspected of being sick. Blood work may be necessary to determine the cause and rule out infectious diseases. The horse should be isolated from the rest of the herd and kept comfortable and relaxed. The TPR should be monitored, and the diet may need to be adjusted.

Colic

Colic is probably the most common health issues facing horse owners. Horse owners should understand that colic is not a disease but rather a symptom of something much larger. It can be the result of eating bad or poor quality feed, not having enough feed or overeating, eating a toxic plant, weather changes, parasite infection, inadequate water intake, inflammation of the bowel, disruption of blood supply, gas buildup, a change in routine, exhaustion and more. It is up to the horse owner or barn manager to try and determine why a horse has coliced, especially one which is colicing often. Many mistakenly assume that a horse that is eating a toxic plant will show symptoms immediately or that all of the horses will be sick- however, not all horses may be eating that particular weed or plant, or your horse may be nibbling just enough over a period of time that there is finally enough buildup of toxins to cause a reaction. Other times, changes in the weather may cause a toxic plant to suddenly release enough toxins to affect a horse.

Signs of Colic:

- Kicking or biting at the stomach
- Loss of appetite
- Lethargic
- Pawing
- Stoic
- Sweating
- Decreased gut sounds

- Lying down and rolling
- Increased respiration and heart rates
- Slowed CRT (capillary refill time)
- Gums blue or black
- Bloated stomach
- Fecal is dry
- No passing of manure

Depending on the cause, the colic can be spasmodic, impaction, or gas.

Spasmodic Colic is painful contractions of the smooth muscle in the intestines, usually caused by overexcitement or stress. It can be compared to indigestion in humans and usually responds well to treatment.

Impaction Colic is also very serious and can result in a rupture of the intestines. Blockages occur because food or sand has become impacted in the intestine, colon, or stomach, although stomach impactions are not as common. The gut will become coiled and looped within the abdomen. Horses with impaction colic are most likely to roll. Other causes of impactions are poor water intake and poor motility of feed. Providing clean water and good quality hay and feed are keys to preventing impaction colic.

Gas Colic occurs when the microbes in the colon produce excessive amounts of gas. Gas can accumulate in the stomach or the intestines, and as the gas builds, the gut distends, causing pain and discomfort. This can result from quickly changing their diet or feeding moldy feed. The prognosis is usually very good with treatment.

Every horse owner should know their horse's vitals, and a stethoscope should be in every barn first aid kit. The lack of gut sounds from both sides of the upper and lower flank areas indicates a problem: a healthy horse will exhibit a noisy gut with gurgles, pings, rumblings, and other sounds. Listen to the heart rate- more than 60 beats per minute indicates distress. A respiration of more than 20 is also a bad sign. Check the CRT and the color of the gums, and take your horse's temperature. Once you have taken your horse's vitals, contact your vet with this information and relay his symptoms.

While waiting for your vet to arrive, remove the feed and try to keep your horse calm. There are differing theories on walking horses. Some believe that keeping a horse moving will exhaust them- however, you do not want your horse to roll, and walking may be the only way to accomplish this. Some vets are okay if the horse is lying down, but you never want to let them roll. Your vet will give you instructions on what to do until they arrive.

Most barns keep Banamine on hand to administer to a horse once they display signs of colic. It is best to contact your vet first though and get their go-ahead before giving any medication. Vitals should always be taken before administering any medicine for pain relief.

> I have boarded in several barns where colic was just accepted as part of managing a barn. One barn I boarded at had an average of one colic per month, and in the three years I boarded there, four horses died from colic complications. My horse was one of the few who did not ever colic. He was also the only horse fed a hay diet consisting of timothy and alfalfa, which I paid extra for. The other horses were all fed a cheap coastal hay diet. Turn out time was also limited to just 2 hours a day. I have boarded at other barns where colic was just an accepted part of doing business. Not once at any of these barns did anyone try to get to the root of the colics. Was it a toxic plant, the quality of hay, or something else? Not once in the four years that I have owned my farm have I had one colic. I attribute this to good quality hay in front of everyone all the time, lots of clean, fresh water, and constant movement.....even at night when they are in their stalls, they still have access to a run off the back of their stalls. I constantly inspect my pastures for potential toxic weeds or plants and have my agriculture agent out yearly to lend her expert eye.

Choke

A choking horse can be terrifying, and the vet should be contacted immediately. While waiting for the vet, remove food and water and keep the horse quiet and calm. Some vets may advise to massage the left side of the neck, to encourage the blockage to move, but never stick a hose in a horse's mouth to try and flush it out, as you may end up causing the horse to aspirate. The risk of aspiration pneumonia increases as time goes by and can be fatal, so do not hesitate to contact your vet.

Horses prone to choking should have their grain dampened to reduce the risk and should never be fed large pieces of carrots or apples, and hay cubes should never be fed to any horse without soaking due to their ability to cause choke.

Lameness Issues

When a horse appears lame, if possible, stall the horse and limit its movement. If you suspect a fracture, minimize movement and apply a splint to the affected leg. Lameness issues can result from something as mild as a bruise or something more serious, such as an abscess, a soft tissue injury, a strain, or a fracture. Abcesses should never be taken lightly because they can become very serious. A nail in the hoof is an emergency call to your vet. Try to avoid pulling the nail until your vet arrives so they can determine what hoof structure is affected. If you must remove it, mark the location and indicate on the nail how deep it was in the hoof. Wrap the hoof to keep it clean until the vet arrives.

Eye Injuries

Eye injuries can deteriorate very rapidly and need immediate attention, especially in the following situations:

- Swelling around the eye or the eyelids

- Squinting or keeping the eye closed

- Red conjunctiva (tissue inside eyelids)

- Cloudy or blueish appearance to the cornea

- Any tear, wound, or foreign object in close proximity to the eye

- Excessive tearing or cloudy drainage is present

Neurological

If you can do so safely, put a neurological horse in a stall or a small paddock by itself. Remove all objects, hay, and feed. To reduce injury, nobody should be in the stall with the horse and try to keep the stall dark and quiet.

Respiratory

If you suspect your horse has difficulty breathing or is experiencing respiratory issues, do not exercise and keep the horse quiet and calm. If you suspect strangles, isolate the horse, and anyone who has had contact with the horse needs to avoid other horses until they have disinfected themselves.

Mental Well-Being of the Horse and Equine Welfare

Equestrians should not only take into account the physical well-being of their horse, but their mental state as well. New studies and research indicates that horse welfare should also be given a priority when evaluating the needs of horses. In her book, "A Horse By Nature", author Mary Ann Simonds dives deep into the horse-human relationships, how to reduce stress and improve communication, the importance of horse-horse learning, friendships and communication as well as the ethics of horse sports.

"No Bored Horses" by Amanda Goble is a book that provides many DIY toys and activities for keeping horses engaged and stimulated. Stalled horses in particular need mental stimulation to prevent them from developing vices, and we now know that interaction with our horses while at liberty strengthens the horse-human bond.

Horses and Humans Research Foundation is dedicated to advancing the knowledge of horse-human interactions through research and education and Equitation Science International focuses on the natural behaviors of horses, their biomechanics and how horses learn.

In her book "Horse Brain, Human Brain," author Janet Jones describes how human and equine brains work together, and shows readers how horses learn, think, perform and perceive, and how humans can work with the horse's brain instead of working against it. How horses see, learn, what they fear, how they trust and focus are topics discussed from both horse and human perspectives.

Brambell's Five Freedoms, The Basic Animal Rights, outline the five aspects of animal welfare. Veterinarians, the World Organization for Animal Health, the Royal Society for the Prevention of Cruelty to Animals and the American Society for the Prevention of Cruelty to Animals have all adopted and follow these guidelines.

The Five Freedoms stipulate that animals should have the freedom from thirst, hunger and malnutrition; the freedom from discomfort which is caused by their environment; the freedom from pain, injury and disease; the freedom from fear and distress; and lastly, the freedom to express normal behavior for their species.

Horses who crib, weave, spook or shut down, may be doing so because any, or a combination of the Five Freedoms is missing from their life.

Competition horses are also at higher risk for stress and therefore the possibility of developing vices, ulcers and even behaviors such as bucking and rearing. New studies are focusing on the relationship that lights and noise have on horses. As a result, the United States Equestrian Federation passed rule GR1215 in 2024, which governs the length of time that lights can be on at horse shows overnight, as well as limiting noise, such as radios and loud speakers. Horses must have at least six consecutive hours of darkness and quiet. This is a policy that should be carried over to horses at home, where barns may keep the lights on at night for security or even to prevent hair growth in the winter. Perhaps that unwanted behavior is due to your horse not getting enough REM sleep!

While there is still much work to be done to educate horsemen about the mental well-being of horses, the tide is changing. Many horsemen are beginning to understand the importance of addressing the mental needs of their horses, as evidenced by the numerous books, schools and websites dedicated to improving the lives of horses through better understanding of their mental status. There is a wealth of information to be learned and shared, and every good horsemen should take the time to educate themselves on such topics for a better relationship and understanding of their horse. Horsemen should learn how to recognize signs of stress in horses, from the obvious of grinding teeth and tail swishing, to the not so obvious signs such as wrinkles around the eyes and tight, pursed lips and a tense mouth.

The Neglected/Abused/Starved Horse

Humans have a moral obligation to look after their animals, but sadly, there are those who do not for a variety of reasons. It may be that they lack money to feed them, lack the knowledge, have mental issues, are hoarders, lack compassion, tend toward violence, or do so for shock value.

No person should ever tolerate any animal being mistreated. If you see something, speak up. At the very least, the animal should be reported to the local authorities. Unfortunately, sometimes, there is nothing the law can do, especially if the owner claims that the animal is under the care of a veterinarian. Other times, what appears to be neglect to one person may not be considered as such in some municipalities. Sometimes, having the media become involved will highlight the issue and force the person to relinquish the animal if the law cannot do anything.

My daughters would often return from trail rides to the barn we were leasing and would mention to me a skinny Palomino mare they saw. I never was able to find this horse when I went looking for her, due to the property being heavily wooded along the road, and unless she was standing at the gate, nobody would know about her. The location was not on our daily commute, so it was not something I was able to look for every day. Finally, though, I was driving past this property, and she was standing at the gate, looking pitifully thin. There were three other horses with her, but she was the only skinny one. I stopped the car, and the first thing I did was photograph her with my cell phone and send the picture to the director of animal services, whom I knew from inviting to our farm to give disaster planning talks to our pony clubbers. She replied that she was sending an investigator, and I returned to my barn to await the call, which came an hour later. An investigator was at the gate, but no horses were to be found. Thankful for taking the photos, they knew she was there and that they needed to act, so they contacted the sheriff's department, who sent out a deputy. Once he saw the photos, he climbed over the gate and went in search of the horses. He found the group and coaxed them back to the entrance. While we all stood around, considering this horse and what actions needed to be taken, I was surprised at how many cars stopped to tell us that they knew about the horse but assumed that she was old, as if being an old horse was justification for being so skinny. The owner was tracked down and given an ultimatum to either leave her job and be there within two hours, or the horses would be confiscated. This deputy was tough! The owner finally arrived, driving an expensive truck, wearing nice clothes, and having had her nails recently done. Her excuse was that there was no water on the property, so she hauled it out there several times a week, and that was as often as the horses were fed. Unfortunately for the mare, due to her age and her placing in the herd dynamics, the other horses chased her off of her limited feed, which was not a proper diet for a senior horse, especially for a horse with only four incisors. It was no wonder she was skinny; she was being starved to death. It never occurred to the owner to feed the horse a special senior diet, to watch her eat it, and to keep the other horses away from her food. When informed that she would be cited and could lose all of her horses, she volunteered to relinquish custody of the horse. Because the other horses were in reasonably good condition…not great, but not skinny, she was allowed to keep them, but with Animal Control performing visits to ensure they were not getting worse. And the mare? She returned to my barn, and a neighbor adopted her, and we started a non-profit rescue! We named her Lady. It was believed that she was 33 years old, and she lived for another two years. She regained roughly 300 pounds of the 400 pounds she needed to put on, had regular dental work, and was groomed and loved for the remaining time she had on earth!

Euthanasia and Disposal of Body

What measures will be taken if the horse is terminal, whether from the infirmities of old age or an injury or disease? How long will the horse be allowed to decline in health before euthanasia?

Unfortunately, many horse owners have a hard time euthanizing their horse, whether the horse is ill, unsound, or has behavior issues. Unlike euthanizing a dog or cat, which can be carried into a vet's office, placed on the table, and given a shot, preparing a horse for euthanasia requires more planning due to its size. Where will the horse be euthanized, and will other horses be allowed to view the body? What about the remains? Will the horse be buried or removed from the farm? Heavy equipment will be required either way. And due to their size, horses just don't lie down and go to sleep. Watching can be somewhat traumatic, particularly if plans don't go right. There are countless ads for people offering up their sick or unsound horse for free, hoping someone will want to take their horse and provide for it rather than deal with euthanasia. Sadly, most of these horses are promised good homes, only to end up in the slaughter pipeline.

No horse deserves this fate, especially one that has been our faithful friend and companion. We tend to inject our feelings into the horse. Horses live in the moment; they do not anticipate or perceive death as we do, and in the end, giving them a peaceful death is the greatest gift we can give any animal. If the owner has a hard time making that final decision, it may be necessary to coordinate a meeting with the vet and the owner. A good barn owner will discourage the owner from passing the horse on to an unknown situation. Euthanizing a horse, even if young, is far better than worrying about its fate. Only a few people need companion horses, especially those requiring much care.

What is your emergency plan in the event of a horse with a broken leg and there is no vet available? What if you have a goat or a mini that has been attacked by a coyote and is bleeding out? Sadly, there may come a time when an animal needs to be humanely euthanized immediately, and no vet is available. A barn owner should have a plan in place. Will you be able to end your animal's suffering with a gun? Several good articles and diagrams address this issue, and it is something that every horse owner needs to be prepared for, "just in case."

What will your policy be regarding the disposal of the body? Do you allow horses to be buried on your property? Some farms have strict policies against burying horses, whether due to a lack of land, county, or environmental policies forbidding such practices, or for their own personal reasons.

This will be an issue that needs to be addressed at some point. Disposing of a body should be done in an acceptable way to the owner. Environmental concerns regarding water quality should be taken into consideration, as well as local ordinances. Horse owners should have a plan in place for when their horse crosses the rainbow bridge, and some barns will address the question in their boarding contract. The disposal should not attract animals, nor should there be a risk of spreading disease.

Disposal options

1. Burial, whether on-site or in an equine or animal cemetery. This must be done in a way to ensure that the water supply is not contaminated. Many horse owners will have peace of mind knowing that they can visit their horse's grave. The cons are that heavy equipment is required to bury the body, and the body must be buried deep enough so that animals will not dig up the carcass. If burying on your property, the cost can range from nothing, if you own the necessary equipment, to a few hundred dollars to pay someone to bury the horse.

2. Cremation. More pet cemeteries are offering cremations of horses as well as whole-body burials. Not all crematoriums can accommodate a horse, so research needs to be done to find a suitable facility (or some pet crematoriums will cut the body up into smaller pieces). Whether or not you get the body back, there is a premium price to cremate a horse, from an average cost of $1500 and up.

3. Euthanizing at a vet hospital. Usually, they will dispose of the body. Some hospitals will offer euthanasia clinics to make this decision even easier. This can be a simple solution, especially if the horse is already at the clinic.

4. Hauling the body to a landfill. Low-cost but necessary equipment will be needed to load the body onto a flatbed truck. It is a very undignified ending.

5. Hauling body to a state lab. Necropsies will be performed, and they will dispose of the body, usually via cremation. Some state labs do offer private cremations. Prices vary from state to state, running from just a few hundred dollars to around $1500. The state lab will perform a necropsy for a minimal charge, so if your horse has passed away due to colic or some unknown cause, this solution can give you answers as to the cause of death.

6. Composting: the most cost effective and environmentally sound method, it is a controlled and sanitary decomposition of organic materials by bacteria. It requires the land necessary and a body can take 6-12 months to decompose. Some may find this a fascinating procedure, while others will be horrified at knowing their horse is lying under a big pile of dirt and leaves and will end up eventually in the garden. It is probably the cheapest method to dispose of the body, but care must be taken so animals don't dig up the body. There are several steps involved in this process as well. Composting is legal in every state except California.

7. Rendering: Check regulations regarding drugs in the system (euthanasia solution, dewormers, etc.). Equipment will be needed to load the body onto a flatbed trailer. Rendering plants are not as common anymore, and the cost averages a few hundred dollars.

8. Zoos and wild animal parks: animals usually have to have died naturally with no euthanasia solution or other drugs in their system. They must be loaded onto a flatbed trailer and taken to the facility.

9. Donate to a vet hospital—especially a horse with a disease that can be studied. The vet hospital will euthanize and dispose of the body.

10. Biodigesters: Found at some vet colleges, it is a method that is becoming more common. It is similar to a pressure cooker and uses alkaline hydrolysis to rapidly kill any potentially harmful wastes in the carcass. The body is turned into an aqueous solution of peptides, amino acids, sugars, soaps, and powdered bone, which are free of harmful pathogens and can be disposed of in landfills or used as fertilizer. The cost is minimal, averaging 30 cents per pound.

As a horse owner, it is imperative to have a plan in place for when your horse becomes terminally sick and needs to be euthanized. Euthanizing your horse instead of passing them on to someone else will guarantee that you will never have to worry about whether or not it ends up in a bad situation. Passing your unsound, sick, or old horse to someone else is not being a responsible horse owner. In May of 2023, Fallon Blackwood was convicted of stealing 63 horses. A vet student, she told unsuspecting horse owners who were looking to give away their horses that she would give their beloved horses a good home. Instead, she sold them to kill buyers to be slaughtered in Mexico. By euthanizing your horse, you will never have to worry if they end up in a similar fate.

By ending the suffering of an animal, you are giving them the greatest gift you can give them.

The Humane Society of the United States has a list of options for disposing of your horse's remains and each state's laws regarding body disposal.

> *It is good to have a backup plan for disposing of your horse's remains in case the first one doesn't pan out. When we made the decision to euthanize our horse Pilgrim, who was suffering from the side effects of Lyme Disease, Tropical Storm Faye had just blown through days earlier, which most likely contributed to the stress on his already taxed body. He needed to be euthanized sooner than later, but Central Florida had suffered epic widespread flooding; even the farm I was leasing, which was high and dry and where I had buried several horses, was 8 inches under water. The flooding did not recede for weeks, and there was just no place available to bury him. I was calling on friends and anyone I could think of who had land that might be an option, but unfortunately, I kept hitting a wall. The only person I could get to handle his body stated that they were going to take him to the dump. I never got over learning as a kid that our pet dog ended up in the landfill after she was euthanized....it was a common practice of vet clinics to do so at the time unless you took the pet home and buried it. I could not stand the thought of Pilgrim going to the landfill. Finally, my vet reached out to someone, who offered to come pick up Pilgrim's body and take it back to his property and burn it. It was the best we could do given the circumstances.*

Both barn owners/managers and horse owners are the stewards of their horses in their care, and to not keep them in good health and provide for them when they are sick or injured is negligent and abusive. Horse owners should be suspicious when scouting new barns if there are sick horses. Be bold and question why the horse is ill, which will also indicate how the barn manager handles sick horses. No reputable barn manager will tolerate an ill or injured horse whose owner refuses treatment. Adding a clause to the boarding agreement will give management leverage if the horse's owner does not seek treatment. Ask about first aid kits, because every barn should have one. Know your horse's habits so that if the barn staff overlooks any issues, you can identify any problems. It is just as crucial that you have a good relationship with your vet; don't be known as the horse owner who just writes the checks. Be proactive in your horse's health! This includes dentals and having your horses hooves attended to regularly. At the end of the day, you are your horse's advocate, and it is up to you to ensure that your horse is in good health, current on vaccines and deworming, as well as dentals and hoof care, and that you have a plan for the day that your horse will no longer be healthy or sound.

Chapter 8
Barn Routines

It's good to have a routine, not only for the benefit of the horses but for the benefit of boarders as well. Boarders like to know when their horses will be fed and turned out so they can plan their barn visits accordingly. Good barn managers will learn to perform their tasks efficiently and quickly and not rely on feed charts or instructions. Staff should be able to adjust routines due to weather, vet and farrier visits, lessons, and other disruptions to their day to ensure they finish all chores by the end of the day. Proper equipment, such as manure spreaders, mowers, drags, and side-by-sides, will help make the tasks easier and faster.

The day should begin early with an established feed time. There is much debate about whether horses should be fed at precisely the same time or if the feed times should be varied. It was once believed that horses did better on an exact feeding time, but we know that life gets in the way. If a horse is expecting to be fed at the same time every day and you are stuck in traffic or have overslept or have an appointment to keep and you are an hour late feeding, then the horse will be more agitated when his meal isn't delivered. In contrast, the horse who isn't expecting his meal at an exact time will be more relaxed and will not paw and kick the barn door. It is best to have a range of feed times, usually giving thirty minutes to an hour of flexibility, so instead of feeding precisely at 7:00 AM, it is best to feed between 6:30 AM and 7:30 AM or even 8:00 AM.

Throwing horse's hay before giving grain is another way to appease them while they are waiting for their grain. It is also believed to be healthier for them, because the fiber from the hay slows down starch digestion and obstructs the absorption of glucose into the bloodstream. This is particularly important for horses, which are metabolic, because a rise in glucose will affect them. Some experts disagree with this theory, so it is a routine that each individual needs to decide upon, and consulting with their vet will help determine what routine to use.

Barn chores should begin after breakfast. For horses that are stalled, daytime turnout horses will need to go out, allowing stalls to be cleaned, while horses turned out overnight will come into fresh-cleaned stalls, whether cleaned the day before or that morning.

Turning out horses can be a challenge, and it is the barn manager's experience and good judgment to decide what horses can go out with others and which should be turned out alone. The length of turnout and even the practice of leading horses out of their stalls should be given some consideration. Leading multiple horses at once will save time but should only be done by experienced handlers, and only quiet and well-behaved horses should be led this way.

There should be an order for turning out and bringing in. The first horse out and the last horse brought in will quite possibly react by galloping in a frenzied manner, so some strategy should be utilized while turning out and bringing in. It is best to start with turnouts closest to the barn or within the eyesight of other horses when beginning your turnout routine, especially when leading one horse at a time. Reverse the pattern when bringing in, starting with the horses farthest away. Nobody wants to deal with a hot and sweaty horse at dusk or right before a meal, so care should be taken to avoid being in that type of situation in the first place.

> *I worked at a barn that had the turnout paddocks along a long driveway. I established a routine of turning horses out by first leading an old pony and its pasture mate out together. The pony was always calm and well-behaved and they were turned out along with another horse in the paddock closest to the barn. This made turning out the remaining horses very easy, as I walked each horse out to the next closest paddock until the last horse was released in the farthest field. When it was time to bring the horses in, I began with the horses farthest away, and it was a very calm and orderly event- until the barn owner hired a new employee who had no regard for my turnout schedule. On her first day of work and it was time to bring the horses in, she began with the paddock closest to the barn, where the two horses and the pony were turned out. She led the two horses together, leaving the pony behind, who panicked and began running frantically. I was*

unfortunately in the process of bringing in the horse that was farthest away, as was my routine, but because the lone pony had now managed to upset everyone, with multiple horses running around and whinnying, I suddenly had a dangerous situation on my hands. It was getting harder and harder to keep control of my horse. I now had a horse that was rearing and trying to break free. I managed to get the horse into his stall without any harm to himself or me, but I was angry to have been put into a dangerous situation because of an arrogant employee.

Having horses turned out will make barn chores easy to perform and get finished. Inclement weather, may mean leaving horses inside, in which case it is safest to lead horses into an empty stall while its stall is cleaned, or if one is not available, putting the horse in the crossties will be safer and make your life easier.

Pastures and paddocks should be large enough to accommodate whatever number of horses you turn out in that space. Horses should be able to run, buck, and play. Footing should be free of rocks, holes, and any other hazards that could injure a horse. Additionally, there should be enough paddocks and pastures to accommodate all the horses on the property. Unfortunately, in areas where land is at a premium, horses have minimal turnout areas, and in some cases, a paddock off of their stall is the only area they have.

Herd management should be practiced and studied. A good manager will understand horse dynamics and gradually introduce a new horse to a group of horses in turnout. The ideal situation is to place the new horse in a private paddock next to the intended area where he will eventually be turned out and let the horses meet over a fence. If possible, bring in a horse from the larger group to be a buddy to the new horse for a few days, and then, if and once they appear to be bonded, turn the duo out in the larger group setting.

There will be several things to consider when choosing what horses to pair up while in turnout. Some barns will only turn out mares with mares and geldings with geldings, while other barns have no issues with mixed-sex groupings. The importance of knowing the horses in your care and how horse dynamics work in your group really cannot be stressed enough. It will be essential to know which horses are the alpha type and which horses get along with everyone. Know which horses are the babysitter types, who is stud-dish or mareish in their behavior, and which horses want to play. New herd groups should be watched closely, and changes will need to be made if there is any aggressive behavior. No horse owner wants to come to the barn and discover that day after day, their horse is being bullied and bearing bite and kick marks all over their body.

Young and senior horses should be carefully placed with the right turnout buddy. Yearlings and weanlings do best with horses their own age or find a horse that will be a good babysitter and not put up with their shenanigans. Likewise, senior horses should not be placed with aggressive or overly playful horses. If senior horses are being fed in a group setting in a pasture, care must be taken to guarantee that they are able to eat all of their feed and hay and are not being chased off by a younger horse.

I boarded briefly at a barn owned by a couple without any knowledge of horses. They decided to build a barn close to town for reasons I am not sure, and they eventually bought a horse. I moved my horses there because I would be on rough board and doing all the work myself, other than dropping feed, and it was only 10 minutes from my house-a big plus with three kids in school! A friend of my daughter's moved her horse to this barn, and then one of our pony clubbers leased one of her horses out to another pony clubber, and this horse also came to the barn. The barn was filling with boarders and there had only been minor issues to contend with at this point. That all changed when the leased horse arrived. The horse owner told the barn owners that this gelding could never be turned out with other geldings because he would fight with them. Unfortunately, not 2 hours after the horse arrived and the horse's owner left, the barn owners turned the horse out with the gelding that belonged to my daughter's friend. I came just as the carnage began. It was like two wild stallions were fighting over a mare. I had never seen such aggressive behavior in two geldings before. And the barn owners just stood there, mouths wide open, afraid to try and separate them. I grabbed a halter, ran into the pasture, and somehow grabbed one of the horses and got him through the gate and to safety. It was probably not my most brilliant move, since I could have been injured, but somehow, I managed to avoid any harm. The same could not be said for the two horses. Both suffered cuts all over their bodies. The barn owners then had the nerve to do absolutely nothing. They didn't even call the owners to inform them that their horses had been injured. I was the one who informed both horse owners of what happened, and because one owner was out of town, I contacted the vet for them, who was also out of town, and following his instructions, I medicated the horse. The owner of the leased horse was livid when she found out and showed up with a trailer to remove the horse the next day. Despite witnesses, the barn owners denied being told not to turn the horse out with other geldings. It got pretty ugly with the owners of both horses, and within a week, the other horse moved. Things went downhill quickly from that point and I also removed my horses.

Stalls should be mucked, and buckets and tubs should be dumped, cleaned, and re-hung. Barn aisles should be swept, either with a broom or a blower, and the entrances should be raked of any debris. If using a blower, care should be taken never to blow debris into the stalls if horses are in them, to avoid blowing dust and debris into their eyes, and to be considerate of anyone tacking up their horse! The next meal should be prepared; the manure should be spread or dumped, buckets refilled, and all other chores should be completed. With an established routine, barn chores can be done effortlessly and without much thought!

Horses should be routinely inspected, beginning at breakfast. A quick visual inspection, as well as an attitude check, should reveal any leg swellings or cuts, particularly if the horse was on night turnout. Is the horse very quiet when he is typically animated? Or is he agitated when he is usually quiet? If stalled, the manure should be examined while mucking the stall. What is the consistency? Dry and hard manure balls indicate a lack of water intake, while cow patties can indicate the horse is being fed an inappropriate feed or another health concern and should be monitored. If there is an excess of slime or mucus, the gut is potentially irritated. Is there a decrease of manure? Lots of grain or long hay stems in the manure will mean the horse is eating too fast or not chewing properly and may need dental work. And, of course, the presence of parasites implies the horse is in dire need of deworming. Did the horse eat all his meal, or is there grain and hay left over?

Any unusually messy stall, with signs of pawing or excessive rolling, can indicate a colicing horse. Experienced horsemen perform these health checks without knowing they are doing them, because they become second nature.

When the horse is led out of the stall, does he come out willingly, or is he reluctant? Listen to his footfalls on the concrete, which will tell you if he is lame. If the horse is being groomed, run your hands down his legs, feeling for any lumps, swellings, or cuts.

These inspections should be repeated when the horse is returned to his stall for the evening, and good managers and employees will give every horse in their care a once-over whenever they walk past them and make a mental note of what the horse is doing or not doing. By learning the routine of each horse, it will be easy to identify when something is amiss and if a call to the vet is in order.

Horses are grazing animals and, as such, should be on pasture as much as possible. If not, they should have hay in front of them at all times. Horses should not go without food for more than four hours. Due to their small stomachs and delicate digestive systems, they are designed to graze constantly.

Acids and enzymes will accumulate in the empty stomach of a horse. When a horse is chewing, it is creating saliva, which is rich in bicarbonate and which buffers the acidity in the stomach. When there is no saliva, there is more acid, and more acid can cause gastric and intestinal ulcers. In addition, the longer the stomach is empty, the more it releases stress hormones, especially cortisol. Cortisol blocks insulin and results in a constantly high blood glucose level, that causes the body to release more insulin, which causes fat tissue to be deposited and results in leptin resistance. This will lead to insulin resistance, which can then lead to laminitis. It's a never-ending cycle unless addressed.

When horses go more than 4 hours without good forage, the good bacteria in the gut is disrupted, leading to poor gut function and as a result, the possibility for colic.

Additionally, over time, muscles can be affected, causing weakness and a lack of energy. This is one reason horses engage in vices such as weaving, pawing, and kicking. By the time they are fed, they are stressed due to starvation. It is just as important that a horse has hay to graze on overnight. They do not sleep the entire night; horses spend most of their time eating, because they need only 20- 30 minutes of REM sleep every 24 hours.

Horses with a constant supply of hay in front of them will actually eat less than a horse that is fed only a flake or two, two to three times a day. They won't eat in a starved frenzy when they know the hay is constantly in front of them. As a result, horses are healthier and happier. Therefore, horses should be on pasture as long as possible, and if there is no grass available, they should have access to hay while turned out, and hay should be readily available while in their stalls.

The weather can impact a barn's routine. Most horses do well in all kinds of weather, but care should be taken for young foals and older or sick horses in extreme weather. Most horses do not mind rain or snow, but shelter should be provided for those who choose to get out of the elements, and in areas with extreme lightning, horses should not be turned out during storms.

Many barns provide a lunch meal; again, try to have flexible feeding times. Dinner should be provided in the evening, and hay should be topped off at bedtime. Water buckets should be checked at all meals, and during extreme weather, they should be checked often and replaced if the water temperature is too hot or too cold.

Sample Daily Stable Routine:

Morning:

- Feed hay and breakfast
- Check horses for any health issues
- Turn out
- Dump water buckets and clean
- Clean feed tubs
- Muck stalls
- Dump or spread manure
- Fill hay bags
- Prepare lunch
- Fill water buckets
- Clean barn aisle

Noon:

- Feed lunch
- Check for any health issues
- Check water
- Prepare dinner
- Any unfinished barn chores should be completed in the afternoon

Dinner:

- Bring horses inside if not already in: check for any health issues.
- Feed hay and dinner
- Top off water
- Pick any stalls if needed
- Prepare breakfast
- Clean barn aisle

Bedtime:

- Add hay to bags
- Check for any health issues
- Top off water

Weekly Chores:

- Remove cobwebs
- Clear drains
- Check fire extinguishers and alarms
- Clean fans
- Order feed and hay
- Scrub buckets and troughs (provided this has not been done daily)
- Pick manure from pastures and paddocks (provided this has not been daily)
- Sweep out hay room
- Order feed and hay

Barn Books and Charts

Feed charts, turnout charts, and any other instructions, which can be updated to reflect any medications needed or changes in turnout schedules, should be posted and followed by employees, particularly new or inexperienced employees. Dry-erase boards are the most common and easiest way to manage barns.

In addition, all barns should have a Barn Book. This is a notebook where every aspect of running the barn is written down. This includes feeding instructions, barn chores, schedules, phone numbers, health records, and anything else one feels should be included. The purpose of a Barn Book is so that if the barn owner or manager is somehow incapacitated, anyone should be able to walk into the barn, pick up the Barn Book, and be able to understand exactly how to run the barn. They should know what horse gets which grain and hay, how much, and when. They will see the name of the feed, where it comes from, how much hay is fed, and what kind of hay. The person reading the book will understand the turnout schedules, what horse goes where and with whom, and when to bring them inside.

The book should include emergency phone numbers and may or may not include the health records of all of horses. If it does not include the health records, there should be a second book that does contain that information, and both books should be kept together, in a place where it can easily be found. This is especially important for barns where there is no help to rely on and if there is an emergency, a friend or relative who takes over should be able to locate the book immediately.

The phone numbers of vets, farriers, feed stores and boarders should all be noted. The book should be detailed and updated at least two to four times a year, usually at the beginning of a season or more often as anything changes. Adding sticky notes will help you note any changes until you can make permanent changes to the book.

> *The barn owner's wife fed at a barn where I worked. She fed every day, seven days a week, both morning and night. She did not have a feed chart, relying instead on her memory. I would watch her mix feed, but she worked so fast that memorizing what every horse got was hard. There were three different types of feed. Some got salt, others got supplements, and some got flax seed or bran. I would joke that the horses were in trouble if something should happen to her...if she were to lose her memory for whatever reason, nobody would know what to feed the horses. It was a running joke, but I was concerned that she was the only person who knew what to feed the horses. As a responsible horse owner, I knew what my horse ate, but as I quizzed other horse owners, nobody else knew what their horse ate, relying on the barn owners to assume that responsibility. No matter how often I brought it up, they never added a feed chart. In my barn, I have 2 dry erase boards, a barn book with instructions and a health record book. One dry erase is located in the feed room and provides easy instructions for what every animal gets. The other dry erase board hangs in my barn aisle, and has a drawn map of the farm property, indicating what fields may be closed off for recovery and who goes where.*

Blanketing

Because this is such a hot topic on social media, blanketing should be briefly discussed. There will be all kinds of advice about whether or not you should blanket. Some advice will give all sorts of arguments against blanketing, while others will provide reasons for blanketing.

It comes down to how well you know your horse, his health, what kind of coat he grows, if he is clipped, and even his breed. Chances are that the Shetland pony or the heavy draft horse will only require a blanket once the temperatures are extreme. In contrast, the thin-skinned Thoroughbred or Arabian, or the warmblood who has been body clipped, will require a sheet or blanket once temperatures dip into the 50s. Horses used to a constant cold will probably not need a blanket. However, horses in the South, where temperatures can hover near 80 during the day and then drop 30- 40 or even 50 degrees overnight, will probably need the extra warmth. A horse that is used to a warm climate will more likely be cold when the temperatures drop below 55° F than a horse that lives in a colder climate and is used to the cold. Horses in poor health and senior horses will also most likely need the extra warmth.

In addition, consider their living conditions: Stalled horses may do just fine with no blanket, whereas horses without shelter may need extra protection.

The lower critical temperature (LCT) is the temperature at which your horse can maintain his core body temperature without requiring additional energy. While some horses will do just fine by giving them extra hay, others will require a blanket in addition to the extra hay, and therefore, it is critical to know your horse well.

If you blanket, don't be the type of owner who goes overboard. Just because you are cold doesn't mean your horse is cold! They may not need all those layers!

One should know what type of blanket or sheet is appropriate and how to put a blanket on properly. Horses should be standing and secure, whether in their stall or tied, particularly if they are turned out in a pasture. To put the blanket on, place the blanket over the back and start by securing the chest straps, then the belly straps, and finish with the leg straps, in that order. To remove the blanket, start in reverse order, beginning with the leg straps. This is so that if the horse should bolt or take off, the blanket will not fall off his back and down his hind legs.

Leg straps should be applied correctly: take one leg strap, pass it between the horse's hind legs, and fasten it to the D-ring on the same side. If you are beginning with the right strap, it should be attached to the D-ring on the right side. Then, take the other leg strap, pass it through the hind legs, and loop it over and under the opposite strap, which is already secure, fastening it to the D-ring on its same side, in this case, the left side. Leg straps should be adjusted so there is room for the width of your hand, approximately 4- 5 inches, between the leg straps and the thigh, allowing for freedom of movement. Straps should never be so long that a horse can tangle his legs in them if he lies down. Leg straps should never crisscross to the other side and form an X.

Chest straps should not be so tight that they constrict on the horse; the same goes for the belly straps. Belly straps should never be loose enough for legs to become entangled, and the horse should be able to reach down with his neck without the blanket digging into his chest.

Blankets should be cleaned as often as possible during use and at the end of the season, when any necessary repairs should be made, before being stored until the next cold season.

There are many types of sheets and blankets, and they should be used appropriately.

Blanket Guide

Type	Use
Stable Sheet	It provides a light layer of warmth, used typically when temperatures are in the 50s
Stable Blanket	Unlike sheets, blankets contain fill in a range of weights, from 0 to more than 300 grams. The higher the gram, the warmer the blanket. They may or may not contain leg straps or a tail strap.
Turnout Blanket	Stable blankets designed for horses to wear when turned out, which have waterproofing and leg straps to prevent slippage when the horse is moving
Show Scrim	Lightweight, open-weave sheets are designed to be used at shows to keep horses clean.
Anti-Sweat Sheet	Open weave, which increases breathability and reduces sweat. They are designed to wick away moisture and can be used as a scrim.
Fly Sheet	Mesh sheet designed to keep flies away when turned out.
Rain Sheet	Used when riding or waiting in the rain at a horseshow. It will provide coverage from poll to tail; it is not designed for turnout because they are not very secure.
Dress Sheet or Cooler	Typically wool or wool blend or fleece, they keep horses warm on a chilly morning at horse shows or after riding. They can be fitted with surcingles (dress sheets) or large enough to cover the horse from its poll to its tail.
Quarter Sheet	Made of wool or fleece, these cover the hindquarters and secure to the billet straps of the saddle. They are designed to keep horses' muscles warm when riding on cold mornings. They can be left on during the ride or removed once the horse is warmed up.

At a high end boarding barn where I worked, the management did not bother instructing new employees on Blanketing 101. I arrived one morning to find that half of the horses were wearing their coolers, which were hung on the front of their stall doors, next to their blankets. Because most coolers do not have belly straps, several horses stood in their stalls with the coolers half off them. The horses who were fortunate enough to have blankets on were incorrectly buckled, with leg straps either dangling or in an X.

Care of the Horse

This is not a manual for how to ride your horse. However, it should go without saying, that every horse should be treated with the best of care, whether it is an Olympic mount, a trail horse or a back-yard pet.

Riders should be instructed in not only how to properly ride their horse, but how to care for their horse before riding and again after they have finished riding.

Horses should be well groomed before being tacked up, with hooves picked, shavings removed from mane and tail and the coat being curried and brushed. Some horses are sensitive to grooming, so it is up to the owner to determine what type of brushes to use on their horse. Grooming products, such as those from Epona Products, have become very innovative over the past few decades and take into account the comfort level of horses.

Small amounts of cool water should be offered often and the horse should be hosed off, with water being continuously applied until the horse is completely cooled off. Studies conducted at the Japan Racing Association's Equine Research Institute in 2018 show that continuously hosing the horse with cool water was the fastest way to decrease the core temperature. It was proven to be faster than intermittent hosing and scraping, walking until cooled out, the use of misting fans, applying cold water, or any other method. Water should be applied under the tail and between the hind legs and if the horse does not appreciate a hose being sprayed into his face (most do not!) then use a sponge to wipe down his head and ears. In cooler weather, cover the horse with a cooler so he does not get chilled and hand walk until cooled out. Brush out any sweat marks if it is too cold to use water. Irish knit sheets under a cooler will help dry horses as well. Horses should never be put away with dried sweat marks and the horse always comes first! Attend to the horse before picking up the cell phone to check for messages.

Tack should be attended to after each ride, to ensure that it stays in good condition. It is just as easy to spend about 10 minutes to wipe down your tack before putting it away. Dip your bit in a bucket of water before hanging it up to remove dried saliva and dirt. Dirty tack leads to leather weakening and breaking and it is gross to ask a horse to accept a bit that is dirty with caked on saliva. Saddle pads should be washed often, as dirty pads can cause skin issues for horses. By spending a few minutes after each ride to wipe down the tack, you will find less effort and time is required to do a deep cleaning of it.

Chapter 9
Pasture and Farm Maintenance

Like any business, there are many "behind the scenes" involved with running a barn, including repairs, mowing, pasture maintenance, and farm cleaning in general!

Most farm cleaning can be incorporated into daily barn chores. Set aside a day each week or month to assign specific tasks, whether removing cobwebs from the walls and ceiling, weeding the entrance area, or mowing pastures.

Daily chores should be performed to keep the stable area clean and well-maintained. Sweeping the aisle way, raking around the entrance, cleaning buckets, and picking manure out of paddocks are all chores that should be done daily. Not only does it make the barn look clean, but it also helps to reduce the fly population.

Other farm maintenance will need to be done "as needed, " such as a fixing a broken water pipe or fence board, which rarely occurs at a good time. Keeping spare boards around is always a good idea in case one breaks. Many broken pipes can be easily fixed if you keep extra pipes and glue around, but in case you are not very handy, it is good to have the phone number of a plumber. Broken boards can pose a hazard to horses and should be repaired immediately. In the meantime, consider the benefits of using duct tape or hay string to fix a board!

Frequent Barn Maintenance Tasks and the Whys For Doing Them

Cobwebs should be removed often. They are unsightly and a potential fire hazard, as is dust, which should also be kept to a minimum. Some spiders can also be the source of unexplained sores on horses. Certain spiders, such as black widows, will make their home under the lips of buckets, waiting for unsuspecting fingers to lift them off their hanger and lurking under benches and in the depths of tack trunks. Spiders, roaches, and other creepy crawlies should also be controlled. Nobody wants to open their tack box to find roaches crawling around their helmet, and nobody wants to find spiders in their boots.

Preventing flies, mosquitoes, roaches, and other pests is also a routine maintenance that should be performed often for the comfort of both horses and humans. Clean barn aisles, not to mention well-mucked stalls, and areas around the barn will go a long way in reducing pest infestations. Care should be used in hanging sticky fly traps because they will also snare lizards, butterflies, and even small birds. Smelly pest attractants should be hung away from the barn to draw the flies out of the barn and not into the barn. Automatic fly systems are worth the investment because they will provide relief from flies all day long. Consider using fly predators, which are environmentally safe and non-toxic. Barn owners can get a subscription, and based upon the number of horses and acreage, a shipment will arrive monthly containing the eggs of biteless and stingless insects that feast on flies in their immature pupa stage.

Care should be taken if blowers are used in the barn so that debris is not blown into horses' faces, because eye injuries can result. At the same barn where the coolers were placed on horses instead of their blankets, the horses were fed in tubs on the ground, just inside their aluminum stall door, that hung several feet above the ground. As morning chores were finishing up, many horses were returning to their stalls for lunch, and more times than not, a blower was coming down the aisle, blowing dust, hay, and other harmful particles not only into their feed tubs but also into their eyes.

Buckets should be cleaned daily. Dirty feed tubs attract flies, and slimy water buckets may prevent horses from adequately drinking. This is a relatively simple task to incorporate into barn chores, and once you find a system that works for your barn's setup, it doesn't take that much extra time. Feed dropped under feed tubs should be cleaned up when mucking stalls.

The area around the barn should not be neglected. Picking manure from paddocks and barnyard areas daily will significantly reduce fly infestation and the spread of internal parasites.

Moist and wet areas will also attract flies and provide breeding grounds for flies and mosquitoes, so managing areas prone to flooding or containing water should be eliminated. This also applies to buckets not in use, old tires, and anything else lying around where water can accumulate. Eliminating the habitat needed for larvae to hatch will significantly reduce the fly population. Eggs hatch in 7 days if conditions are ideal, and one fly can produce 300 million offspring in just 60 days! Fly breeding season begins once temperatures exceed 65º F, and they continue breeding until the first frost. Manure that has been spread or dragged and manure compost bins that are covered will go a long way in reducing fly habitat. Flies also like to lay eggs in decaying organic matter, including spilled feed, manure in pastures or paddocks, and in grass clippings.

Rodent control should also be addressed regularly, whether by enlisting a barn cat, a terrier, or a snake. Rats and mice will be attracted to any spilled grain. Rats will nibble on the coronary band of sleeping horses, chew open bags of feed, and leave behind the potential for disease. Eliminate rodent breeding grounds, such as trash piles, stacks of lumber, weeds, and stacked bags of grain. Crawl spaces should be sealed up. Poison should not be used to kill rodents, due to the risk of poisoning birds, pets, and other animals that come upon the carcass. Many lethal options on the market do not involve poisons. Snakes are perhaps the best rodent control option, and any time you find a non-venomous snake hanging around your barn, be happy about it! They will leave you alone while keeping your barn free of rodents. There is also the chance that they will keep venomous snakes at bay.

At a barn I leased, there was a small crawl space between the feed room and the hay loft, which was only about 6 inches tall, too small for my barn cats to get into. Rats had taken up residency, and their population soon became too overwhelming for my two cats. It was not uncommon to find drowned rats in water buckets. I was frustrated. I had tried putting out traps, but they didn't work, and I wasn't about to try poison due to the risk to my cats and birds. I joked that I needed a snake to control the rat population. One day, I walked into the barn, and lo and behold, a corn snake was curled up on a shelf. Summoning up my courage, I knocked the snake into a bucket using a broom. Before he could escape, I took him to one of the openings in the crawl space. Not sure how to get the snake to go UP, I tipped him out of the bucket onto the tines of a pitchfork and then turned him up and away from me. His first instinct was to slither back towards me. Using my free hand to shake a broom at him, I encouraged him (or her?) to somehow find its way into the crawl space. Well, he must have heard (smelled? felt? sensed?) something because suddenly, that snake shot upward like he was being shot out of a cannon! He entered the hole, and within SECONDS, there was a tremendous commotion as rats were abandoning their home from openings that I didn't even know existed! It was like the sinking of the Titanic. Rats were scurrying everywhere. I was sickened at how many rats there were, yet amazed that one snake could cause such panic. Considering how snakes send my youngest daughter into cold sweats, I shouldn't have been surprised! There must have been nests of babies that could not evacuate, and I did feel a bit sad, but not for long. That snake must have thought he hit the lottery! He stayed up there for over a week! Occasionally, I would see him peeking his head out of one of the holes.

Meanwhile, I prayed that my snake-phobic daughter didn't happen to look up and see it! I only told her about the snake a year later! The rats NEVER came back! I saw the snake in the crawl space just once more, about six months later. I guess he was in the neighborhood and decided to check it out and see if he could get an easy meal again. He didn't stick around because there was no free meal up there!

The farm I own now is home to a pair of black racers and a coachwhip. Occasionally, I will find the coachwhip in my hay stall under the pallets, which explains why I rarely see rats.

Pasture Maintenance

Pastures should be inspected often, not only to find broken boards but also to identify any toxic weeds or plants that may have appeared, find and fill in any holes, pick up any trash, and monitor the health of the grass. Scouting pastures often is the foundation of a sound pasture management program.

Grasses produce a seed head, which is necessary for reproducing, and the net movement of energy is up. Once a seed head forms, it moves from the reproductive state to a vegetative state, and the net movement of energy is down. Plants want to store enough energy in the base or roots to survive winter. Now is a good time to mow, because once the plant develops seed heads, the quality is low. Removing the stem and seed head will help stimulate new growth, which will be in the form of leaves. The leaves will be of high quality for grazing, and they will aid in capturing sunlight to provide energy for the plant.

Grass should never be mowed or grazed down to under 3 inches in height. Horses should be removed if the grass becomes too short, and the pasture should be allowed time to recover. If grasses are not allowed to recover after mowing or from grazing, they will not be able to recover over winter, and weeds will take over.

Pastures should be scrutinized for weeds. Identify the number, location, and type of weeds present. Note the dominant species. Weed management should focus on controlling the dominant species while preventing the spread of the less common weeds.

While grass may be difficult to grow in some regions, that is no excuse to allow weeds to take over. Horses should be turned out on fields and paddocks that are free of weeds, trash, and holes. If grass is inadequate, work should be done to keep weeds away. It not only looks better, but it is safer for the horse.

Utilizing your county extension office is a free service, and the information you receive from your agent is invaluable. They will provide you with a report regarding your soil, grass, and weeds and help you develop a plan for maintaining your pastures.

Identifying weeds is the first step in weed control. Your extension agent can provide information about the common weeds in your area and what is growing in your pastures. Some weeds may look alike, and it is important to know which ones are toxic and problematic.

Before applying fertilizers and herbicides and seeding to pastures, testing the soil will take the guess-work out of which products and seeds to use and prevent spending unnecessary money. It is relatively inexpensive to test and only needs to be done every three years. The soil test results will indicate the pH level, whether or not lime is required, and what other nutrients your pasture lacks. Aeration may be necessary before doing anything else if the soil is heavily compacted.

After soil testing, your next course to develop lush pastures is to practice weed control. Weed prevention is necessary in safeguarding pastures. Weeds can be transported via hay, harvested grass seed, sod, spreading manure, animals, equipment, water, and the wind. When purchasing grass seeds, buy only those guaranteed not to be contaminated with weed seeds. Grass seed should be certified as weed-free.

Weed control can be accomplished by mowing, hand pulling, or the use of herbicides. If herbicides are used, they must be used at the right time of year. Care must be taken to keep runoff from water supplies, and most products require horses and all grazing animals to be kept off the pasture for a specified length of time. It is important to note that weeds are not the issue; they are a symptom. They are a sign of underlying problems that need to be addressed. Once weeds are under control and pastures are fertilized, established perennial grass will help to prevent weeds from becoming established. Not all weeds respond to the same herbicides, so again, it is essential to know what weeds are growing in your pasture and to be able to treat them with the correct herbicide: otherwise, you are wasting money. In addition, some grasses will not tolerate certain herbicides. For example, Argentine Bahiagrass will not tolerate Roundup, while Pensacola Bahiagrass cannot be sprayed with metsulfuron-containing products like Cimarron. In addition, weather conditions can affect the potential for herbicide injury to grass and the rate of herbicide applied.

Determine whether you will spread fresh manure or if you will compost the manure before spreading it on your pastures. Composting manure first by microorganisms in a controlled environment will deliver a nutrient-rich organic material that will be free of potential weeds, parasites and odors. Composted manure applied to pastures will go a long way to create a healthy pasture, which means less money spent on fertilizers and supplemental hay.

When planning your pasture program, whether it is new or established, there are several items to consider:

- Determine the species of grass that can be grown in your area, which will depend on climate and soil.

- Take into account the drainage. Certain grasses will not tolerate soil that drains poorly and remains wet.

- What is the growing season and peak demand for quantity and nutritional value?

- Will the pasture be used for grazing or to produce hay? Will it be used as a primary source of fiber?

- Consider the level of management required to produce optimum pasture production.

- It is possible to extend your grazing season by mixing different grasses. Over-seed cool-season forages into summer grazing pastures to extend grazing into the fall and, in some climates, even winter.

- Due to prussic acid poisoning, never plant Sorghum or Sudangrass hybrids.

Rotating pastures is essential to pasture health. It will enable grasses to become established, and it is vital for the health of pastures to have breaks. Excessive grazing, which results in grass under 3" in height, will damage not only the plant but also the root health. Roots in poor health will be slow to recover if they are able to do so at all. Roots in poor health will be less resilient to disease and unable to store water and nutrients. It is a vicious cycle, with overgrazing and poor grass health enabling weeds to take over. Bare spots are also areas where weeds will generate, so it is best to over-seed those areas.

It is best to address pasture management in the fall when the rainy season ends. Now is an excellent time to take horses off the fields to allow the pasture to rest and begin and to address the weeds, hopefully giving the pastures a good start come spring.

Once you have a hard freeze, the growing season is over, and regrowth will not occur until spring. Temperatures under 28° F degrees for several hours will elevate the sugar levels in the grass; therefore, the risk of colic and founder increases. Remove horses from the grass if the height is less than 4 inches for a period of one week until the sugar levels decrease. If the pasture is already stressed and under 3 inches tall, grazing should be halted until spring to prevent poor re-growing conditions. In addition, frost-damaged leaves from known toxic trees, such as red maples and cherry, are also at their greatest risk of causing poisoning, and therefore, such areas should be avoided for at least 30 days. Pastures that contain Sorghum-Sudangrass or Johnsongrass should also be avoided for the remaining season due to the risk of cyanide poisoning.

Only certified seed and only grass seed that is known to grow in your conditions should be used. Take into account the zone in which you live, the soil condition, and how much shade or sun your fields will receive daily. For seeding to be successful, the fields should be properly prepared, and the timing of seeding needs to be taken into consideration. Offering your horses a variety of grasses will help build a stronger gut, which will be better able to withstand small amounts of toxins. Good pastures will be seeded with a variety of seeds, which should all be indigenous to your location. By seeding with a mixture of grasses, you will also develop a more durable pasture for grazing.

Goals of Good Pasture Management:

- Establish a decent grazing period throughout the year

- Minimize infection from internal parasites

- Eliminate toxic and noxious weeds

- Prevent overgrazing

- Remove seed heads

- Rest periods

By establishing a pasture journal, you can keep track of your pasture management plan from year to year. Note what seeds were planted and at what time of year. Note the weather conditions and results. How long were the horses turned out each day, and for how many months? Did you rotate, and for how long were the pastures allowed to rest and recover? What was the rainfall for each month? What fertilizers and herbicides were used? Were weeds under control, or did you have an excessive amount to deal with? What were the results of soil testing? Include a map of the grazing area and make note of areas that were overgrazed, underutilized, excessively wet, or full of weeds. What was the grass height? Photos are also helpful to keep track of your pasture from year to year. By creating a pasture journal, you can keep track of your progress from year to year and adjust your pasture management plan every year based on your results.

Good grazing management and planning will affect your grass's pasture yield and nutrient value. While a general rule of thumb has always been one horse per acre, the truth is closer to 2 to 3 acres in order to sustain one horse grazing full time. The type of grass, quality, rainfall, amount of weeds and fertilizer are all things to consider when determining the stocking rate. Combining multiple forage species will also aid in providing nutritional needs of horses than grazing on just one type of grass. Maintaining a lush pasture is hard work, but there are many excellent resources that will guide you. Each state has a county agriculture extension office, or contact your soil and water conservation district, which offers free to low-cost services to help manage your pastures, from fertilizing to seeding, as well as identifying and preventing weeds. Several good sites on social media are dedicated to improving pastures. The success of your pasture will depend on the preparation and choice of grasses. Starting with a clean, weed-free, and tilled base is essential, and it is cheaper to control the weeds from the very beginning than to try to and address weeds later in the season.

> *At the high-end barn I worked, (the very same barn where the horses were blanketed with coolers and blowers that blew dust into the horse's eyes as they ate– where every morning following night turnout, several horses would return to their stalls with oozing and crusty sores around their mouths.)– many horses in the barn suffered from various stomach ailments. The boarders were supplying their horses with a wide range of products to combat the issues, none of which helped with diarrhea, colics, and other ailments. I suggested that the barn manager contact the local agriculture extension agent. She had never heard of them! She said she would talk to the farm owner when I explained what they did and that the service was free. A few weeks later, I inquired as to whether or not they had contacted the agent. It was explained to me that the owner did not want the agent out for fear that word would spread that there were toxic weeds on the property, making horses sick! My response was, why would they want to be known as the farm with so many unexplained sick horses? Their response to a situation that could be fixed so easily was mind-boggling.*

Toxic Plants

It is a misconception that horses will avoid eating plants that are poisonous. If grass is scarce, a horse that is hungry enough will eat anything that is growing. While some plants are not palatable, others may be pretty tasty, especially in the early stages of growth when the tender young shoots are sprouting. Young foals, especially, will explore anything growing in their field. Other factors can influence the toxicity of plants and weeds, including the horse's health, size, immune system, the amount of plant digested, previous toxic events, soil composition, water intake, weather, and seasons. Some weeds also have a cumulative effect, and a horse can eat it for weeks or months before there is a reaction; by then, it may be too late for treatment: therefore, removing toxic weeds and not overgrazing pastures are essential. If grass is not abundant, offer hay, whether by placing a round bale or block in their field or tossing flakes of hay. It is best to place the hay in a tub or on rubber mats to prevent the horse from ingesting sand.

Weather can also cause plants to produce toxins. Certain weeds and grasses may suddenly produce toxins, particularly after rains in the fall, when it follows a dry summer. These rains can cause new growth, which is toxic. These type of weeds include the following:

- Sudangrass

- Johnsongrass

- Redroot pigweed

- Black nightshade

- Horse nettle

- Russian thistle

- Kochia

- Lambsquarters

Additionally, toxic weeds and toxins are known to find their way into cut hay and grain. Therefore, it is best to purchase only high-quality hay and feed from a reputable grower or dealer. Sadly, there have been cases where hay has been contaminated with botulism and toxic weeds, and horses have become very ill or died as a result of eating it.

The effects of poisonous weeds and plants can include skin irritation, colic, organ failure, weight loss, and death. Depending on the plant, the poisoning can occur with just one mouthful, or it can take eating the plant over a long period before any symptoms are noticed. Death can be instant, or the horse can suffer for weeks or months until euthanasia is the only option. Symptoms may often go undiagnosed, such as when a horse colics. Owners are so worried about resolving the colic that they don't focus on what is causing it, which may be the result of a poisonous plant.

Managers and owners should do everything possible to remove toxic plants and weeds from pastures. Just because one horse has never had an issue with a toxic plant or weed doesn't mean other horses will not react. Remember that Google is your friend before planting any plant or flower near a barn, fence line, or pasture! Existing toxic plants should be removed. Pulling toxic weeds will ensure you get the roots, thus preventing future re-infestation. Pulled plants should be placed in the trash can; never leave them on a compost pile or in a pile on the ground, because some can regenerate from their roots.

Most Common Toxic Weeds, Plants and Trees:

Plant Name	Toxic Parts	Region	Symptoms	Treatment
Angel Trumpet	All parts, seeds	Southern U.S. and tropical climates	Anorexia, weight loss, thirst, diarrhea, excessive urination, death	Activated charcoal, if caught early, along with supportive drugs
Apple Tree	Fallen apples on the ground, when consumed in large quantities	Throughout the U.S. and Canada	Cyanide poisoning and death	Mineral oil and laxatives to remove excess quantities from the digestive tract
Avocado	Fruit, skin, leaves, bark	Tropical climates	Colic; death	NSAIDS & analgesics
Black Locust	Bark, seeds	Eastern and Central U.S.	Weakness, diarrhea, severe gastro irritation, posterior paralysis	Recovery is good if the horse has not eaten too much. Activated charcoal and supportive therapy.
Black Walnut	Roots	Eastern and Midwest, south to Arizona, Texas, and Georgia	Affected by shavings used from Black Walnut: laminitis, depression, respiratory	Remove the horse and wash the legs. Call vet ASAP to treat laminitis
Bracken Fern	Plant	Worldwide	Takes 1 month for symptoms to appear. Depression, muscle tremors, paralysis, colic, rapid heart rate, and temperature	Thiamine and supportive care

Cherry Tree	Seeds, leaves, bark, wilted leaves, and new growth are the most toxic	Oregon, Washington, southern and eastern US, south Canada	Fatal cyanide poisoning. Drinking water after ingestion releases cyanide into the bloodstream. Slobbering, increased respiration. and convulsions	Treatment must be started ASAP.
Common Boxwood	All parts	Throughout the U.S. and Canada landscape	Weakness, convulsion, respiratory failure, death	Sodium nitrate and sodium thiosulfate IV, sedatives and laxatives None
Jessamine Jasmine	All parts. Winter and spring are the most dangerous times	Eastern and southern U.S. and in landscape	Increased heart rate and respiratory rate, muscle weakness, colic, and death. Symptoms occur within hours of ingesting	Activated charcoal, supportive care, fluids
Jimsonweed	All parts	Throughout the U.S. and in landscape	Bloating, staggering, seizures, high temperatures, labored breathing, and death; symptoms occur within a few hours of ingesting	None
Milkweed	All parts	Throughout the U.S. and in landscape	Convulsions, neuro and gastro disorders, congestion in lungs, heart and spleen, bloating	Intensive care with cardiac monitoring
Nightshade	All parts	Throughout the US	When ingested in large amounts, tannin kills the surface cells of the digestive tract and enters the bloodstream, causing anorexia, abdominal pain, thirst, bloody diarrhea, and kidney failure.	Activated charcoal, supportive care
Oak Tree	Leaves and flower buds in spring, acorns	Throughout the U.S. and Canada	Diarrhea, paralysis, cardiac arrest, death	Calcium hydroxide via nasogastric tube, intensive IV therapy

Oleander	All parts. Red flowers are the most toxic	Southern U.S. and West Coast	Rapid respiration, weak heartbeat, death from suffocation	Activated charcoal, IV fluid, supportive care
Peach Tree	All parts contain cyanide	East from Texas and north to Canada	Oral irritation, colic, bloody diarrhea, death	Sodium nitrate and sodium thiosulfate IV, sedatives and laxatives
Pokeweed	All parts	Southeast Canada, Eastern US to Minnesota, Texas	Severe anemia, weakness, depression, death	Activated charcoal, saline cathartics, blood transfusions
Red Maple	Wilted or dried leaves, especially in fall	Eastern U.S. and Canada, west to Minnesota and Texas	Kidney and liver damage, death	Fluid, oxygen, blood transfusion
Rhodo-dendron/ Azalea	All parts, nectar	Eastern and Southern U.S.	Acute and chronic cyanide poisoning, death	Activated charcoal, ASAP, IV fluids
Sudan grass or Johnson grass	All parts: cyanide poisoning when grass is stressed	Southern U.S., north to New York and west to Iowa	Fatal. Liver damage in horses who survive.	IV solution of sodium nitrate and sodium thiosulfate
Water Hemlock (also known as poison parsley or poison parsnip)	All parts: considered one of the most toxic plants to humans and animals.	One of 4 species in the Apiaceae family will be found in all states except for Hawaii and is found in Canada. Prefers wet and moist areas.	Water near the roots may also become contaminated.	No treatment due to the rapid speed of toxins' effects.

Social media is full of photos of lovely barns with lush landscaping in the barnyard, hedgerows of shrubs along fence lines, and containers of flowers throughout the barn. Remember that many of these photos may have been staged for a beautiful picture or even photo-shopped, but that doesn't mean they belong in a barn. Many ornamental garden plants and vegetables are also toxic, and care should be taken to avoid planting these near horses. These include foxglove, tulips, daylilies, hydrangea, lantana, morning glory, daffodil, iris, wisteria, clematis, bleeding heart, English ivy, lupine, and privet, to name a few.

Barn Yard Friendly Plants, Trees, and Shrubs:

- Alyssum
- American Hazelnut Shrub
- Aster
- Black Eyed Susan
- Black Gum Tree
- Black Hawthorn
- Blazing Star
- Blueberry
- Catnip
- Chamomile
- Cornflower
- Crepe Myrtle
- Eastern White Pine Tree
- Echinacea
- Flowering Dogwood Tree
- Impatien
- Jacob's Ladder
- Marigold
- Nasturtium
- Oregano
- Pagoda Dogwood Shrub
- Pansy
- Peppermint
- Petunia
- Podocarpus Shrub
- Poplar Tree
- Red Bud Tree
- River birch Tree
- Rose
- Sage
- Snapdragon
- Spicebush
- Sunflower
- Thyme
- Valerian
- Viburnum
- Yarrow
- Zinnia

This is just a partial list of horse-friendly plants. The ASPCA and you local county agent have a very extensive list of plants that are safe to plant near your barn.

I love to garden and have a variety of plants, flowers, trees, and vegetables growing around my farm. Before I purchase any plant, if I see something I like, I research that plant's toxicity to horses. If the plant is going in my backyard or somewhere else that is not accessible to my horse and donkeys, then I next research if the plant or flower is toxic to dogs, chickens, ducks, and goats!

Horse owners should be wary of barns with pastures that contain many weeds. Be proactive and able to identify poisonous weeds, trees, and plants, and avoid barns that are oblivious to such growing on their property.

Barn and Pasture Maintenance By Season

Spring Pasture:

Once the grass has grown to a minimum of 5", gradually introduce horses back onto your pastures, especially horses, ponies, and donkeys that have metabolic disorders. The spring grasses contain the highest levels of sugars, starch, and fructans (non-structural carbohydrates or NSC), which can trigger laminitis. Fifteen minutes a day of grazing is a good place to start, increasing their turnout time daily. By offering hay to your horse before turning him out, he may be less likely to overindulge on grass. In addition, grazing muzzles may be used to restrict the amount of grass eaten.

Contact your local state extension agent to have a good walk around your property, search for toxic weeds and plants that may have popped up, have your soil tested, and devise a plan for applying fertilizer and herbicides. Nitrogen, phosphorus, potassium, and lime are all products that may need to be added to your pastures.

Nitrogen should be applied in the spring to jump-start grass growth. Your fields may require more nitrogen than what is contained in your fertilizer. Typically, nitrogen is applied in April and can be applied annually. Phosphorus and potassium can be applied anytime after the first grazing but no later than June. They can be applied annually. Lime can be applied at any time of the year but should only be applied every three years, not annually. It takes 6-12 months to react in the soil, so plan accordingly if you are reseeding and apply it 6-12 months before.

Not all pastures require nitrogen, phosphorus, potassium, or lime, so it is important to check your soil before needlessly applying any of these.

If pastures contain more weeds than grass, now is the time to reduce the weeds, whether by applying herbicides, hand pulling, or mowing. Use care when utilizing herbicides and read instructions thoroughly.

Seeding should be done as the rainy season begins. Use grasses indigenous to your area, and consider shade and the amount of sunlight your pastures will receive daily. Applying seed without soil testing is a waste of money. If pastures contain less than 50% desirable grazing grass, start over and reestablish them; otherwise, the recommended course of action for pastures with more than 50% grass is over-seeding by adding new seed to the existing pasture. Prepare pastures for seeding by mowing the pastures short to prevent the taller grass from shading out the new seeds. Pastures can also be tilled, particularly if you are starting over. The seeding will depend upon your climate but should be done while temperatures are still cool at night. Typically, seeding is started in April and finished by late May. The longer horses can stay off of newly seeded pastures, the better it will be able to withstand grazing and hoofs. Six months to a year is optimum. Pastures should be mowed often. Regular mowing before grass goes to seed will encourage plants to replace leaves instead. Mowing will also help control weeds. Grass should never be cut under 3" because this can damage the grass and prolongs the recovery time.

In addition, remove tree debris from fields and inspect fencing for broken boards and look for holes and trash. Once pastures have been restored, grazing can resume. The optimum situation involves rotating pastures and moving horses off grass when it is down to 4- 5 inches in height.

Spring Barn Maintenance:

- Check electrical wiring for rodent damage

- Clean fans before operating

- Clear cobwebs from barn ceilings and rafters

- Make sure well-traveled paths and walkways are prepared for rain and mud. Add gravel or other well-draining material

- Check that the plumbing is in good order

- Replace any troughs that may have cracked from the freezing winter temperatures

- Clean gutters

- Inspect smoke detectors: replace batteries

- Inspect fire extinguishers

- Restock first aid kits

- Inspect footing in arenas

Summer Pasture Maintenance:

Horses should be grazing by now, and the grass will be growing unless drought or other conditions prevent it. Nitrogen can be applied again in June, provided the grass receives plenty of moisture, whether from rainfall or sprinklers. Lime, phosphorous, and potassium can also be applied in the summer if they were not applied in the spring.

Continue to monitor pastures for trash, holes, broken boards and weeds and remove any new weeds.

Summer Barn Maintenance:

- Blankets should be washed and put away. Any blankets that need repairs should be attended to before being put away

- Check electrical wiring for rodent damage

- Clear cobwebs from barn ceilings and rafters

- Clean fans

- Inspect smoke detectors and fire extinguishers.

- Clean gutters

Autumn Pasture Maintenance:

Reseed pastures in early fall for cool-season grasses. The month you reseed will depend upon your climate and rainfall. Continue to mow when you see seed heads forming. Removing the stem and seed head will stimulate new growth.

Weeds can be sprayed with an herbicide at this time and another application of nitrogen in September will enable more growth during the cooler weather. Now is a good time to spread composted manure.

Continue to check fencing for broken boards or rotted posts, which may need to be replaced before a winter storm knocks it down.

If you have not had your agriculture agent out in more than a year, this is a good time to have them out and test your soil and develop a plan, especially if you think your pastures need a fall fertilizer.

Autumn Barn Maintenance:

- Clean out areas where manure and other organic material have accumulated, particularly in high-traffic areas. This will reduce the chance of these areas becoming muddy in winter and spring

- Freshen up the footing in high-traffic areas to reduce muddy conditions later in the seasons

- Clean barn gutters

- Check electrical wiring for rodent damage

- Inspect smoke detectors: replace batteries

- Inspect fire extinguishers

- Remove cobwebs from ceilings and rafters

- Blankets and sheets should be taken from storage and be ready to use

- Plans should be in place to care for your senior horses in the coming winter months

- If you live in a climate where you can purchase and store hay and grain for the winter, this should be completed by the end of September

- Any necessary barn and fence repairs should be wrapped up before the first snowfall

- Pipes should be wrapped in preparation for freezing temperatures

The cooler weather means this is a good time to work on projects you could not tackle due to rain or heat! Constructing your manure compost pile, addressing the muddy areas, constructing a sacrifice paddock, or removing weeds and dead branches are best addressed before winter arrives.

Winter Pasture Maintenance:

Depending on your climate, your pastures may be unusable, sitting under a foot of snow or crisp from frost, or there may be signs of winter rye grass popping up between the last blades of summer grass. It is an excellent time to be thinking about what management practices you can utilize in the coming spring.

Horses should be kept off winter pastures in the north to prevent horses from damaging the remaining grass and root system, which will result in delayed recovery in the spring. Many farms have a designated winter turnout area, whether it is a sacrificial pasture or dry lot paddocks. These paddocks will need extra care as they recover in the spring. Ideally, drainage will have been improved in these areas to avoid becoming shoe-sucking mud holes once the snow begins to melt.

Manure should not be spread over frozen ground. The grass is unable to utilize any nutrients in the winter, and it will only encourage the area to become a muddy slop come spring. Horses should be kept off pastures for at least a week after a hard freeze or frost (several hours below 28º F.) Pastures after a frost or freeze are higher in non-structured carbohydrates, which can lead to laminitis. Horses with any metabolic disorder, that are especially prone to laminitis, are especially at risk after a frost or freeze.

Keep in mind there will be no more grass growth after a freeze, and horses should not be grazed once the height is less than 4 inches, even if your grass is still green. If pastures are allowed to go shorter than 4 inches after a frost or freeze, the recovery time of your pastures in springtime will be much longer than if horses were removed and the pastures were allowed to rest.

Continue to inspect fencing and pastures for any potential damage or broken boards from winter storms.

Winter Barn Maintenance:

For many equestrians, winter is their downtime. Unless you are fortunate enough to have access to an indoor riding arena or you can travel south, where the weather will allow you to continue riding, the shorter days, freezing temperatures, and hard ground mean that most riding will come to a temporary end. Continue to monitor your horse's condition and health, especially senior horses. If your horse has grown a long coat, running your hands along their skin and continuous grooming will enable you to check for weight loss that may otherwise go undetected. It will also allow you to search for ticks and keep tabs on the condition of the skin. Many skin problems will arise when the conditions are muddy, such as scratches or rain rot, so it is important to keep grooming as part of a regular routine, even when not riding.

- Tack should be well-cleaned and conditioned, especially if not being used. Store in a temperature-controlled room

- If you have not established a disaster plan, now is a good time to do so. Identify the possible scenarios Mother Nature may dump on you and devise a plan for each catastrophe. If you have a disaster plan in effect already, go over it, make any adjustments, give new copies to boarders, have a disaster drill, and include your employees and boarders. (see Chapter 12)

- If you do not have a fire prevention plan, now is the time to create one. Hold drills with your employees and boarders. (see Chapter 11)

- Check electrical wiring for rodent damage

- If a professional electrician has not evaluated your barn in recent years, now is an excellent time to schedule an appointment with one

- Remove cobwebs from ceilings and rafters

- Winterize farm equipment and store anything that will not be used until spring

- Now is a good time for cleaning, removing junk, and any other barn chores that you have been putting off

- Keep your horse engaged with boredom busting games

As a horse owner, it is your responsibility to inspect all of a potential boarding barn's facilities, not just the barn itself. Is the fencing in good repair? Do you notice many weeds in the fields, or are they well managed? Be able to identify common toxic weeds known in your location. Walk the fields. Are there holes and rocks that may cause injury to your horse? Is the barn clean, free of cobwebs, and well-maintained? Extension cords, especially those not rated for outdoor use, are a red flag because they can be a fire hazard. Look around for any potential risks. A barn that practices routine barn maintenance will be a safer haven for your horse and give you peace of mind.

Chapter 10
Safety in the Barn

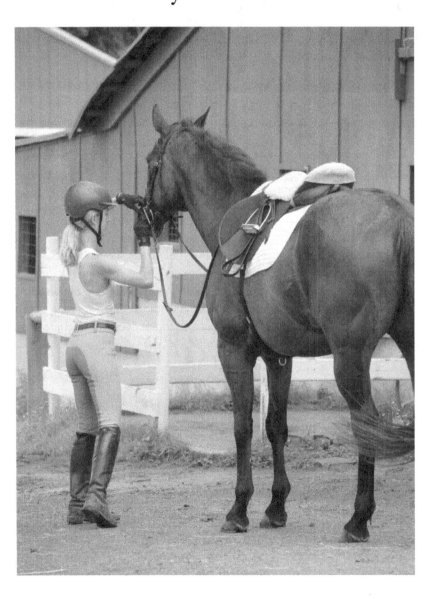

All employees and boarders must understand basic safety around horses. Employees should never be turned loose on their own to lead horses, catch them in a pasture, or bathe them if they do not have the experience and are uncomfortable with doing anything beyond mucking stalls. Handling a horse properly will go a long way in preventing accidents because horses are unpredictable and can react to any situation with lightning-fast speed. One should also know how to keep horses safe from injury, because they can be highly accident-prone and are able to injure themselves on seemingly thin air in the 30 seconds you turn your back on them.

Handling Horses

Horses can and will spook at the most benign and silliest items. We have all seen the memes of horses spooking at plastic bags and balloons. Wild horses learn to survive by being aware of their surroundings at all times and, therefore, will smell, see, and hear things long before a human does. Horses learned to survive by their "flight or fight" reaction. This trait never left the domesticated horse! New situations and places can make them nervous, and there is always that one horse in the barn that will run you over at the gate to get to dinner, and a rattling truck going down the road can easily send your calm horse from a quiet walk into a bucking frenzy.

The horse is designed to be highly aware of peripheral motion. This is its survival mechanism. One must recognize basic horse physiology and know that a horse has blind spots when it comes to his vision: directly behind his head and body, with an arc of about 20 degrees. He also has blind spots directly under his head, in front of the forehead and below the body in front of his face. Horses use two types of vision, binocular and monocular. Monocular vision allows horses to see on both sides of the head, which means the right eye and the left eye work independently of each other and see different views. Each eye sees across an arc of 200-210 degrees around the body. The monocular fields straight in front of the horses face overlap and that results in a binocular field, between 65 and 80 degrees, which is responsible for depth perception. The horse sees in front of his nose with both eyes but can only see to his left side with his left eye when facing forward, and the same goes with his right eye. A horse cannot see what they are grazing or eating in a bucket and they can't see you if you are directly behind them. By changing his head position, they can increase their line of vision. A horse should always know where you are in relation to its body, whether by patting or talking to it. By lowering its head and moving it from side to side, a horse can scan a 360-degree horizontal periphery. Raising its head will help it focus on distant objects. When the head is perpendicular to the ground, the visual field is lowered and the focus shifts to the immediate ground in front of the horse.

An experienced horseperson can read a horse's body language. Always pay attention to the horse's ears, tail, head, and legs.

Many barns insist that barns should be quiet, but if a barn is too quiet, a horse will never learn to handle noises when they do occur. While running and shouting should not be tolerated, go ahead and play music, run the blower, and carry on as much as normal in a barn. Horses should be allowed to encounter as many objects as possible to desensitize them to anything strange they may encounter at a horseshow or on the trail, including bikes, bouncing balls, tarps, umbrellas, and even gunshots, and fireworks. Many horses are sent into a frenzy on holidays such as Independence Day and New Year's Eve, but if horses are slowly desensitized to the noise and bright colors, they will most likely get through those days without injuring themselves or the need to be sedated.

Common Sense Horse Handling Rules:

- Speak to horses as you approach so they know you are there, especially if they are facing away from you

- Never approach a horse from the rear without them knowing you are there

- Walk toward a horse's shoulder and not toward his face, so you are better in his sight

- Stand close to the horse's body

- When leading, never wrap the lead rope or reins around your hand or arms in case he should suddenly bolt

- Lead on the horse's left side, between their head and shoulder

- Never drag the lead rope or reins on the ground

- Horses should never be tied to an object that can break if he suddenly pulls back, such as fence boards

- Horses should be tied with a quick-release knot. If using cross ties, attach the ties to a piece of hay string, which will break if the horse panics and tries to break free

- When tied, horses should never have the rope so long that they can get their leg caught, and it should not be so low that they can lower their head and get caught

- When releasing a horse into a field, turn its head to face you and the gate before removing the halter. Horses should be taught to stand patiently while the halter is removed and not to bolt, and they should never be allowed to be released before they are through the gate, because this can encourage bolting

- When blanketing a horse, start with the chest straps first, then the girth, and secure the leg straps last. When removing the blanket, start in the reverse order so that if the horse moves, the blanket will not slip down and become entangled in his legs

- Always wear closed-toe shoes with a closed heel. Sandals and flip-flops are never acceptable in a barn

- Don't lock stall doors with a person in the stall with a horse. If the horse spooks, the person needs a quick exit

- Never duck under the lead rope of a tied horse

- Don't leave equipment such as pitchforks in the aisle way or anywhere else the horse can become injured on them

In today's world, there should be some discussion regarding the use of cell phones because most people have one. It is just plain dangerous to be talking on your cell phone while riding, not to mention disrespectful if either an instructor or a student uses one while in the middle of a lesson. By talking on a cell phone, you are not paying 100% attention to your horse and your surroundings, and it distracts other riders. There should only be one reason to have a phone on your body when riding: you are riding alone or out on the trail and need it for emergencies. If you ride with your phone, keep it silent and never answer any calls. Use it strictly for emergencies! Sadly, we are seeing more and more phones in warm-up arenas, which means that riders are not paying attention to other horses or riders, and that can be a potentially dangerous setting. Some riders like to ride with earplugs and listen to music or podcasts, but that means your attention is, again, not 100% on your horse or your surroundings, and you should save the music for when you are back on just 2 feet and working in the barn.

In addition to being safe around the horse, care should be used so that the horse will not harm itself.

Halters should never be left on a horse unless it is a breakaway or leather halter. They should fit snugly but not too tight and not too loose as to trap a hoof or get caught on a fence post. The throatlatch should always be secure when on. Leading a horse without securing the throatlatch is unsafe, because it can catch on any object as it is loosely flapping.

> *A friend was leading her horse into its stall, not bothering to secure the throatlatch of the halter. To this day, I have no idea what happened, but within a matter of seconds, he was screaming in pain as the dangling strap managed to get caught on something, resulting in a horrible deep cut to his throat, that required many sutures.*

Common sense should be utilized when trailering horses. Trailers should be in good repair. Unfortunately, there are no standards for manufacturing trailers, so not all are as safe as they should be. When purchasing a trailer, it is best to consider one with a steel frame and not aluminum, which will be sturdier and protect your horse in case of an accident. Walls should be double-layered to prevent a horse from kicking through the wall. Ceilings should also be double-layered and painted white to reflect the heat. Consider installing fans as well to keep your horse cool. Floors should be solid and durable. Treated lumber or synthetic Rumber material is best to prevent the floor from failing. Older trailers should have their floors inspected often for rotted wood, including the underside, and to check for any areas of rust along the frame. Butt and chest bars should have quick-release pins, which should work even if your horse's full weight is pushing on it. The more open and airy the trailer is, the more inviting it will be for your horse to want to load and haul quietly. There should be good lighting and airflow, and outside noise should be minimized. Horses should never be allowed to travel with their heads hanging out open windows. There have been instances when horses have tried to escape through the windows with disastrous results. In addition, horses with their heads outside the window while in movement are at risk for injuries, whether from flying debris from passing vehicles or even from being hit by vehicles passing too closely.

The tow vehicle should be properly rated to pull the weight of your trailer, and the truck should be able to stop! Just because your vehicle can pull your trailer doesn't mean you should! The hitch ball should be the correct size, and the hitch itself should be in good condition and properly connected. The wiring should be inspected to ensure it is in good working order. Tires should never be old or bald, because there is a risk of a tire blowout. Bearings should be inspected and packed yearly.

Before loading up your horse, inspect your trailer. Look for signs of rust, faulty wiring, bees that may have taken up residence since your last voyage, and any other signs that may be cause for concern. Ensure the tires have the correct air pressure, and check that birds have not made a nest in the underside of goosenecks.

There is debate about whether a horse's legs should be wrapped. In case of an accident, the wraps will provide extra protection. Shipping wraps will offer the most protection, but if you do not know how to apply them correctly, consider using shipping boots. Bumpers will protect a horse's head if it should bump its head on the trailer's ceiling.

Care should be used when hauling in extreme weather. In summer, avoid hauling when temperatures are more than 90° F and with high humidity. Avoid making prolonged stops, try to avoid traffic, and keep the trailer moving to create airflow. When hauling in winter, use blankets only in extreme cold or when horses are body clipped, because the inside of a trailer will become very warm, especially with multiple horses inside, even in cold weather. Horses should not be hauled with their tack on, because there is a risk of the leathers or any part of the saddle catching on the trailer. Horses are also at risk of becoming dehydrated, especially on long trips, so be sure to offer water at least every 3- 4 hours.

Unfortunately, many drivers on the roads today are not considerate and will cut off horse trailers. It is best to drive carefully and under the speed limit. In rain or snow, extra care should be taken while driving.

> *A horse trailer accident on the interstate resulted in the death of one of two horses. The trailer was being pulled by a vehicle that was not rated for hauling a horse trailer, and when someone cut them off, the trailer began to fishtail until it flipped over. The surviving horse was wearing shipping wraps, which the owner had applied. The other horse, owned by another person, was not wearing any protection. The vet who euthanized the horse stated that he probably would have survived had he been wearing shipping bandages.*

Fencing should be safe for horses, which means no barbed wire. Several styles of wire fencing are excellent for keeping predators and dogs out of the pastures. Be sure to use no-climb fencing with 2-3 inches spacing. A hoof can get caught if the space is 4 inches or greater.

> *I will never forget driving down a road and seeing a horse lying on its side, its leg caught in fencing. It was amazing that the horse was calm, because I have read of other instances where horses panicked and ended up pulling their hoof off. In this situation, I was close to a friend's barn, and several other cars had stopped. While I stayed with the horse to keep it calm, someone drove to the barn to summon help and tools, and we were able to cut the horse free without any additional harm to itself.*

Leave it to horses to find that one nail sticking out of the fence, the stall latch not completely shut, the bolt sticking out of the gate post, snaps facing the wrong direction, and the space between the gate and post. Horses are masters at finding ways to injure themselves, some more than others. Good managers will constantly inspect their barns and property and look for any hazards that can harm a horse.

We had a Thoroughbred who was a champion at hurting himself in the most unusual ways. When he went to college with my daughter, he somehow somersaulted over a branch. He ended up with a puncture hole that went into his elbow and exited 2 inches behind the entrance wound and also pierced his hind pastern. When I arrived to take him home to begin his rehabbing, I discovered that this barn had placed a strip of wood with nails sticking up along the back side of a door that went from the barn to a pasture. Our horse was not turned out in this pasture, or he would have most likely injured himself on the nails. Why would anyone think this is a good idea? Weeks earlier, while at home for Christmas break, he managed to get loose while I was leading him in for dinner and he ran into the barn and into his stall while dragging his lead rope. As he went to run out the back door of his stall and into his paddock, he stepped on the lead rope, which caused him to hit his head on the top of the door jamb. He gave himself a concussion, with a bloody nose, that lasted three days and required multiple Vitamin K injections to try and clot the blood. He also had a pretty good swelling on his head but no lasting damage.

Chapter 11
Preventing Barn Fires

Everyone knows that barns are combustible, yet so few barn owners practice safe fire prevention other than banning smoking. Every year, hundreds of horses are killed or injured due to barn fires, most of which could have been prevented. In this chapter, we discuss barn fires: wildfires will be discussed in Chapter 12.

Some sobering statistics:

- 80- 85% of barn fires are caused by human error: smoking in the barn, welding near combustible material, outdoor burn piles left unattended, or electrical in nature. The most common cause of fires is electrical, with heating devices and malfunctions being the most common cause of electrical fires

- Lightning strikes, fireworks, and spilled gas are also leading causes of fires in barns

- Arson accounts for nearly 15% of fires

- According to the Animal Welfare Institute, barn fires in 2021 killed nearly 700,000 farm animals. From 2018 to 2021, 539 fires killed almost 3 million animals, the majority of which were poultry and pigs. In this time frame, the annual economic loss was estimated to be roughly 48 million dollars in property damage

- It is estimated that barn fires cause roughly 100 injuries, 10 fatalities, and nearly 300 million dollars in property loss each year

- Between 2009 and 2014, nearly 200 horses and four people died in barn fires, including Olympian Boyd Martin's barn, who lost six horses

- Animal Welfare Institute also states that in 2022, more than 500,000 animals died in fires in agricultural buildings. Of that staggering number, at least 140 were horses; the number may be even higher due to poor reporting numbers, which include cattle, pigs, poultry, goats, etc. That number was down from 2007, in which 304 horses and nearly one million animals perished in fires

- In 2007, of the 203 barn fires, 4 were arson; the rest were caused by human error and preventable. However, barn fires are rarely investigated unless there is a human fatality, so this number is most likely inaccurate, and the number of fires is probably much higher

- In 2023, arson killed 30 Standardbreds, and one person was injured in a barn fire at Tioga Downs, New York. Also, in 2023, a barn fire destroyed 26 horses in Georgia, and another ten perished in a barn fire in Texas, resulting from welding near the barn

- Barn fires kill horses more often than any other disaster type

- Fires are the number one emergency affecting horse owners

- Most barn fires are fully engulfed in less than 7 minutes after ignition, with dangerous smoke levels by 5 minutes

- The most common scenario in a barn fire is that horses are long dead from smoke inhalation by the time firefighters arrive

- Economic loss is high: in just one report of 14 fires, the loss of horses and property was estimated to be around 5.6 million dollars

- A barn fire in 2007 killed one person trapped in an apartment above the barn, as well as claiming the lives of 22 horses. The fire was caused by a faulty electrical issue inside the apartment, which was revealed years earlier in an inspection but never addressed

These statistics are sobering and should be a wake-up call for every barn owner, manager, employee, and horse owner to take a good look at their barn and do whatever needs to be implemented before there is a fire.

Because horse barns are considered agricultural buildings, the standards are lax in management and construction. These lax rules can contribute to the ability of fires to ignite and spread. The National Fire Protection Association NFPA 150-Code for Fire and Life Safety in Agriculture Buildings provides the best practices for designers, architects, and barn builders to increase human and animal safety and evacuation for barns of any type.

As already stated, a barn can be fully engulfed by fire in 5- 7 minutes, with dangerous smoke levels at the 3-5 minute mark. It is, therefore, unrealistic to think that the fire department, especially in rural areas, will arrive in time to extinguish the fire and save the lives of horses or any other animals in a burning barn. The horses will be dead from smoke inhalation before they are rescued. And if the fire department does manage to arrive in time, horses are in full panic mode, and the sight of firefighters in full dress, with helmets and air-breathing tanks, will send them further into a heightened stress mode; they will be reluctant to be haltered and led out of a burning barn. And that is if the firemen can locate the horses in a dark, smoky barn, find halters, and open gates or doors.

Barn Design

Everything about a barn construction screams fire hazard: from the wood construction often used to bedding, rubber mats, hay, and landscaping, every barn is a potential fire waiting to happen. Prevention is critical through management practices, facility design, emergency planning, and drills.

Most barns are designed for aesthetics, based on tradition, while fire safety takes a back seat. Fire marshals are not consulted, let alone any other fire safety expert. Many barns were built before the NFPA (National Fire Protection Association.) updated their codes in 2013 for animal housing and have not been retrofitted to accommodate the changes. Additionally, not all jurisdictions require these standards, so not all new builds are guaranteed to meet the codes. NFPA Standard 150-Animal Facilities should be consulted when building a barn, especially when considering layout for evacuations.

If living quarters are being planned in the barn, NFPA Standard #101-1973- Life Safety Code should be followed. It is important to note that insurance is unavailable in most states for barns with apartments above the stalls unless strict fire protection is provided during construction.

Many construction materials used in barn design are conducive to fires. If building new, consider using materials that will not ignite or burn as fast, such as masonry, heavy timber, or fire-retardant woods. Many barns will use varnishes on their wood walls, which will only help to spread the flames of fire. However, fire retardant varnishes are on the market, which will help slow the spread of smoke and flames. Only these products should be used in a barn. Temperatures will reach 1,800° F at the ceiling level within minutes and within 3- 5 minutes to approach the flash point, where all combustibles within that space will ignite. In most barns, this is usually the loft, where hay and bedding may be stored, and this further fuels the fire. That is why compartmentalization (such as a separate barn for shavings and hay and storing tractors and the like in a different building) is recommended.

Most fires start 3 feet off the ground, whether from a cigarette butt or a sparking outlet. Flames will climb quickly to the roof through insulation or combustible materials. Even concrete barns will burn, because the rafters and trusses are wood, as are the doors, not to mention bedding, hay, and rubber mats. Concrete contributes to the insulation of heat after it starts due to heat in its walls, and steel rafters will weaken from the heat of trapped air and will fail and collapse. Falling rafters and ceilings are the most significant hazard to rescue personnel in a barn fire.

Metal absorbs heat faster than wood. Many new barns use lightweight wood trusses with metal gusset plates or joint connectors instead of nails. They are stronger and cheaper and offer more clear span, but they have a poor fire rating.

When building a barn, things to take into account include:

- Attempts should be made to increase the time a fire takes to reach the flash point. This can be achieved by modifying building materials, finishes, and contents, compartmentalization with fire-resistant barriers, and separation of combustibles, high ceiling heights, and/or large room volumes

- Flame rate spread should be taken into account when building a barn. This is the time it takes for flames to travel the surface of the material and is rated from 0 to 100 with 0 being the best rating. For example, concrete block has a value of 0, while dry red oak has a value of 100. Using flame- retardant-lumbar decreases the spread of flames by 75% to a rating of 25

- Low Smoke Development Ratings measure material that produces less smoke as it burns. Less smoke means better visibility, fewer noxious gases, and fewer sparks.

- Fire Ratings are how long a material may block the progression of a fire. The better the rating, the slower (minutes) fire spreads. It is a complicated rating, however, because metal siding will have a low (good) flame spread rate, but it is a good heat conductor, which is a poor fire rating because combustible items touching it may ignite

- Suppression methods, such as fire extinguishers, hoses, water connections, water availability (hydrants, dry hydrants), and sprinkler systems (wet, dry), should be evaluated and maintained.

- Fundamentally, many barns are built without concern about how to evacuate horses in the event of a fire. Center aisles with no doors on the back side of each stall will trap horses in a burning barn, especially horses located closer to the center of the barn

Fire trucks should be able to easily find the property by a reflective number at the road and they should be able to enter the property. Vehicles or trailers should never be parked near the barn, preventing fire trucks from having easy access. There will be no time to move vehicles out of the way once there is a fire, so it is imperative to have designated parking spaces, especially in boarding facilities. Fire trucks should have access to water, preferably from a hydrant but otherwise from an accessible pond or swimming pool (less than 10 feet from a gravel parking area and no more than 10 feet lower than the truck.) If there is a gate, there must be a plan for how the fire truck can access the property. Gates should be wide enough for emergency vehicles to enter, with reflective street numbers and the fire department and local police should have a copy of the key if the gate is locked, or know the gate code to gain access. In addition, the ground should be hard enough for a 20-ton fire truck to sit on and not worry about getting stuck.

Barns should be kept clean and free of debris in the aisle ways. Cobwebs and dust are combustible and can prevent sprinklers from being 100% effective. Dust and cobwebs should be removed often, and while doing so, fans, electrical systems, and detection systems should be inspected and cleaned.

The best-designed barns with fire safety in mind will have several entrances and exits, located not only at each end of the barn but with several more located throughout the barn, as well as doors exiting to the outside located in tack and feed rooms and lounges. Doors should be on the backside of every stall. There should be openings every 50- 75 feet, and there should never be a dead end. Openings should be wide and tall enough to lead a horse through. Horses will not want to leave the safe confines of their stall when there is smoke and flames (their lungs can't take it, and neither can yours!) and there is total chaos all around. It is never safe to be in the interior aisles of a burning barn due to the risk of falling structures, so having an egress on the back of each stall will increase the chances of the horses being rescued. Having a small paddock for each stall on the outside wall is even better, giving the animal a chance to self-evacuate. Holding areas or fire lanes will provide a safe area in which to release horses. Roof vents will slow the heat build-up, allowing gases and heated air to leave, but are rarely considered in barn construction. Through modification or in new barn builds, every attempt should be made to increase the time it takes a fire to reach its flash point. Barns should be constructed to limit fire spread, maintain the structure's integrity, and maintain fire escape routes.

7 Principles of Barn Construction for Life Safety

1. **Construction Materials**

2. **Compartmentalization**

3. **Egresses/Exits**

4. **Interior Finishes**

5. **Building Services**

6. **Detection Systems**

7. **Fire Protection Systems**

Electrical

One of the leading causes of barn fires is electrical in nature. According to the Animal Welfare Institute, most barn fires are caused by a heating device, such as a heat lamp or space heater, with other electrical malfunctions also contributing to fires.

If building new, use an electrical blueprint to ensure sufficient electrical service to the barn. Only certified/licensed electricians should be used, and they should be made aware of what types of appliances the typical barn uses, from hot water, air conditioning, bucket heaters, lightning rods, infrared heaters, microwaves, washers and dryers, and fans. An electrician should be hired to review the existing barns' wiring, panel box, and outlets to ensure that everything is up-to-date and safe. Electrical boxes should be in an easy-to-access location, always closed and free of dust, cobwebs, and humidity. Combustible material should never be stored near an electrical box. All employees should also know where the panel box and breaker are located. In addition, consider installing a main electrical switch on the barn's exterior, which will allow electricity to the entire barn to be cut off all at once, if needed.

Most issues that are electrical in nature include exposed wires, chewed cords, lack of conduit, wires within reach of horses, use of extension cords, incorrect use of fans that are not rated for barns, lighting, lack of outdoor panels or outlets, and an insufficient/overloaded sized panel. These are all red flags and are ignition sources for barn fires. While bringing everything up to code may be costly, many insurance companies will offer a lower premium for making the necessary safety changes.

For established barns, especially those much older, consult with a certified/licensed electrician to bring your barn up to date and to code. Most insurance companies will offer a rebate or lower your premiums, which will help to offset the cost. One barn in Virginia fully upgraded four large horse barns, several equipment and tractor barns, several living areas in the barns, a large home, and several employee homes for $500,000. Still, they reported that the premium dropped so much that it paid for itself within five years.

Only outdoor-rated fans with a closed motor should be used, and they should be cleaned and inspected often and installed by a licensed electrician. Box fans should never be used in any barn setting, because they do not contain a closed motor and they are not rated for barn use. Box fans have been the source of many a barn fire. All wiring should be UL Listed (Underwriters Laboratories). The use of extension cords should be kept to a minimum, and only outdoor-rated and heavy-duty cords should be used. They should never be accessible to a horse, either by mouth or by stepping on the cord. Cords that are wrapped up while in use will generate heat, so always use extension cords that are fully stretched out. When not in use, they should be disconnected, and only one cord should be utilized rather than connecting multiple short cords to one another. Light switches should also be out of reach of horses and should have a protective cover over them. Portable heaters should never be used in a barn setting. If they are utilized in a tack room or lounge, they should only be used when people are present and always unplugged when not in use. Never use near tack or blankets, because the heaters will radiate heat, and with combustibles nearby, they can ignite.

Electric bucket heaters have caused their share of deaths. In Lebanon, Ohio, 35 horses perished in 1989 when an electric water bucket heater started a fire. A disconnected prong that was still warm had been placed near some rags, causing a fire. In November 2000, 20 Standardbreds died when a portable submersible electric water heater was placed in a plastic bucket and left unattended. After the fire, officials recovered what remained of the heater, with plastic melted to it, against a wooden wall where the fire started.

Any heater can fail and cause a fire. If you are going to use one, you must never leave it unattended, unplug it when not in use, and use care when setting the appliance down. They can blow over or radiate heat onto bedding, rags, blankets, hay, and tack and create an environment for a fire by drying the object out. A faulty electric hot water tank was the cause of a barn fire in Clarence, New York, in 1991 that left 40 horses dead. Rescue spokespersons for the fire department stated that the barn was fully engulfed when they arrived, with only three horses being rescued.

Many barn owners mistakenly believe that barns should be heated and closed up tight in the winter, but the truth is that the heat from the horse's bodies will usually suffice and keep the barn from getting too cold. While horses should never be in a draft, there should be fresh air, and it should be able to circulate. Fires often go undetected in a barn that is closed up tight in the middle of the night. These fires are often detected only due to somebody driving by and noticing the flames. If you are concerned about your horses staying warm, use blankets and feed extra hay to help keep them warm.

Because lightning is a major cause of fires, lightning rods should be professionally installed. Well-ground rods will reduce fires and injury or death from strikes by diverting energy to the ground.

Lastly, a main shut-off switch should be installed near the barn, which can be modified to exclude the water pump and sprinkler system.

Suppression and Warning Systems

Barn fires involving combustible material will double in size every minute so prompt action will depend on early warning systems.

Many barns do not incorporate detection systems, mistakenly believing they are useless in a barn setting. After doing everything possible to prevent barn fires, detection systems are the next best way to combat fires.

Material can smolder for hours, even days, without an open flame. Having smoke detectors located in multiple areas of the barn will alert everyone to a potential problem. At the very least, barn owners can install smoke or heat detectors throughout the barn, especially in areas where hay and bedding are stored and in feed and tack rooms and lounges. Cheap detectors are not sufficient for use in barns! By having professional installation, there can be direct communication with a security system or to 911, which will increase the response time, especially at night, when nobody is in the barn to hear the alarm. Most systems will also alert the staff or owner, allowing for time to rescue horses.

It is imperative to keep smoke detectors clean of dust and cobwebs. They should be inspected often, tested, maintained, and monitored. It is not uncommon for dust to set off most smoke detectors, so consider installing them just in enclosed spaces, such as tack rooms, feed rooms, lounges, and living quarters. For more open areas, consider installing photoelectric or ionization types of smoke detectors.

Suppression systems are also underutilized with the belief that they will not save horses or are too expensive. In 2014, 35 horses were saved at Plainridge Racecourse in Boston, Massachusetts, when a suppression system was activated during a fire. Alternatively 9 barns at a racetrack in San Luis Rey, California, caught fire from cinders from a wildfire 2 miles away and lost 48 of the approximately 475 horses on the property in 2017. There was no suppression system in place.

Because suppression systems can add 20- 25% to building costs, they tend to be ignored. However, once again, the payoff will be in lowered insurance premiums, as much as 50%, not to mention the lives saved and the value of the animals and the structure involved. Another argument is that suppression systems will not work in certain climates, but there are systems designed for both hot and cold climates.

Wet systems will not work in sub-zero temperatures due to pipes freezing and potentially bursting. Dry systems can be installed for such climates though. In a dry sprinkler system, pipes are filled with compressed air or nitrogen, which keeps the water out of the pipes by way of a valve. When the sprinkler head opens due to a temperature variation, the valve opens, releasing a flow of water. The only drawback is that the system needs a separate tank and pump to provide enough water and pressure. They can be costly, but, the lives potentially saved and the structure cost cannot be ignored.

Sprinklers are the best method of suppression. They give rescuers time to rescue horses and prevent further structural damage.

Another form of suppression is using fire extinguishers. Use ABC classification for barns; one should be placed at every entry, every 50 feet, and located inside tack and feed rooms, lounges, and wherever hay and bedding are stored. They should weigh no less than 10 pounds and be maintained monthly by turning upside down. Everyone should be instructed on how to use an extinguisher properly and make sure to check the expiration date.

Alarm systems have also been shown to work. They are also best installed by a professional. They are activated by heat, and while they are reliable, they need to be close to the source of heat to be activated, reducing the response time. Fixed-temperature line thermal detectors are recommended for barns to increase the floor area coverage. Flame detectors are another reliable system but are more costly than heat detectors. They react to electromagnetic radiation emitted by flames and are not subject to false alarms. Rate-of-rise heat detectors are less expensive and yet highly reliable.

Alarm systems should be tested often and monitored, and using the simplest system available will reduce any chance of failure by the alarms.

Anatomy of a Fire

For a fire to burn, there must be three things: an ignition source (spark or intense heat), a fuel source (combustible material), and oxygen. The fuel source will smolder, sometimes for hours, depending on the availability of oxygen, the location of combustibles, and the fuel.

In tests using a 12 x 12 stall with two bales of fresh straw, the fire took only 1 minute to create an air temperature of 374° F, 15 feet above the floor (UL and Union Carbide's 1950s research).

Straw bedding reaches a burning temperature of nearly 300° F in less than 5 minutes, during which it will burn an area 10 feet in diameter, develop as much heat, and burn at the same rate as gasoline. It is impossible to survive more than a short exposure to 150° F, and the tissues of the lungs will be destroyed. Therefore, animals must be rescued within 30 seconds for no injury. After one minute, the lungs are seared, and by 3 minutes, the animal or human is dead. (NFPA 150, 1993.)

With flames, more heat is being produced and the fire grows exponentially. Temperatures will reach 1800° F at the ceiling level within minutes and 3- 5 minutes to approach the flash point, where all combustibles within that space will ignite. In most barns, this is usually the loft, where hay and bedding may be stored, further fueling the fire. This is why limiting the combustible fuels (bedding, hay, etc.) in barns is vital.

Toxins, mainly carbon monoxide and hydrogen cyanide (known as the Toxic Twins), are released by the process of burning and will cause severe lung damage. In 2005, a fire in Fair Hill, Maryland, claimed 24 horses, and all were deemed to have died from smoke inhalation. The fire crew reported no sounds from horses when they arrived, meaning they were already dead despite no flames. A similar fire started in electrical equipment in Connecticut in 2018, killing more than 18 horses, with no flames present.

Once flames appear, the heat and fire increase. Having a properly designed barn and suppression systems in place is essential, hopefully slowing the spread of flames.

Prevention

Several steps can be taken in both new builds and existing barns, which will go a long way in preventing fires.

The first preventative measure should be to compartmentalize all combustible items by separating each type, such as farm equipment, manure, chemicals, gas, hay, bedding, etc. Firewalls and doors can be used to separate areas to store such items and living spaces in barns.

Farm equipment and fuel should also be in a separate building, and manure in a compost pile should never be located near a barn. Manure, hay, and bedding are all extremely combustible and ignition sources.

Many older barns have haylofts that should never be used to store hay or bedding. Haylofts increase the fuel loading and increase the speed of fire. Ideally, hay should be stored in a secondary building, and regardless of where it is stored, barn owners should utilize a firewall, detection and suppression systems, and an alarm. Never store pesticides, fuel, herbicides, etc., in the same area as where hay is kept. Keep the majority of hay in the secondary building and bring in small amounts at a time to the main barn, typically just enough bales to use each day. It should be taken seriously to compartmentalize and properly store hay. Safety should override convenience.

When storing hay, take the time to stack the bales properly, with air space between rows and stacks of bales. Keep in mind that green hay is highly combustible, as is recently baled hay, which may have a high humidity content. A probe will indicate the internal temperature of hay; below 130° F will present no issues. Hay that shows temperatures between 130 and 140° F should be monitored; hay at 150° F is at risk of fire and should be moved around to circulate and monitored. Hay measuring 175- 190° F is in imminent danger of fire; bales should not be moved, and the fire department should be notified. With temperatures above 200° F, the situation is very critical. The fire department should be called, water should be applied before moving hay, and when moving the hay, a hose should be on standby. Thermal imaging cameras can be utilized to trace any smoldering hay.

And it bears repeating: smoking should never be allowed in or near a barn! It is just not worth the risk! The same also goes for burning brush near a barn or welding where there is combustible material.

It is imperative to understand that ventilation, suppression, and compartmentalization are the keys to slowing down the spread of fire and allowing first responders to remove horses.

Key Prevention Steps:

- Smoking should never be tolerated around a barn

- Keep flammables and machinery out of the barn. This includes tractors, side by sides, generators, gas cans, welding equipment, etc

- Keep debris off the roof

- Keep vegetation away from the barn. You should maintain a 40- 50-foot firebreak around your property

- Remove cobwebs. Not only are they unsightly, but they are also fire hazards, as are oily rags, dust, and trash lying around. Store hay and bedding in a separate building. Stack hay loosely and make sure it is properly cured and dry. Never store chemicals, pesticides, etc., near hay

- Use only UL-Listed appliances and outdoor extension cords

- Don't leave extension cords exposed to horses

- Don't run cords across floors where a shod horse can step on one. If you have a cord patched with electrical tape, toss it. Your horse's life is worth more than the $15 it costs to replace it

- Don't set heavy objects on cords, which can generate heat

- Extension cords should never be coiled up if they are too long, because they will generate heat

- Refrain from refueling equipment in the barn

- Do not allow birds to build nests in light fixtures

- If you have dryers in the barn, make sure they are clear of lint

- Space heaters in tack rooms can dry out leather and blankets and cause a fire to ignite

- Open outlet boxes and remove dust and cobwebs

- Water bucket heaters should be in good working order and never left unattended. When not in use, they should be stored carefully to ensure that they are completely cool

- Fire extinguishers! Have them at both ends of the barn, one every 50 feet and within ready access. Ensure you know how to use one and that they are tested monthly. Put extinguishers in the tack room, lounge, feed room, and hay room. Make sure to check them monthly and that everyone knows how to use one properly

- Install smoke alarms, flame detectors, and carbon monoxide alarms

- If possible, install a fire sprinkler

- Have hoses outside the barn

- Is your wiring up to date and safe from critters chewing on it? Make sure all wiring is enclosed in metal conduit and is up to code. Replace any frayed wires

- Is the master switch to the power readily accessible outside the barn?

- Install lightning rods.

- Do not use electrical heaters in the barn!

- Do not use Lasko brand or other house box fans. They are not designed for barn use! Use only heavy-duty metal fans with enclosed motors and have them installed by a licensed electrician

- Hay rolls! Just as baled hay sitting in a barn can combust, so can a hay roll. Sitting outside and exposed to rain can cause heat to build up. Pull layers back after a rain and check for heat

- Consider installing fire curtains in the roof trusses, which will slow the transfer of super-heated air and smoke

- Remember shavings! Bagged shavings and bulk piles are combustible and should be stored safely

- Manure piles can also "cook. " They should be far from the barn and spread thin, and manure compost bins should be far from structures

- Scan your barn. Do you have rags, assorted cans, fertilizer, pesticides, gas, and other contaminants lying around?

- Invite your local fire department to assess your facility

- Write down your plan and practice it monthly. Include all employees and boarders. Make changes as needed

- Use the most non-combustible materials in barn construction

- If applying varnish, make sure it is flame retardant

- Tack rooms, living quarters, and lounges should be brought up to the Life-Safety Code

- Install additional exits. Install doors on the back of each stall

- Electricians should inspect your barn occasionally and make any upgrades if necessary.

- Are all electrical circuits protected by Arc Fault breakers or a complete Arc Fault breaker panel, and are all electrical outlets GFCI protected?

- Do not park trailers or vehicles near the barn

- Unplug appliances when no one is around

- Halters and leads should always be outside the horse's stall. Spare halters and leads should be stored in a separate building with easy access

- Hold drills to help horses handle noise, flashing lights, and smoke

- Leave flashlights in the secondary building where accessible, because the fire department will shut off the power

- Don't leave aerosol cans in the sun; they can build up heat, explode, and start a fire

- Swimming pools, ponds, hydrants, and hose bibs should be unobstructed so the fire department can utilize them as water sources

- Latches should be in good working order. Rescue personnel will be wearing heavy gloves, so latches should be able to be quickly opened

- Barns with long interior aisles should mark stalls with glow-in-the-dark or reflective lettering

- A list of emergency contacts should be posted in the barn and secondary buildings

- A 20-ton fire truck should be able to navigate your gate and driveway and get as close as possible to your barn

- Download apps such as Pulse Point, which alerts you to emergencies near your location

- **And because it bears repeating: Smoking should never be tolerated on a farm, especially in or near the barn**

Emergency Planning

All barns should have an emergency fire plan, which should be posted for all boarders and employees to see. Every boarder and employee should be familiar with the plan, and it should be practiced several times a year. Many barns now require boarders to participate in drills and include a copy of the plan in their boarding contract. Not only should your boarders and staff be included in your drill, but your local fire department will be more than happy to participate. By inviting your local rescuers, they can also provide a fire assessment of your barn; they can learn about haltering and leading horses if they are not familiar with doing so, and your horses can become familiar with their scary equipment. In addition to posting your emergency plan, a copy of your emergency contact list should also be included, and provide both copies to your first responders.

Having your local fire department perform a fire assessment saves valuable time and money. Training and assessment can take just two firefighters two hours to visit your barn, compared to 30 firefighters coming to your barn to fight a barn fire, which, for large barn fires, can quickly add up to 300 or more man-hours. You do not want the fire department to see your farm for the first time when responding to a fire! By having an assessment, they will learn the layout of your property, know approximately how many horses are stabled, know how long your driveway is, and be able to send the correct trucks.

By writing down your plan and practicing it, you will be able to identify any areas where improvement is needed and make changes. Time yourself and your boarders. Remember that a barn can be fully engulfed in as little as 5 minutes, and smoke can be dangerous in 3 minutes. Can you run into your barn, halter and lead your horse out to safety in that time period? If not, what is the plan for your barn?

Teach your horse to lead with just a lead rope around his neck. Practice not just leading around the barn, but as they become proficient at it, throw in challenges, such as leading at night in the dark, with loud noises, and any other chaotic challenges you can create. By asking your local fire department to visit, they can acclimate your horses to their clothing, helmets, and oxygen tanks. Lead your horse with a lead rope during these visits. Be sure to have an area where your horses can be safely released without them running to the road or getting in the way of rescuers and hoses. The last thing anyone wants is for someone to be kicked or run down by a frantic horse or for a horse to be saved from a fire only to be hit by a car or injured by the equipment.

Keep extra halters, lead ropes, and extra fire extinguishers in a separate building close to your barn and within easy reach. No one wants to be searching for any of those items. They should be hung immediately inside the doorway and be used only for emergencies.

Boarders should insist that barns have emergency plans and perform drills. Unsafe practices, such as using box fans instead of safer fans with closed motors, may be costly. Boarders can offer to pay for new fans for their stalls, which is a small price to pay for peace of mind, and the barn owner will be very appreciative that such an important matter could be resolved.

Do your boarders know your barn address? Many do not! Have your address posted along with your Disaster Plan, and when you hold drills, ask your boarders to recite the address. Do you know the length of your driveway? Providing this information to the 911 dispatcher may save valuable time by ensuring that the correct fire trucks are responding.

Despite Your Measures, You Have a Fire. What Do You Do?

Once you are aware of a fire in your barn, it is imperative to stay calm and alert, think rationally, and act decisively.

- The first course of action is to call 911. Be sure whoever calls knows your address. Next, call your vet.

- If you are able, use a fire extinguisher. It should always be aimed at the base of the fire. Never turn your back to a fire.

Start removing horses that are accessible, but never go inside a burning barn due to the risk of collapse or smoke inhalation. Horses in burning stalls are most likely to die from smoke, even if rescued, so focus on the horses you can safely remove. Never attempt to recover tack or equipment. It isn't worth your life.

As the fire department arrives, assess the situation. Is there anyone in the building? Is everyone accounted for? Have one person be the spokesperson to the fire captain to avoid any confusion. Lastly, was your fire plan executed?

Be aware of your surroundings and conditions. Changes in wind direction or speed, a change in air temperature and humidity, and an increase in smoke and ash are all signs to leave the barn immediately. As already stated, you will have roughly 1 minute to save a horse with no health risks. After 1 minute, the lungs become seared, and suffocation begins. At the 3-minute mark, they will most likely be dead: therefore, practicing your drills is imperative so horses can be quickly haltered and led away from a burning barn. Horses will be more likely to be frightened by sirens and panicked humans than by the smoke itself. Blindfolding should never be considered: Blindfolds are a Hollywood fallacy and only work in the movies! Attempts to blindfold a horse take longer to get on the horse, and horses can become very dangerous and unpredictable as a result. If a horse gets loose while wearing a blindfold, it can injure a person or itself. Instead, teach your horses to leave their stall and to lead well. Ensure that all barn personnel have advanced handling skills.

Once you have removed horses, remove any blankets, fly masks, boots, etc, and hose them off entirely. If anything has melted onto the horse, wait for your vet to remove it. Cinders will continue to burn under their hair, so it is imperative to hose off the horse and inspect their coat thoroughly. Even if your horse appears uninjured, a vet needs to do a thorough exam, including checking for smoke inhalation. Carbon monoxide and carbon dioxide are by-products of fire, and can cause asphyxiation. It is not uncommon for horses to crash days after a fire due to pneumonia. Your vet needs to treat horses rescued from fires aggressively.

Have flashlights available, because once the fire department arrives, they will turn off the power source. Large facilities should have a diagram of their property with marked animal confinement areas and the location of water, gas, and power sources. Provide a copy to your local fire department and post a copy in all buildings.

If arson is suspected, which occurs in roughly 15% of barn fires, due to anger or profit motive, an investigative unit is involved. Usually, the State Fire Marshal is also called upon. Insurance companies will become involved within 48 hours. Once the investigation is complete, the fire department files a report.

> *At one of the barns where my daughter kept her horse during college, we were told that the owner's husband had his office upstairs in the hayloft and kept his supplies in part of the loft. I never gave the hayloft a second thought until months later when my husband saw the barn for the first time and was given a tour of the hay loft. The owners had a business that involved making plastic road barriers and cones and storing the materials over the horses' stalls. All very combustible and flammable items, sitting in a hayloft inside a wood barn! My husband, a mechanical engineer, P.E. who works in fire protection, was taken aback by what he saw. He shared his concerns with me as we drove home, and I was horrified to learn that we had placed our horse in a potential fireball waiting to happen. Unhappy with additional issues, we took the opportunity to bring the horse back home until we could find a new barn.*

There is no predictability to the time, location, facility, or climate when it comes to fires. They happen as often in cold weather as they do in hot weather. It is extremely important that all barn owners and managers implement every aspect possible to prevent the risk of a fire. The chances of a fire can be reduced through education, better facility design, or retrofitting existing barns, installing alert and suppression systems, planning, and drills. Human and animal lives will be saved, not to mention the impact of economic losses of structures, trailers, tack, equipment, and the animals themselves.

Chapter 12
Disaster Planning
(Wildfires, Hurricanes, Tornadoes, Flooding, Local Emergencies, Etc.)

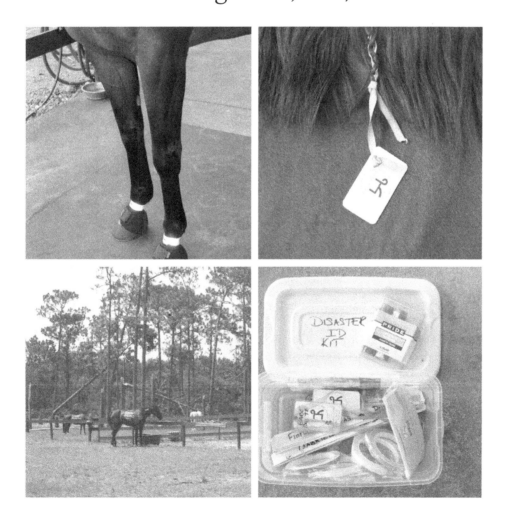

No matter where you call home, your farm will be subject to some natural disaster or local emergency, whether it be from hurricanes, tornadoes, wildfires, floods, a hazmat disaster, or an outbreak of a contagious disease. Being prepared is the best way to lessen the impact of any potential effects.

Other types of disasters include high wind events, heat waves, blizzards, earthquakes, mudslides, hail, and power grid failure. All of these events affect horsemen worldwide: however, your location or climate will dictate which events you may experience. Some will experience only one type of natural disaster, but local emergency types of disasters can affect anyone, anywhere. Some may experience more disasters more often than others, due to their location and climate.

> *With the prevalence of wildfires in California, many farms practice fire drills. In Florida, it is not uncommon to prepare for a hurricane, only for the hurricane to switch its path at the last minute. I call this having a drill!*

Boarder Considerations:

As a potential boarder, one should ask the following questions:

- How does this facility prepare for disasters?

- What is your evacuation plan?

- What are the responsibilities of the horse owner in a disaster?

- What are the responsibilities of the barn owner?

- How will the property be prepared?

- Is there a written disaster plan to be shared with boarders?

- Is there a monthly or quarterly Safety Committee meeting to discuss relevant preparations, planning, and review of management and maintenance issues?

- If the horses are not evacuated, what will the barn owner do to ensure their safety?

- Do I need a Power of Attorney to allow someone else to make decisions for my horse if I cannot be contacted or reach the location?

- Do I need to sign a waiver or a legal document to ensure a mutual understanding of how my horse may be evacuated in case of a disaster?

Planning

As a barn owner/manager, it is your responsibility to identify which weather disaster you may be subjected to and have a plan for how to deal with it. Determine if your county has an Emergency Plan that includes animals, specifically livestock. Your boarders should be made aware of your plans by way of safety meetings and in their contract, so that they will know how to prepare their horse in accordance with your plan and also so that they can partake in emergency drills. Having a plan in effect will help you deal with each disaster's challenges in a calm and organized manner. A disaster plan is just as important as having a fire plan.

All horses should be able to load, and training days should be held often, including loading at night and in the rain. A horse that won't load will risk being left behind in a disaster or released to fend for itself. Unfortunately, horses tend not to do well when left on their own.

Hazard Assessment

Identify what type of disaster or disasters are common in your area and then formulate a plan that will work for you and your boarders. Enact a plan, share your plan with your boarders, and have drills. Identify your risks and vulnerability if you shelter in place. This includes water, natural gas, electricity, transportation, vet services/medical care, feed, and forage.

Identify potential local or regional evacuation facilities based on location and disaster. Identify a shelter close by in case of a barn fire evacuation, another location across town for a disaster that will affect only a small area, such as a power outage or chemical spill, and locate an evacuation site much farther away in the event of hurricanes or wildfires. Remember that in the event of hurricanes and wildfires, the location you choose may also be affected by changes in the direction of the winds or flooding. Many people have had to evacuate two or three times when trying to get out of the way of these major disasters.

Be prepared to pay a fee for emergency stabling, because another facility will incur costs for helping you in an emergency, although some facilities will waive all fees. Those who decide to evacuate should plan on staying with their animals and being a gracious guest, taking care of your animals as if they were at home and cleaning up after them. Don't take advantage of the hosts and leave your stalls a mess when you leave, or they may not be available the next time you need them. Don't expect to leave your animals either. Someone will need to feed and water your horses and clean their stalls.

By basing your disaster plan on the most common disasters that strike your location, you will be able to expand on your plan, whether the orders are to leave immediately or to shelter in place. Having the right app or website for your jurisdiction's communications will help you make your decision in an orderly amount of time.

An "all-hazards" approach will mean that one good disaster plan can be applied to other less-common events, especially because some disasters will create smaller events, such as tornadoes and flooding resulting from hurricanes.

Write the plan down, drill it, and make changes as needed. Make sure that every boarder has a copy as well as phone numbers for contacts and post it next to your fire plan. Hold drills at a minimum every few months and change the time and condition. What if the horses are all out in their pastures? Can you be as effective at night or in the rain or snow? The goal is to ID, load, and evacuate in the quickest amount of time for evacuation plans.

For shelter-in-place drills, the goal is to identify and prepare the facility for disaster such as removing possible flying debris, filling water tubs, moving trailers, etc. Just like having a fire plan, a disaster plan will help when things are chaotic and your thought processes are not clear. If you are not sure what disasters may affect your location, contact your local Emergency Manager or Emergency Operations Center for an assessment and resources.

Evaluate the possibility of hazards that can impact your barn or facility. Are you close to railroad tracks where freight trains are hauling hazardous material? Are you near interstate highways where big trucks are hauling chemicals? What if the train derailed or the truck overturned, releasing hazardous chemicals, and you only had minutes to leave?

What are your weaknesses and vulnerabilities?

- Do you know your closest shelter if you had to evacuate today?

- What is your backup for power?

- How will you provide for water? For one day? For one week?

- How long does it take to hitch your trailer?

- Is your truck fueled?

- How will your barn be affected by having no power for one day? Five days?

- How will you manage a barn if employees and boarders are unable to make it to the barn?

- How many days of feed and hay do you have on hand? Can you feed everyone for a week? Can you purchase hay and feed for all the horses if the owners are displaced and unable to provide the necessary finances?

- How will you communicate with boarders and staff if cell service and the internet are down?

- If you can't reach the boarder and their horse is injured or has to be euthanized, who makes the decisions? Do you have a Power of Attorney? Do you have the owner's credit card information?

- What is your business continuity plan after the disaster?

These are all questions that need to be answered in your disaster plan.

Identify the effects of a disaster afterward. Flooding will bring possible chemical leaks, raw sewage, and floating ants and snakes (or alligators, depending upon where you live), and hurricanes or tornadoes can leave downed power lines and broken fencing, resulting in horses having changes in their daily routine.

Your plan should be reviewed and updated as necessary. The process should include everyone who could be impacted, from employees and boarders to family members. It cannot be said enough: *Practice, improve, take ownership.* The goal is to preserve welfare, life, and quality of life and to be a resilient community that can be self-reliant and respond independently without taking away valuable resources from the community. This will help provide for the continuity of the business after the disaster, even if the "business" is your personal homestead.

Barn owners may want to have a credit card on file for each horse's owner, insurance information, and a waiver authorizing the barn owner to make decisions regarding the horse's welfare in case the owner is incapacitated or unavailable.

Have a disaster kit and evacuation kit in place and ready to use. Disaster kits should include at least two methods of ID for each horse (have a day where all boarders get together to not only have a drill but to make ID's for their horses.) Keep the kit where you can easily find and label it so others will know what it is. With the exception of feed, hay, and water, items for your evacuation kit should be in your trailer and ready to go. Doing so will save valuable time if it is already in the trailer. Create a checklist with tasks to be performed and assign each task to someone. One person can be responsible for ID'ing horses, another for unplugging appliances, and another can fill every container with water. By enlisting boarders in a drill, they can help execute every aspect of implementing your disaster plan quickly and efficiently; they become a part of the plan instead of being affected by it.

> *I boarded at a stable where every time we had a hurricane, most of the boarders showed up to help. I was in charge of making IDs, which I had done months in advance, and I enlisted another boarder to help place IDs on each horse. Another boarder would close back windows, while others would fill buckets, remove possible flying missiles, etc. The day after a hurricane, everyone would show up as soon as they could navigate the roads, help clean up debris, and restore the barn to its pre-storm condition. We were a team and we were in this together!*

Permanently identify horses before a disaster strikes, whether by tattoo, freeze brand, or microchipping. During Hurricane Katrina, most horses were reunited with their owners because Louisiana required all horses to be microchipped as part of their Coggins testing. In the EU, all horses must be microchipped, and many show and breed registries, including the FEI, now require that horses have a microchip.

Keep an emergency binder. This should include where you will most likely evacuate, health papers for every horse, and photos and videos of horses, property, and equipment. Include owner and vet information, maps, and feed charts. Owners need to be made aware of disaster plans in their boarding contracts, and many barns require owners to permit the barn owner or manager to make health and life decisions in an emergency situation in event the owner of the horse is unavailable. Do you have a contract or Power of Attorney that spells out your rights and obligations in an emergency when the owner is unavailable?

The best disaster plan is devised in advance when no threat exists and resources, such as generators, are available. It is practiced with all boarders participating, and any changes are made based on the results of the drills. Invite your local fire department to visit your farm, make an assessment, and look for any issues that arise and which you can improve on. Ask for a copy of your county Emergency Operations Plan and check if any annexes deal with horses.

By incorporating safety practices into daily routines, barns will be better equipped to deal with emergencies. These include:

- Enforcing the No Smoking policy

- Holding safety meetings and drills regularly

- Making sure that all horses are current on vaccines and Coggins

- Ensuring that all horses can be caught will lead in all kinds of situations, stand tied, and load willingly into a trailer.

- All drivers should know how to hitch and pull trailers

- Trucks and trailers are maintained and fueled

- Phones are equipped with weather apps

- Security of the farm is enforced (locked gates and tack rooms, security cameras)

- Bio-security measures are practiced with every new horse

- All animals have at least one type of permanent ID

A good plan will be devised just before the disaster strikes, but resources, including gas, water, generators, and feed, will be limited. There will be no time for drills.

A poor plan is where there is no plan in effect, and the barn owner is making decisions while the disaster is either imminent or in the throes of the emergency itself. These types of poor choices are the kind that people and animals pay for with their lives. In December of 2017, the San Luis Rey Training Center in California, had no real plan or disaster preparation in place when the Lilac Fire ripped through the facility and 48 horses died, many were injured, including three people with severe burns. Nine barns were destroyed. Many of us will never forget seeing the news footage. The "plan" was to turn the horses loose, resulting in chaos with more than 400 Thoroughbreds running loose. The local fire department responding to the chaos had no idea what to do to be effective and had to navigate their way around frightened horses.

Before a disaster strikes, it is time to review your insurance coverage and ensure it adequately covers your business. A good plan will address the following:

- Cover business interruption

- Cover extra expenses, including relocation

- Provide for loss of income

- Adjusts for inflation

- Covers fire and water damage

- Covers for debris clean up and removal

- Civil ordinance coverage (an example is COVID)

- Comprehensive building and structure replacement

- Covers leased equipment

- Interruption of power, heat/air, sewer

- Coverage of Workers' Compensation

- Custody or control

Hurricanes, Flooding and Tornadoes

If you live in any state that touches the Atlantic Ocean or Gulf of Mexico, you will likely experience a hurricane at some point. In recent years, even the West Coast has experienced its share of hurricanes. Even if you live inland, the remnants of a hurricane will affect you with heavy rain, winds, and tornadoes. Flooding typically goes hand in hand with hurricanes but can also result from broken dams or levees. They can be slow-rising or fast flash floods, leaving little time to evacuate. Another spin-off of hurricanes can be tornadoes, or they can suddenly appear out of nowhere with very little notice to prepare. Luckily, with today's technology, most of us live where we can receive tornado warnings on our phones or over the TV, which will give us some time to get ourselves to safety.

Hurricanes provide the luxury of having days to prepare because the weather forecasters track them from their inception. Hurricane Charlie in 2004 taught us that hurricanes can and do switch paths at the last moment though, with those in Central Florida finding themselves with just 6 hours to go from casually preparing for a glancing blow to having to prepare for a direct hit.

Hurricane Andrew left farms in South Florida so devastated that the building codes were changed. Nothing was safe in the high winds, and many barns collapsed, leaving horses unaccountable in the aftermath. That disaster was the inception of better disaster planning for animals in the United States.

Hurricane Katrina taught us the effect that flooding would cause, with many horses suffering horrible fates of drowning when they were left in their stalls. Most recently, Hurricane Ian in 2022 taught Floridians that no matter where you are in the state, you will feel some impact with a hurricane that size. The damage shocked people in Lee County, because the projected landfall was farther north near Tampa. When the storm changed its course ever so slightly, those in Lee County were not prepared for the destruction they were about to experience, and sadly, there were reported deaths of horses that were not evacuated from low-lying areas. Despite all the talk on the news, people failed to consider the size of the cone. If you reside within the path of the projected landfall, you will be impacted, one way or another.

Because of the unpredictability of landfall of hurricanes, evacuating is challenging to plan. Where can you go that a hurricane won't follow? With the more horses and animals you have to evacuate, this is a serious question that needs to be answered. This is where Horse TLAER (Technical Large Animal Emergency Rescue) Math comes into play. One must consider how many trips and hours will be required to move horses. Suppose a barn has ten horses to move and only a two-horse trailer and the evacuation facility is a 100-mile round-trip excursion, not to mention the time involved in loading, unloading, and setting up, plus traffic. In that case, the barn needs to begin evacuation very early on. For example, plan 30 minutes to load, and if the trip is an hour and a half (with no traffic) each way, plus another half hour to unload, you need to plan 4 hours for every trip. As the hurricane gets closer, traffic will increase, and your travel time will unfortunately increase as well. In addition, roads may be closed and fuel limited as the hurricane or wildfire approaches, preventing your return to load up more animals. Early evacuation is crucial; if possible, enlist the help of as many people as possible.

Evacuating:

If you decide or are given orders to evacuate, you must do so once the evacuation orders are issued. You should identify the reason for evacuation other than mandatory evacuation orders. Is your barn in the path or cone of a catastrophic storm? Is it in a flood zone? You are at risk for flooding if you live near any lake, river, or swamp. In Central Florida, the north-flowing St. Johns River continued to rise for weeks after Hurricane Ian, causing significant flood damage throughout several counties, with scores of horses needing to be rescued. How is the construction of your barn? Do you have trees or power lines overhead that could fall on it? Will a good gust of wind at greater than 65 miles per hour reduce your shelter to a pile of lumber? These are all questions that should be answered as you develop your evacuation plan.

If you didn't plan ahead, try utilizing social media platforms to find locations to evacuate. If show grounds are full, social media can help direct you to good good sites where private residents will offer safe refuge. After the storm passes, social media is also a helpful resource for putting out SOS posts for missing horses, found horses, where to locate hay and feed, and other useful advice.

Even if you feel your horses would be safe at home, it is still a good idea to learn where you would evacuate in case of mandatory evacuation orders or some other major catastrophe would cause you to leave. Once you pick your location, be sure you have contact information, an address for this spot, and how to get there so you are not left scrambling at the last minute. Have several locations picked out beforehand, and you must call the one you plan on evacuating to, to make reservations. Many evacuation sites fill up quickly, so have your backup locations ready just in case.

Be sure your truck is gassed up and you know the back roads to your destination. Major highways will quickly become parking lots. The last thing anyone wants to deal with is being stranded on the road with a trailer load of horses, which happened to several people during Hurricane Katrina when snarled traffic caused vehicles to run out of gas. Evacuees were forced to ride out the hurricane, stranded on the interstate with their animals inside of trailers.

Take ALL of your animals with you. Don't leave any animal behind, because you don't know when you will be able to return, and you don't want to rely on neighbors or friends, since roads may be impassable for any number of days. It seems that with every hurricane, there are stories of animals tied up and drowning or being found in a barn with a collapsed roof around them days later when the owner returned. On the other hand, responsible owners who consider their animals as family members are more than likely unwilling to evacuate if no shelter or resources are available. Now is the time to decide how to evacuate all the animals in your care. Will it require multiple trips? Can you enlist friends or boarders to haul horses? Goats, barn cats, and other animals can usually fit inside trailer dressing rooms to free up space. Most sites will accommodate all animals. The World Equestrian Center in Ocala, Florida, took in not only horses and donkeys but also kangaroos and tortoises during Hurricane Ian in 2022! And keep in mind that with a hurricane looming, this is not the time to start teaching your horse how to load into the trailer! Even if you know your horse loads, but it has been a while since you have gone anywhere, practice loading before a disaster looms.

Many times, states will waive the health certificate requirements to evacuate across the state border, however, you still need to ensure your animals are up-to-date on vaccinations and their Coggins. Shelters will require current vet records, and you'll need to keep in mind that it can take weeks for a horse to build up immunity from a vaccine, so it will be useless if evacuating to a large public site within a few days of injection. Most evacuation sites will also require vet records. It's a good idea to have copies of your documents in your evacuation binder and keep a file either in your truck or in the dressing room of your trailer so you won't waste time trying to locate the records before leaving.

Be sure to bring along several days' worth of grain and hay. The last thing you want to worry about during an already stressful situation is the inability to feed your horse its usual diet. It's also a good idea to have stored water in case you are stuck in traffic for any length of time.

Lastly, it's a good idea to always have your evacuation kit ready.

Once an impending disaster is announced and danger is imminent, take the following steps to ensure a successful evacuation:

1. Get ready. Have your evacuation plan binder and evacuation kit ready—gas up the truck, hitch trailers, and load feed and hay.

2. Identify the evacuation site.

3. ID horses.

4. Evacuate sooner rather than later. Take into account the number of horses, trips, and distance. It is better to start a few days early for a stress-free evacuation. And if the disaster doesn't strike, consider this a successful drill.

The response of a farm and its community will contribute to the outcome of a disaster. Everyone involved should be flexible and be able to address the problems as the crisis changes. This will lead to the recovery period, which can last days, weeks, or months and includes repairing buildings and fencing, providing veterinary care for horses, clearing debris, and assessing how well the plan worked and what changes, if any, need to be made in the future. Always consider your plan a work in process, allowing for course correction as you hone your efficiency.

Shelter in Place

If you decide to stay put, much work still needs to be done! Some regions will have shelter-in-place plans, and one should know what they are. For example, in California, some canyons have only one escape route and require FireWise preplanning with CAL FIRE (California Department of Forestry and Fire Protection) to defend your property.

One of the most debated questions is what to do with your horse. Are they better off inside or outside?

Look at your barn construction. Is it well-built and up to code, or is it just a bunch of boards nailed here and there to give some shelter? Will the roof collapse inward or blow off? Is there a hayloft full of hay and equipment that, if it collapses, will land on top of the horses? Are you in a flood zone? What happens if water rushes your property and floods the barn? And it's not just your barn to be worried about with flooding. One horse died during Hurricane Ian when water rushed the property with such force that he was swept away from his field; his remains were found a week later, just on the other side of the fence line.

If you turn your horse out, you must consider that in hurricane-force winds of greater than 65 or more miles per hour, even the tiniest item becomes a missile that no animal can outrun. Tree branches, jump cups, buckets, blown-off rooftops, and your neighbor's kids' toys will all cause severe and even fatal injuries to horses. What about electrical wires? How is your fencing? If you leave your horse out, ideally, there should be at least two perimeters of fencing, as downed fencing is a reality. In addition, make sure that the horses can reach higher grounds in the event of flooding. Make sure that there are no electrical wires in your fields. During Hurricane Andrew and in its aftermath, horses that survived the storm were electrocuted or hit by vehicles because of broken fences and downed power lines. These realities should be considered for any significant storm and approaching tornadoes. Don't assume your horse can outrun a tornado. They can't! If your horse leads a pampered life and is not used to being outside during bad storms, leaving him out in a hurricane may not be such a good idea.

After the storm or disaster, where will your horses be allowed to graze or be turned out? The areas will need to be free of hazardous materials, floating ants, downed power lines, etc. The bottom line is that whether you leave your horse in or out is a decision only you can make based on where you live and your facilities.

Most barns have wells that rely on power. In an emergency, you will most likely lose power. Therefore, providing enough water for every horse and animal on your property is critical. The typical horse will drink 8-15 gallons of water daily. In the heat of the summer, that number may be higher. Realistically, plan to store at least 15 gallons of water *per horse per day* for one week. Rain barrels make excellent water storage containers, typically holding 50- 90 gallons. Barns with many horses should invest in as many barrels as necessary. Rubbermaid totes and muck buckets also hold large amounts of water. When not in use, barrels can be used as jumps or for storing tarps and other disaster equipment.

Hurricane/Disaster Shelter in Place Preparation Checklist

(This checklist applies to most disasters!)

Once you decide to ride out the storm, you have a lot of work to do:

- Fill every bucket, trash can, and other containers with fresh, clean water. At a minimum, plan on 15 gallons of water per horse per day. Therefore, consider investing in barrels to be used for water storage. You cannot rely on the fire department to provide water

- Pick up enough hay and feed to last a week in case roads become impassable or the feed store is damaged and can't open. Cover with a tarp to keep dry and safe

- Pick up and store away every item that isn't tied down: flower planters, flags, barn decorations, chairs, tools, etc. Even if this turns out to be just a drill, at least your barn is getting a good cleaning and organizing! Knock over jumps and any other object that can blow over

- Identify potential low areas around the barn and fix them. Make sandbags and add dirt, rock, etc., to low-lying areas

- Identify your horses using at least two methods of ID:

  a) Body marking with livestock paint. Available at Tractor Supply and from most livestock supply companies. Be aware that these dry out, so check and replace them as needed. Put your address and phone number on the sides of your horse

  b) Write your info on the hooves with a Sharpie

  c) Neck banding

  d) ID tag on halters, making sure that when leaving halters on, you use a breakaway halter only

  e) Braid ID into mane or tail. Use a small baggie with emergency info inside, or make a laminated tag. Laminated luggage tags from any office supply store work well. With a baggie, you can include more info, such as dietary concerns or medical issues, in case your horse is lost

- When using a phone number, be sure to include a second number, either a landline or the number of a friend or relative from out of state. Just be sure to let them know. It is not uncommon for phone lines to be down in a major hurricane or after a tornado

- Never attach your horse's Coggins to his body because if your horse becomes lost and is picked up by an unscrupulous person, they can claim they own the horse

- Microchipping is the best bet to identify your horse. It is becoming more common with breed registries and will aid in getting a lost horse back home

- Keep current photos of your horse- along with their Coggins and vet records- in your personal files so you can identify them should they become missing. Store this in a safe place

- Attach reflective tape to your halter. Some livestock supply stores also carry reflective paper strips to apply around the hooves and neck. These will help make the horse visible to cars should it get loose

- Inform others of your plans

Floods

There are many precautions a barn owner can take to prevent flooding. These include:

- Identify if your property is in a flood zone. If you live near a major lake or river or along the coast, you will likely experience flooding at some point and you must realize the risk

- Many realtor sites now list the environmental risk level of a new home, including the risk of flooding

- If you are building a barn, it is a good idea to make it at the highest part of the property, or if that is not possible, elevate the barn by at least one foot

- If grazing in a floodplain, keep horses safe and away from that area until danger has passed

- Identify where to move livestock in the event of flood. Where is the highest point of the property?

- Identify where to move equipment

- Move hay, grain, and medications to a safe location

- Test sump pumps

- Turn off the power when a flood is imminent

- Horses should never be stalled or tied when there is a threat of flooding

- Make improvements to your property, such as widening and cleaning out culverts to prevent washouts

- In the event of flash flooding, there may be no time to do anything except remove horses from their stalls

- Open gates so animals can move freely

- Horses stuck in flood waters are at risk of several dangers, including:

a) Drowning

b) Injury from fencing, equipment, and other debris hidden by the rising water

c) Becoming stuck in the mud

d) Difficulties in locating dry spots in which to stand and provide adequate food and water during flooding. Photos post-hurricanes show horses seeking refuge on rooftops or porches and standing in stagnant water for days if no dry ground can be found

e) Snakes and floating ants

f) Stress from standing in water and the inability to eat properly may cause colic and laminitis

- Other health issues include:

  a) Rain scald

  b) Mud fever

  c) Pneumonia

  d) Open wounds

  e) Waterborne illnesses such as leptospirosis

  f) Drinking contaminated water, which can lead to diarrhea, intestinal illness and death

  g) Cellulitis or Phythiosis

  h) Skin infections, which in turn cause the skin to slough off

Tornadoes

If you receive a tornado warning, there is very little you can do to prepare. Just like with hurricanes, there is much debate as to whether or not the horse should be left inside or out, and it all comes down to your facilities.

A turned-out horse cannot outrun a tornado and will be subject to flying debris, and downed fences, or downed power lines. If turned out, horses should wear halters and fly masks to reduce eye injuries from flying debris, and if there is enough time, they should have some form of ID attached to them. A horse in a stable may be at risk of collapsing roofs, walls caving in, or trees falling on the barn.

Because a tornado is imminent, having a tornado plan and knowing what to do when you hear an alert is essential. It is far more important that you keep yourself and family safe during the tornado so that you can do something useful to help your horses and animals after it passes.

Wildfires

Wildfires are one of the most frightening of all disasters, because you seldom have time to evacuate. All it takes is one careless person tossing their cigarette butt out of their car window during a dry season or a slight wind to make a burn pile get out of control. Sometimes it's as insignificant as a lone spark from a truck dragging a metal chain and all of a sudden, you have a full-blown fire.

The best you can do in the case of wildfires is to prepare ahead of time, have an evacuation plan, be able to receive the disaster orders and evacuate as soon as the order is given. Fire officials may close the roads, making evacuation impossible, so it is a good idea to be aware of the fire danger level in your area and have your trailer ready and hooked up to your truck. Have your evacuation kit packed and in the trailer. Some areas of the country are constantly threatened by wildfire. It has become an everyday part of life, so it is a good idea to have drills. In other parts of the country, it is seasonal, usually in the winter months when it is drier and there is little rain.

To safeguard and protect your farm, it is best to do so months in advance:

- Identify the risks around your property and address them early on

- Trim shrubs and trees at least 50 feet from your property. Remove the vegetation under them as well. Reduce or remove anything combustible. Remove vegetation along fences and buildings. Trees should be trimmed 6-10 feet off the ground, and limbs should not touch fence lines or hang over structures

- Avoid planting highly flammable vegetation, such as junipers and cypress, which contain a high volume of resins and oils. Plant and maintain fire-resistive landscaping

- Avoid using wood mulch. Instead, use fire-resistant materials such as stone or gravel around the perimeter of structures

- Inspect buildings for anything that may ignite from embers, including oil cans. During wildfire season, remove mowers, tractors, etc., from the barn area and keep the roof and gutters free of debris that may ignite from embers

- As mentioned earlier, it is best to store hay, shavings, and other combustible items in a structure separate from the barn

- Install sprinkler systems in the barn and even on the roof of structures

- When building a new barn, use fire-resistant materials such as stucco and metal instead of wood

- Ensure vehicles are gassed up and in working order

- Prepare your evacuation plan with evacuation routes and facilities. Plan more than one route, in case that route may be blocked by fire or smoke

- Have your emergency binder with all health records up to date and store it in a truck or trailer.

- Make sure you have working fire extinguishers and smoke detectors. A rule of thumb is one extinguisher at every entrance and every 30- 50 feet

- Practice trailer loading

- Study the FIREWISE programs online for suggestions

- By this time, hopefully, you've already done your due diligence. Now, there is a wildfire in your area. What should you do?

With a wildfire approaching:

- Decide whether to evacuate or shelter in place. If you have been following the news reports, you should have your trailer hooked up and ready to go at a moment's notice

- If you evacuate, do it as soon as possible. Do not wait for smoke or flames to impact your horses. Blocked roads can prevent people from fleeing, leaving fire to overtake them and their horses. It is better to leave too early than too late.

- Be sure to have your evacuation kit already in the trailer.

- If you do not evacuate, post signs at the entrance of your property and the barn informing first responders you are there and listing the number and types of animals sheltering in place.

- Use social media to connect with equine evacuation routes and sites to find assistance

- Speak to your veterinarian about having tranquilizers ready. Low-flying helicopters, smoke, and fire trucks may agitate your horse and make loading difficult. If loading proves to be difficult and time is running out, what is your next plan of action? Turn the horse loose or start walking the horse out?

- If the horse is turned loose, ID the horse with at least 2 ID options. It is best to turn them loose without a halter, as halters can catch fire

- Close structure openings to prevent ember ignition

- Remove flammable items away from the structure. Remove propane tanks and grills from the area

- Open gates connected to fencing for easy access by firefighters or animal rescues

- Turn on lights so structures are visible to firefighters, unless your jurisdiction suggests turning them off

- Connect garden hoses to spigots

- Shut off the gas at the meter and pilot lights if applicable

- Have carriers or crates ready for your small pets, whether cats, dogs, rabbits, poultry, or goats. Dressing rooms make excellent spaces for pets, but it is best if they are confined. Large dog crates will hold goats or just about any farm animal in a pinch

A friend lived about 20 miles from where her horse was kept. My barn was a few miles away from her barn and I could see smoke in the direction of her barn so I let her know that there were wildfires in the area. She said that the barn owner had notified her that they were on standby for evacuating and would keep her updated. The call finally came around 5:00 that evening that they indeed had to evacuate. My friend was still at home and would have to waste precious time driving to the barn! Once she finally arrived, the firefighters would not allow her access to the property for about an hour. Eventually, she was allowed to get her horse, but with all the widespread commotion of smoke, fire, helicopters, and firefighters, the horse would not load. Finally, after about a 20-minute struggle, she loaded, with no time to spare, because at that point she would either have to turn her loose or walk her out. The moral of this story is not to wait! Be ready! It's better to leave too early than not to be able to evacuate at all!

Earthquakes

Just like tornadoes, earthquakes are difficult to predict, probably the least predictable of all disasters. The majority tend to strike in certain regions, so someone living in Florida or Maine probably will not be as concerned about preparing for an earthquake as someone who lives in California.

Like all disasters, it helps to have a plan. But how does one prepare for an earthquake?

The best way is to build your structures with earthquakes in mind. Barns should be designed to keep your horses safe should an earthquake strike, and barns should be routinely inspected for their structural soundness. One cannot evacuate from an earthquake, but one can take steps to deal with the aftermath :

- You should be able to evacuate in the aftermath if there is much destruction and keeping horses on the property is not safe. Know where you can evacuate to

- Keep sufficient food and water supplies

- Be able to evacuate horses from barns as soon as possible. Keep halters and lead ropes accessible

- Shut off water, gas, and water valves

Blizzards

It is best to prepare for blizzards in late summer or early fall. Horses should have adequate shelter, and roofs should be built to be slanted to avoid snow accumulation, which can result in a collapsed roof if too much snow accumulates.

Hay can be stored in large quantities in the north without fear of it molding, so most horse owners have stocked up for the winter by the time autumn has arrived. By having extra hay and feed on hand, in the event that roads are not passable due to snow or downed power lines, there should be no worries about horses having to go without food. Horses must consume more calories when temperatures are freezing, and while there is often debate about when to blanket, it is usually a good idea to blanket when the weather is extreme for your area. By extreme, that can mean a 40° F degree drop in Florida, from a high of 80, down into the 40s or even 30s in a 24-hour period, or in the extreme northern states, where the temperatures drop below zero. Extra care should be given to elderly horses, as well as sick horses, clipped horses, and foals. Fresh and cool water should be available at all times. Horses do not like to drink frigid water; if ice is on the bucket, they will not drink. Horses that cannot drink are at risk of colic. Adding warm water to their grain will help keep them hydrated and warm them up internally.

A Warming Climate, Heat Waves and Droughts

Undoubtedly, our weather is getting more extreme, with powerful hurricanes occurring more frequently and more wildfires out west and everywhere experiencing extreme heat. Data is showing that the last twenty years are the warmest yet since it has been measured and recorded.

Triple digits are now the norm for most of the country for a good chunk of the year, and not only is it making it harder to keep our animals cool and comfortable, but it is also affecting our hay and feed, the quality of air, and the rise of infectious diseases. Horses should be provided with shade and access to cool and clean water at all times to help them handle the extreme heat.

The study of how the climate affects horses is only in its infancy stage, but it is a looming disaster that should be watched closely, because we are all living in the middle of it. Continuing droughts are and will affect hay production. Almost 50% of the acreage used to grow hay is currently affected by drought. Water is needed to produce hay and grain, but too much (flooding and hurricanes) or too little (droughts and wildfires) will seriously impact how and what we feed our horses, not to mention the price to feed horses will continue to rise. The rain totals will also impact how our horses graze their pastures, because the quality of grass will suffer. As pasture grasses die off, toxic plants will take hold, so care should be taken to remove them.

Smoke from wildfires will decrease the quality of the air we breathe, not to mention temperatures soaring into the triple digits. These will impact horse sports, because extreme heat and poor air quality are not conducive to any athlete, two- or four-legged, performing at their best. Moving events and competitions to evening and even overnight instead of in the middle of the day will become the new norm.

We will see the toll that a changing climate takes on horses through skin issues, respiratory disease, poor hoof quality, more parasites, and increased invasive creatures. Storm damage will be more significant, and there will be weather-related riding limitations.

Extreme heat should give caution to the rider before tacking up their horse for a ride. Pay attention to the humidity and temperature, by adding the two figures together to determine safe riding conditions. Less than 130 is safe riding conditions. If the number is between 130 and 170, the rider should exercise caution and common sense and any number over 170 is dangerous riding temperatures.

Lastly, extreme weather patterns will drive wildlife out of their normal homes, which means more risk of interacting with our pets and horses. This means a greater chance of zoonotic diseases, while more water-driven disasters will result in vets treating more cases of waterborne pathogens such as Leptospirosis, Pythium insidiosum, and Encephalitis.

Extreme weather patterns are affecting us all, and we need to pay attention to them in order to manage a stable of horses effectively. We can adapt to these changes if we alter our management practices to maximize our horses' health and reduce property damage.

Local Emergencies: HAZMAT Evacuation, Power Failure, Contagious Disease Outbreak

Barns, particularly where horses are constantly coming and going, should have a written standard for handling outbreaks of certain diseases, such as strangles or EHV. The risk of disease or injuries also increases after disasters, whether from contaminated water, exposure to hazardous materials, or injuries due to debris in pastures.

Unfortunately, one cannot predict when there may be a contagious disease outbreak, a HAZMAT evacuation due to a derailed train carrying chemicals, or a power outage, which will shut down wells and all access to water for a week. If you already have a disaster plan in effect and drill often, you will be better prepared for whatever emergency comes your way and be able to respond proactively, no matter the hazard.

Evacuation Kit

- 3- 7 days' supply of grain and hay for each animal

- Blankets, if needed

- Cash

- Copies of vet records, Coggins, and proof of ownership. Keep copies in the truck or dressing room ahead of time: Keep them in your Emergency Binder

- Dog/cat carriers

- Duct tape

- Emergency contact list: vets, friends, relatives, evacuation sites: Keep them in your Emergency Binder

- Emergency or weather radio

- Fans

- First Aid Kit

- Flashlights

- Fly Spray

- Filled gas can

- Heavy work gloves

- Identification for each horse, a minimum of 2 methods

- Instructions for feeding and medications

- Knife

- Leg wraps

- Map of local and alternative evacuation routes (phone service may not be working)

- Medications

- Extra halters and leads

- Plastic tubs to store water and feed

- Rope

- Supplements

- Tack and supplies

- Tarps

- Temporary Fencing

- Tools in case the vehicle gets stuck (shovel)

- Twitch

- Water for several days: at least 15 gallons per horse per day

- Water and feed buckets

- Wire cutters

- Water purifier

Barn owners, managers, and horse owners must take responsibility for the horses in their care. Not only will the disaster itself be traumatic, but the days or weeks following will be chaotic, with the possibility of impassible roads, no access to feed or water, and no electricity. Barn owners should be self-reliant and not rely on outside help, which may or may not be immediately available, because horses will not be given priority in a disaster, especially the more rural the facility. This fact makes it all that more important for a barn to have planned ahead of time. Employees and horse owners may be unable to commute to the barn, so you may be on your own, caring for all the animals. What will your plan be in such a situation?

You can develop a well-thought-out plan based on the assessment of your local fire department or emergency manager. In addition, FEMA offers several online courses, and several Facebook groups are designed to help you prepare and handle disasters, such as the Technical Large Animal Emergency Rescue group. In addition, CERT (Community Emergency Response Teams) offers training sessions for handling animals in disasters.

Daily management routines in your barn will also increase the efficiency and confidence in how your barn handles disasters. By following basic fire safety rules, your barn will be able to react in a more proactive manner in case of wildfires. Barns that practice good vet management should be able to prevent the transmission of diseases, which can not only result in sick or dead horses but can also result in a barn being placed under quarantine.

Chapter 13
Going Green in the Barn
(Being a Good Steward of Our Environment)

More barns are making a conscious effort to be mindful of their environment. It is just as important to be good stewards of our planet as it is to be one at home. Ways you can go green at the barn include:

- Put recycling bins in the barn and encourage boarders to use them

- Buying supplements that come in recyclable containers or eco-friendly packaging

- Use biodegradable products to keep chemicals out of the environment

- Donate Smartpak containers. Schools and art programs can use plastic trays for paint, glue, and other crafts

- Make jumps out of natural items, such as trees and branches. Reuse pallets as jumps

- Conserve water and reduce water runoff. Turn the hose off when not in use and eliminate leaky hoses and faucets. Install gutters and a rain barrel system

- Use the water from buckets and troughs to water your plants. Plant grass or vegetation around the wash rack to absorb water and filter soaps and other contaminants

- Buy feed and hay in bulk to reduce delivery trips

- Old fence boards can be repurposed for various projects, from ship-lapping tack rooms to building chicken coops

- Supplement containers make ideal storage for nails and screws, and other small items

- Baling twine can be used in the garden to create green bean trellises, temporarily hold up broken fence boards, and have many other uses around the barn

- Composting manure will keep it out of landfills. Use the composted material in your garden or on your pastures

- Keep mud to a minimum to prevent contaminating nearby streams or ponds

- Keeping pastures weed-free will reduce the need for herbicides. Hand pulling and mowing are green methods of controlling weeds, as are eco-friendly herbicides, such as a mixture of Dawn dish detergent, salt, and vinegar

- If installing pavers in the barn aisle, use recycled tire rubber

- If you're building your barn, consider using wood certified by the Forest Stewardship Council. This organization certifies that wood products are grown and harvested from managed forests for sustainability

- New barns should incorporate natural light wherever possible to reduce the need for electricity and provide natural ventilation

- Pick up and remove manure in turn-out areas often

- Plant native plants in shallow areas to capture runoff from downspouts and driveways

- Use natural fly control such as Fly Predators or a natural fly spray

- Welcome barn swallows into your barn, because they will eat flies and other pests

- Reuse feed bags and boxes in the garden to prevent weeds

- Use reusable cloth bags instead of plastic bags and buy items with less packaging

- Donate worn-out saddle pads and towels to the local animal shelter for bedding

- Provide water fountains or coolers for boarders and discourage wasteful plastic water bottles

- Reduce electricity use by installing dimmers and timers and switching to fluorescent or LED lighting rather than incandescent

- Reduce damp or wet areas, which are breeding grounds for flies and mosquitoes

- Reduce, reuse and recycle

It is just as important to incorporate practices at the barn that are good for our planet as we do at home or work. Horse farms have been notorious for being bad for the environment. Herbicides, pesticides, fertilizers, and manure piles can result in runoff into waterways. Overgrazing leaves land barren and unable to regenerate. Horse show competitors and boarders who don't practice recycling and reusable water bottles contribute to the growing pollution of landfills and polluted waterways. But the tide is changing, and more and more farms and even horse show management are working to do better by Mother Nature. By going green in your stable, your payoff will be not just for a better planet but for your wallet as well. Sound environmental practices will help you and your animals live a healthier (and hopefully longer) lifestyle, reduce the amount of pollution entering our soil, water, and air, preserve animal habitats, and reduce the amount of energy used. It is everyone's responsibility to do their part to contribute to a healthier and more sustainable planet, and that includes horse farms.

For more ways to go green in the barn, contact your local conservation district for free assistance: www.nacdnet.org

Chapter 14
The Boring- But Oh So Important- Stuff
(Contracts, Barn Rules, Insurance,
Employees and More)

Most horse people would say that the reason they bought a barn and opened it up to boarders was because of their love of horses. They will also likely tell you that the reason they hate their business is because of the people.

If given the option between having a barn full of horses and never seeing a human being in their barn, many would choose the latter. But that is not practical or feasible.

Having boarders will mean, at some point, drama and conflict. There are even Facebook groups that deal only with barn drama. Unfortunately, barn drama is almost a given as egos flare and personalities clash. The drama may often be warranted, because many boarders want what they are paying for but are receiving mediocre care, but often times, the drama seems to center around boarders not getting along with either one another or with the barn management.

> *When I was 18 years old, some friends and I moved our horses to a private barn, where there was one other boarder. She had been there by herself with her two horses for a long time and she felt that she was entitled to more rights than the rest of us because of that seniority. One day, I turned my horse out in the jump field after a lesson while I ran to the store for a snack. There was just one other boarder at the barn when I left, who assured me she would keep an eye on my horse and bring him inside if anyone showed up and needed the field. My saddle was left on my stall door, so it was obvious that I would be returning. In the time that I was gone, the boarder who felt entitled arrived, and before the other boarder could bring my horse in, the entitled boarder immediately grabbed my horse, led him into his stall, and threw my saddle on the ground. There was no reason for this, since she rode dressage and had her own riding area with a dressage ring, and her horses had their own turnout paddocks. The next day, my friend was mucking her stall. We only had one wheelbarrow to share amongst us. While my friend ran to the bathroom, the entitled boarder entered our barn, dumped the wheelbarrow into the freshly mucked stall, and took it. This began an all-out war between the boarders! Since the entitled boarder had her horses in a separate barn, my friend would take the manure from her stall and place them in piles in the entitled boarder's paddocks, after she had already cleaned for the day.*

> *The barn owner, a friendly retired man, was quickly losing patience. Despite the new boarders trying to come up with ways to appease the entitled boarder, such as relocating the jump ring to a different field, the war between her and my friend continued. Don't mess with a 17-year-old who suffers from severe PMS! Eventually, I moved to a different barn with no drama. The funny ending to this story is that many years later, as a Pony Club District Commissioner, I could not figure out why one of the parents looked so familiar, and then it dawned on me. She was the entitled boarder! I don't think she ever recognized me!*

The current trend in boarding barns is to require contracts. Unfortunately, the days of a handshake and a verbal agreement are no longer as common. While a contract won't solve every issue, the more issues you anticipate in writing, the less room there will be for dispute.

> *In all my years of boarding, which I can't even begin to list every barn over 50 years, only ONE has had me sign a boarding contract. And that barn owner was one of the craziest barn owners I have ever had to deal with. There were several barns where I wished there had been a contract to spell out what I was entitled to as a paying customer. Some barns posted rules, which tended to be general and not too extensive, but otherwise, barn rules and what was expected of me as a boarder was conveyed verbally.*

Also changing is the way barns hire help. It used to be that barn owners relied on neighborhood kids who wanted to be barn rats and would love to hang out in a barn all day, swapping mucking stalls for a lesson. Additionally, many barns would trade board or lessons for working off board, illegal immigrants were hired under the table, and top riders could benefit from working students.

The tide is changing for many when it comes to hiring employees, including providing insurance, filling out tax forms, asking for immigration status, and paying a decent wage.

These and more are the not-so-fun aspects of running a barn, but they should be addressed.

Establish Who Is in Charge!

Barn owners must establish who is in charge when running a boarding barn. It is not only essential to have contracts and rules, but there is good advice on social media platforms for running a barn! These include:

- Don't let the boarders run the bar

- Set boundaries

- If costs increase, increase the board. Do not operate at a loss! You should not be subsidizing anyone's hobby, whether it be for peace of mind, money, or your time

- Keep your standards high

- A questionnaire for potential boarders will help weed out those who may not be a good fit

- Background checks or references, such as asking other boarding barns, farriers, vets, and other pros, will also help weed out the bad

- It is possible to have friends among boarders, but don't confuse the two

- Establish barn hours

- Like any other business, there should be rules

- It's okay to part ways with a boarder

- Keep a credit card on file, even if they pay by check or cash. Charge the card if they are delinquent. You can also use the card in the event of an emergency or disaster if the owner is not available

- Make sure that the boarder signs the boarding agreement before they move in. This can save you a lot of headaches and trouble down the road

Unfortunately, just about every barn has to deal with boarders complaining. When you get a group of horse people together, you are bound to run into one or two who think they know everything and are not afraid to voice their complaints to the manager and other boarders.

And they may be right about their complaint, but there is a right way and a wrong way to go about conveying their concerns.

A private conversation regarding any issues is the best course to take. If there are legitimate concerns, a good barn manager will find a way to solve the problem. Now is the time to convey that complaining loudly and in front of other boarders is unacceptable, and any concerns should be handled in an orderly manner; however, some boarders are just plain toxic and must be dealt with swiftly. These types of boarders will ruin the mood for everyone else, can destroy your reputation, and cause you nothing but anxiety and stress. A complaining boarder is clearly unhappy with the situation, regardless of who is in the right, and should be asked to leave as soon as possible. A simple "Our barn is not right for you" should be all that you need to explain to them.

A good boarder will respect and honor the barn manager's boundaries, rules, and way of running the barn. If there is no mutual respect, it is time to move on, but before becoming a boarder who moves every few months, ask yourself if the problem is the barn manager or if you are the problem! Are you placing unreasonable demands on a barn, such as requiring blanket changes at every 10-degree intervals? Are you the type of boarder who bullies other boarders? Do you gossip? Unfortunately, there are not only bad managers but bad horse owners as well.

Contracts

Contracts are becoming more common. While there are laws to protect the barn owner from a boarder who doesn't pay, it is expensive and time-consuming to file a lawsuit, and you may not recover the total amount owed to you. At the very least, having a boarding contract is a way to tackle gray areas before they become a problem. A written agreement will protect the barn and horse owners and lessen any disputed risk. By spelling out each party's obligations, many headaches can be avoided. It can be a straightforward form, just one page long, or highly detailed, going on for multiple pages. A good contract will spell out each party's responsibilities and potential liability issues and address any emergency situation, including the death of the horse or even the death of the owner or the health and care (or lack of) for the horse. The rights and responsibilities of each party (the "bailee" or stable owner and the "bailor" or horse owner) should be thoroughly spelled out.

A contract between a "bailee" and a "bailor" is known as a "bailment" arrangement, in that physical possession, not ownership of personal property, is transferred from one person to another. In this case, it is between the horse owner and the stable owner. The bailment relationship is implicitly created regardless of a written contract, so it is best to go ahead and have a contract. Legally, the parties owe specific duties of care and assume certain risks that go along with safeguarding someone else's property. Without a contract to spell out the obligations of each party, default property rules will apply. The boarding contract will specify each party's rights and responsibilities.

What are some items to include in a contract?

1. Introduction: Include the parties' names, the horse's name, and a thorough description of the horse; a photo of the horse is helpful. Also, include both parties' contact information, the stable's address, and the agreement's date.

2. Fees and payment terms: State the boarding fee, if additional services are charged, the date payment is due, the day it is late, and any late fees.

3. Because there are so many options for transferring money, list what payment options you will accept, whether cash, check, or via an app. Stipulate whether or not a deposit is required and, if so, how much and what it is for. If you require a credit card for late payments, indicate this too. Credit cards can also be used during disasters or emergency ordinances, such as COVID, when the Owner cannot come to the barn or be contacted.

4. Facilities and services provided: Include the type of feed provided, how often and how much the horse is to be fed, the turnout schedule, who is responsible for damages from the horse, and what level of health and care shall be provided to the horse. Is blanketing included or an additional fee? Is there a fee for parking the horse owner's trailer? If there are any extra charges, these need to be listed. These could include holding the horse for the farrier or vet, grooming, administering medications, bandaging, or exercising the horse. Include days and hours of operation.

5. Risk of loss: A statement stating who is responsible for any loss or damage to a horse (death, theft, disease, injuries). Some barn owners may require a boarder to have health insurance for their horse, which the horse owner is responsible for. Usually, the horse owner is required to assume these risks.

6. Hold harmless: states that the horse owner will assume responsibility for any damages to property or other animals. Some barn owners may require the horse owner to have liability insurance on their animals at their expense.

7. Emergency care: If the barn owner cannot reach the horse owner in case of an emergency, the barn owner is permitted to contact a vet and provide emergency care, with the horse owner responsible for all costs. Barns in areas where disasters are common, such as wildfires or hurricanes, may ask owners to sign a release, allowing the barn owner to make decisions about the horse in the event of a disaster in case the owner cannot be contacted. This includes vet services and euthanasia.

8. The health of the horse: Some barn owners want a guarantee from the horse owner that the horse is healthy and free of a contagious or transmittable disease and current on vaccines, farrier work, dental, deworming, and has a negative Coggins test within the last 12 months. Some barn owners may include that the horse owner must keep the horse in good health by staying current on the aforementioned. Failure to do so can result in the termination of the contract, or the barn owner may enlist a vet or farrier at the horse owner's expense.

9. Stall rest guidelines and expectations, from medicating, rehabbing, and the cost of extra bedding.

10. Stable rules: A list of barn rules for horse owners to acknowledge, usually as a checklist and requiring initials. Failure to follow the rules will result in the termination of the boarding contract.

11. The right to update the contract at any time.

12. Notice of termination of board: States how many days' notice must be given to leave the barn, whether from the barn owner or the horse owner. Usually, a 30-day notice is given.

13. Default: Any breach of contract by either party will result in immediate termination of the agreement, and the non-breaching party will be entitled to recover any expenses caused by the breach.

14. Right of Lien: If the horse owner fails to pay board fees for a stated time, the stable may assert a lien on the horse (s) and/or equipment. Liens on animals vary from state to state.

15. Abandoned horse: If a horse is abandoned by its owner, the barn owner has the right to file a lien.

16. Arbitration: If parties cannot settle their differences, they can elect arbitration or mediation before filing a lawsuit.

17. Boarders are required to plan for disasters. They should know the drill, practice it, and be ready in an emergency. Boarders should also know the barn's disaster plan.

18. In the event of a disaster and evacuation, the owner of the horse is responsible for all costs associated with evacuating.

19. Signature of both parties.

These are standard clauses in a boarding contract. A well-written contract should protect both parties from surprises, so barn owners should carefully consider the items they want in their contracts.

Now, let's talk about the not-so-common clauses:

- Horse owners are not permitted to alter the barn, stall, paddock, pasture, or riding area to suit themselves. This includes constructing shelter, removing fencing, moving jumps out of the arena, and moving the round pen fencing

- Including a clause to deal with the death of a horse. What is to be done with the horse's remains? Some farms allow horses to be buried at the property, while others require the body to be removed. If the barn owner has the necessary equipment to bury the horse, is there a fee?

- There is a $10- 25 clean-up fee for not cleaning up after your horse or not putting your tack away

- If the horse owner dies, who is responsible for the horse? Some barn owners can be held accountable for the horse until the probate is resolved, which can take several months to several years

- If the horse leaves for training, what is the expectation for holding the stall?

- Is there a multiple-horse discount?

- Private residences are off-limits. This is a hot topic, as apparently there are boarders who feel they can wander up to the barn owner's residence, walk in without knocking, peer in windows, and be rude and intrusive

- Keep out of the swimming pool!

- Rules regarding consumption of alcohol on property

- Charging for repairs to damage that horse causes

- No outside dogs are allowed. Dog bites and damages could cost the barn owner legal or medical fees

- Many lessons were learned from COVID. Consider adding wording stating that the barn will follow any mandates regarding health issues and to include the horse owner being responsible for any extra costs associated with such a mandate

- Adding the phrase "This will be determined at the sole discretion of the barn owner" in places so if the boarder or trainer is unsafe, cruel, or not properly caring for a horse, the barn owner can terminate the contract

- Adding wording stipulating that the barn owner can update the contract at any time and the boarder has a stated period of time to sign and return, or their contract will be terminated

- Vehicles on the property are the sole responsibility of the vehicle owner

- Ask permission before hosting a clinic

- Guests must sign a release

- Require a deposit

- Charge a fee for cribbers

- Any tack or equipment left for two weeks after the horse has departed becomes the property of the farm

- Feeding protocols: Who is allowed to feed? Don't take hay or feed without permission. Will the barn supply the hay and grain if a horse is at a horseshow or away for an extended amount of time?

- If asked to leave, the boarder will have 14 days to remove the horse, and the board is forfeited.

- Posting photos of other boarders or their horses on social media is prohibited without their permission

- Adding a social media clause regarding bad-mouthing of the facility, other boarders, horses, etc.

- The barn owner is available to take calls or texts during certain hours unless there is an emergency. Do not call or text after hours

- Cover extra charges for stall rest: extra bedding, hand walking, extra cleaning, etc.

As a potential boarder, don't be afraid to question some of these items in a contract. A boarding stable is under no obligation to provide anything more than the absolute minimum level of care, and sadly, that is what many do. A well-written contract that both the boarder and barn owner can agree upon is essential to avoid stress and conflict.

It is not uncommon to ask potential boarders to fill out a questionnaire. This will give the barn owner an idea of what the potential boarder is looking for in a barn and help determine whether or not the horse owner is a good fit for their setting.

A Sample Boarding Questionnaire for Prospective Boarders:

- Horses name:

- Horses age:

- Horses breed:

- Why are you looking to move from your current barn?

- How many barns have you boarded at previously?

- How long have you owned this specific horse?

- How would you describe your horse's personality?

- Please describe your horse's previous/current turnout situation (hours out, type of paddock, alone or with a herd, mares, or geldings).

- How does your horse react to being stalled?

- Does your horse have any vices, such as cribbing or weaving?

- What does your horse like and dislike?

- Does your horse have any medical history or chronic conditions that we should know about (colic, allergies, cellulitis, lymphangitis, strangles, a metabolic disorder, chronic diarrhea, laminitis, heaves, choke)?

- Does your horse require special turnout equipment, such as fly boots or mask, fly sheets, brushing boots, etc?

- What discipline do you currently ride?

- How long have you been riding?

- How long have you owned horses?

- What is your level of expertise?

- How often do you ride/exercise your horse?

- Who else comes with you regularly to the barn?

- Do you lease your horse out to another person, or do you have plans to do so?

- What type of grain does your horse eat, and how much?

- What kind of hay does your horse eat, and how much?

- When was the last time your horse saw a vet? What was the issue?

- Do you plan to keep the same vet if you board here?

- When was the last time the farrier visited?

- Do you plan to keep the same farrier if you board here?

- Is your horse safe to ride?

- Is your horse safe to lead/groom/remove blanket/crosstie?

- Is there any other information we should know about your horse? (sensitive to flies, needs a chain lead, is food aggressive, easy to lead, grumpy when in heat, dunks his hay, paces, kicks the wall, herd bound, must be turned out alone, etc.)

Sample Boarding Agreement/Contract

This Boarding Agreement ("Agreement") is made and entered into on this day of 20, by and between FARM NAME and ("Owner" or "Horse Owner"), and if the Owner is a minor, the Owner's parent or guardian.

FARM NAME agrees to accept the Owner's horse(s), as listed on the attached horse information sheet(s), for boarding on a month-to-month basis, and it is the plan and intention of the Owner to board this horse. For and in consideration of the agreements from now on set forth, FARM NAME and Owner mutually agree as follows:

1. During the time that the horse (s) is/are in the custody of FARM NAME, FARM NAME shall not be liable for any sickness, disease, theft, death, or injury that the horse may suffer. This includes, but is not limited to, any personal injury or disability the horse may receive while on FARM NAME premises. Owner fully understands and hereby acknowledges that FARM NAME does not carry any insurance on any horse(s) not owned by FARM NAME, including, but not limited to, such insurance for boarding or any other purposes for which the horse(s) is/are covered under any public liability, accidental injury, theft or equine mortality insurance, and that all risks relating to boarding of horse (s), or for any other reason, for which the horse (s) is/are in the possession of FARM NAME, are to be borne by the Owner.

2. The Owner of the horse has examined the facility and understands and accepts the inherent risks involved in turnout and stabling at this facility. This includes normal interaction between horses that are turned out together. FARM NAME is not responsible for any injuries caused by horses being turned out together.

3. The Owner further acknowledges that the facility meets the horse(s) 's special needs and does not require any alterations.

4. The Owner agrees to hold FARM NAME completely harmless and not liable for any injury whatsoever caused to the Owner and/or any loss or damage to personal property.

5. It is the Owner's responsibility to carry full and complete insurance coverage on the Owner, the Owner's horse(s), and all personal property.

6. Trailers or equipment stored at FARM NAME are at the Owner's risk, and FARM NAME assumes no liability for damage that occurs to said equipment

7. The Owner hereby acknowledges receipt and understanding of the current FARM NAME Rules, which are incorporated by reference in full, as if fully set forth herein. The Owner agrees he/she and his/her guests and invitees will be bound and abide by these Rules and accepts responsibility for the conduct of his/her guests and invitees according to these Rules. A copy of the Rules will be provided to the Owner and posted on the wall in the tack room.

8. FARM NAME will provide the Owner with a copy of the disaster plan. The Owner is expected to review and participate in drill practices, or the boarding contract can be terminated. A copy of the disaster plan will be posted in the tack room.

9. All riders under the age of 18 agree to wear a riding helmet while riding a horse on the property. The horse's Owner agrees to enforce this policy with any guests or minors. All riders must wear appropriate riding apparel.

10. The Owner agrees to pay for the repair cost for any damages sustained by the Owner's Horse(s) above normal wear and tear.

11. The Owner shall pay FARM NAME for boarding services, as selected on the Horse Information Sheet. 12. Published Barn Rates are subject to change with thirty (30) days advance notice to the Owner. 13. In the event a pasture-boarded horse requires a stall board for any reason, the daily stall rate (or monthly rate, whichever is less for the invoice period) will be charged in addition to the regular pasture board. The stall rest fee is on top of any other boarding fees.

12. Pro-rated board is due when the horse is delivered, and timely payments are strictly enforced on the first (1st) of each subsequent month. A late fee of $25 per horse will be applied for any invoices not paid in full by the 10th of the month. If payment is overdue by 90 days, FARM NAME is entitled to a lien against the horse and personal property for the amount due. It shall enforce the lien and sell the horse and property for the amount owed, according to the appropriate laws of the state of NAME OF STATE. The sales of horse and personal property may be sold by private sale to satisfy the lien, or FARM NAME may take possession of the horse and/or personal property

13. This Agreement can be terminated by either party with thirty (30) days advance written notice provided to the other party. If the Owner causes an unsafe situation or disruptive, toxic, or abusive atmosphere or fails to follow posted rules, FARM NAME may terminate the agreement with 24 (twenty-four) hours' notice.

14. Any personal property left at the facility for more than 30 days after this agreement is terminated will become the property of FARM NAME.

15. The Owner acknowledges that the image of the horse(s) may be present in various marketing materials, including social media posts. The Owner grants authorization for such use.

16. Horse shall be free from infectious, contagious, or transmissible disease. The following are required as a condition of boarding: A. Current negative Coggins test (required for horses coming onto the property); B. Health, worming, and immunization record, as prescribed by veterinarian; C. Regular foot care as prescribed by professional farrier; D. FARM NAME reserves the right to refuse the horse if it is not in proper health upon

arrival.

17. FARM NAME reserves the right to notify the Owner within seven (7) days of the horse's arrival if a horse, in FARM NAME'S opinion, is deemed dangerous, sick, or undesirable for a boarding stable. In such case, the Owner is responsible for removing the horse within seven (7) days and is liable to pay for all fees incurred during the horse's stay. After all costs have been paid, this Agreement is concluded.

18. The Owner will be responsible for all veterinary, farrier, deworming, vaccinations, grain, and feed supplements. The Owner will arrange regular veterinarian and farrier attention, which the veterinarian and farrier will invoice directly to the Owner. In the event of sickness and/or accident to the horse, after reasonable efforts have failed to contact the Owner, FARM NAME has permission to contact a veterinarian for treatment at the Owner's expense as outlined in the horse information sheet.

19. If the Owner does not provide regular vet and farrier services, FARM NAME can terminate the boarding agreement.

20. Services provided as part of the board:

    A. Stall board with daily turnout (weather pending)

    B. Morning / evening feedings of barn-supplied hay and feed

    C. Daily basic wellness check

    D. Daily stall cleaning, including cleaning of water and feed buckets and fresh water, offered as often as necessary throughout the day and evening

    E. Horses will be blanketed as needed with no more than two daily blanket changes at no additional cost.

    F. Horses who require the use of fly masks, fly boots, brushing boots, bell boots, etc, will be provided such at no additional labor cost. These items will be provided by the Owner of the horse

21. The Owner agrees to provide humane care as recommended by the Veterinarian for the safety and well-being of the horse. If a special diet is required, the Owner agrees to pay to provide that diet.

22. FARM NAME manages pasture and paddock turnouts. Horses may be moved to other pastures or paddocks as needed, as determined by FARM NAME.

23. In case of a horse's death, the Owner must arrange for removal within 24 hours. It is suggested that the Owner has a euthanasia plan in effect.

24. Should either party breach this Agreement, the breaching party shall pay for the other's court costs and attorney fees related to such breach.

25. This Agreement is made and entered into in the State of NAME OF STATE and shall be enforced and interpreted under the laws of this State. Should any clause be in conflict with State law, that individual clause is null and void, not the entire Agreement.

26. The Owner agrees to receive text and email alerts for various events. FARM NAME agrees not to share your contact information with any third parties not involved in day-to-day operations. The Owner agrees that their contact information may be posted in public areas around the farm (for example, stall doors) so they can be contacted in the event of an emergency.

27. FARM NAME may install surveillance cameras and related equipment, including video recording, for security and animal welfare purposes.

28. This Agreement represents the entire agreement between FARM NAME and Owner. No other agreements or promises, verbal or implied, are included unless expressly stated in this written Agreement as described as follows: A. None.

29. When FARM NAME and Owner or Owner's parent or guardian, if the Owner is a minor, sign this Agreement, it will be binding on both parties, subject to the above terms and conditions.

Terminating Contracts

A barn owner may terminate a boarding agreement for no reason unless it is stated in the contract that an explanation must be given. Landlord/tenant laws do not apply to horses and boarding stables. Common reasons for evicting a border include:

- Not paying on time.

- Not getting along with other boarders or owner or employees/too much drama

- Boarder is too demanding

- Boarder does not follow barn rules

- Boarder handles the horse in an unsafe manner

- Boarders horse is dangerous or destructive

- The horse is not being cared for properly

    One of my first boarders was a young woman with a cute horse on whom she ran barrels. She understood that we were eventers and were not geared towards barrel racing, and she would not be allowed to practice barrels in our riding field. She was okay with that, regularly going to her trainers every other Friday and returning late Sunday. Unfortunately, she would return with a horse caked with dried sweat and spur sores. It was apparent that he was never cooled off, instead loaded into the trailer to come home while sweaty. She would give me updates on their lessons, which would include lots of galloping and tight, non-stop circling. Without fail, he would colic on Monday morning. She could not make the connection between his "training" and his colics, and nothing I said could convince her otherwise.

After several months of this, I finally had enough. I felt so bad for the horse and the stress of those Monday colics that I finally gave her a 30-day notice.

If a boarder is asked to move, they must. They have no legal grounds to stay, even if they have been a model boarder for many years and paid their bills on time. Barn owners have been known to go to such lengths as tying horses up at the gate when a boarder refuses to leave, which, while wrong for the poor horse, certainly gets the point across.

In all my years of boarding, I was only asked to leave a barn once. It was at the same barn where the geldings were put together, which resulted in a very dangerous situation. By the time this event happened, I was already looking for a new barn, because this facility was not working for anybody. One day, I arrived at noon, and the owner was walking around the barn, talking on his cell phone. He saw me arrive and dashed for the feed room, where he proceeded to feed the horses....their breakfast! Not only was he 4 hours late in feeding them, but he had the feed tubs mixed up and was about to feed all 3 of my horses the wrong breakfast. Each horse had a different diet. I had a yearling draft cross, a 20-year-old quarter horse, and an upper-level eventing Thoroughbred, each with their own nutritional requirements. I grabbed the buckets from him and fed my horses, and because I was so upset, I felt it best to remove myself from the farm and return after I had cooled down. When I did, I found an envelope on the bulletin board with my name on it, and inside was an eviction notice for "having a bad attitude." I was given just two weeks to leave, but I called my trainer, loaded up two of my horses, and left the next day, with plans to return for my yearling within the week once I found a barn to take him to. A few days later, I came to the barn to find his water trough empty. It was hot and in the afternoon, and he was banging on the trough. It was apparent it had been empty for some time, and other troughs were also empty. Not one to keep my mouth shut, I just had to say something. And as a result, I was promptly told to have him off the premises by the end of the day! I somehow managed to get him removed that day!

Within a few months, they either evicted everyone or those not evicted left on their own. The barn sat empty, and they eventually sold the land to be developed.

On the flip side, some boarders have tried to leave when the environment became toxic and have had to have a police escort in order to retrieve their horses and belongings. In situations like this, it is best to have your barn bill up to date, pay the next month's board, and inform the barn owner you are leaving. If you can, have your belongings already packed up, so all that you need to do is load your horse and make a quick exit.

> *The second barn my daughter boarded at when she went to college was on the recommendation of a friend who also boarded there. After about a month, her Thoroughbred began to lose weight. Impromptu visits revealed he was being fed coastal hay instead of the alfalfa/timothy we were paying for. Then she discovered that his good quality feed had been replaced with an All Stock feed. No wonder he was losing weight! There were lies about his turnout, and we learned he and other boarders were being left outside in thunderstorms, including one lightning storm when the weather was chilly (he was clipped) while the owner's horses were in the barn and occupying his stall. At this point, our relationship had become hostile, between our phone conversations and texting. The feed room was now locked to prevent my daughter from giving him the good hay we were paying for, and he was losing more weight. My daughter told me that the owner would be away at a horseshow for the weekend, and I hooked up the trailer and drove the 2 hours to pick him up and bring him home. I left a board check for the next month and a note stating we would not be returning with our horse.*

A boarding agreement will spell out the rights and obligations of both parties. The horse owner should feel that their horse will be well cared for, and the stable owner will know that their rights are clearly stated. We know that boarding horses can be stressful for both the stable owner and the horse owner, and a contract will help ensure that both parties understand what is expected of each other.

Barn Rules

Barn rules should be created first and foremost for safety reasons and, secondly, to prevent chaos in the barn. Every boarder should know the rules before they sign a boarding contract; they should be given a copy, and the rules should be posted in the barn. Rules should be created to keep a safe environment and reduce your workload. It can be brief and straightforward, such as *No Smoking and Clean Up After Your Horse*, or it can contain a whole list of rules. You will need to figure out what works best for you and your staff, and it may need tweaking at times, usually because a boarder created the need for a new rule.

> *One barn we attended for pony club clinics had three pages of rules, laminated and located throughout the barn. These included outrageous requirements, such as requiring all horses to wear the same blankets of not only the same colors but from the same manufacturer and requiring all horse owners to purchase the same tack trunk in the same color as the blankets. Horse owners were expected to adhere to a strict dress policy regarding their apparel, with no tank tops allowed, and riders had to wear a polo with the barn logo on it for lessons. Other rules included no hand grazing the horse anywhere in the barnyard area, including at the trailers if you shipped in, all manure left in the barn area was to be picked up immediately, and there was to be no trace of shavings from a horse trailer left in the grass. It was so stressful to haul in for pony club events that the parents insisted we find a new clinician! This was the same high-end barn with a hidden hay room and would only allow for half a wheelbarrow load of manure and urine to be removed from stalls.*

Barn rules not only establish some order where there may be chaos, such as knowing proper arena etiquette, but some may also be necessary for safety reasons, such as no smoking.

Two friends of mine moved into a barn, which had been going downhill since they moved in. Every day, a new rule went up, all meant to address the two boarders, who were the only boarders at this newly established (and short-lived) boarding barn. They had to yell "GATE" as they approached the outdoor arena so that the owner had no doubt they were about to enter the ring, even though there were no other boarders. After a few weeks of boarding, they were informed that they were required to use the owner's husband as their farrier; their farrier was now prohibited from coming on the property. Barn hours suddenly appeared, and the list went on and on. As each new rule appeared, the more the barn owners acted like dictators, until one day, in the heat of an argument, the barn owner's husband, who not only claimed to be a farrier but an international show jumper star, pushed one of my friends down, where she fell onto a gate, resulting in an injury. Both friends returned that afternoon with horse trailers and not one but two deputies as police escorts for them to remove their horses and belongings.

Common rules include:

- NO SMOKING!

- Kids must be supervised at all times/no minors under 18 without an adult present

- Act professionally, with no running or yelling

- Helmets must be worn by all or by those under the age of 18

- No dogs allowed

- Pick up and dispose of trash

- Clean up after your horse and yourself

- Do not use anyone's tack or equipment without their permission

- Owners must provide routine horse care

- Close gates

- Respect the Barn Owner's privacy

- Be kind

- NO DRAMA

- Dress appropriately: no tank tops, sandals, etc…

- Respect barn hours

- Pay on time

- Don't leave the horse unsupervised

- Know arena etiquette and practice it

- If entering an indoor arena, shout out that you are approaching

- Inhumane treatment of horses will not be tolerated

- State where boarders can and can't ride, jump, lunge, graze, bathe, and groom

- Waivers must be signed by visitors

- Designate approved areas for parking cars and trailers

- No speeding in the driveway

- Attend evacuation and disaster drills

- No abusive language; no bullying towards horses or boarders

These are a lot of rules, but sadly, in today's world of not too much common sense, they are the kind of rules that need to be written. Some of these rules can be considered as part of the boarding contract with a brief list posted instead, such as:

- NO SMOKING!

- No dogs

- Clean up after yourself and your horse

- Don't use other people's belongings without permission

- Close gates

- Respect hours

- Helmets are required

- All visitors must sign a release

- All children must be supervised

A barn that has too many rules and some that are just plain silly may be a red flag to a potential boarder. These are some of the not-so-common rules found on social media:

- Manure must be picked up immediately in the arena or riding area

- Do not touch anyone else's horse

- Do not kneel when picking hooves

- Before use, boarders must water the arena, round pens, turnouts, and pastures

- Pastures are limited to 3 turnouts per week

- Pick manure from your pasture

- Clean your buckets

- Jumping is only allowed while taking a lesson

- The trainer must approve lunging

- Do not place anything on the jumps (drinks, blankets, coats, etc.)

- Do not ride through manure

- Hooves must be picked before exiting and swept back into the arena

- No food is allowed in the arena

- Boarders must have approval from the barn owner before bringing guests

Some boarders do not respect the farm and treat it poorly. Some rules make you wonder what kind of boarder instigated such a rule in the first place! These interesting rules were found in a Facebook group:

- No humans may shower in the wash stall

- Don't jump the furniture with your horse

- Please don't park on the owner's lawn or camp out on their lawn to use their Wi-Fi, and don't ask for their password

- Do not pee in the stalls

- No naked photo shoots

- No mounting or riding in the barn

- No sex is allowed in the tack room, in stalls, or anywhere on the property. We are here to ride!

Barn rules are necessary, but don't get carried away with the rules as a barn owner! Too many rules will come across as a barn that has forgotten why they are in business in the first place. Boarders want to be able to come to the barn and enjoy themselves and not worry about constantly breaking some silly rule.

Some rules are necessary; others just become petty. It is best to tackle gray areas before they become a problem, so having your rules in place would be best rather than adding to them as an issue arises. And sometimes, if a boarder is doing something you find unsafe or disagree with, taking them aside and speaking to them privately may resolve the issue. Barn owners and managers should always be able to speak with their boarders, rather than taking to social media to vent their frustrations!

While on the topic of barn rules, horse owners should know basic riding etiquette, mainly for safety reasons. These include:

- Announce your entrance in a covered or indoor arena where visibility is limited. Shouting "GATE" is the most common way to announce yourself

- Riders having a lesson will take precedence over anyone else in the arena. Ask for permission to use the ring at the same time as the lesson, and if it is okay, ride in an area where the student will not be utilizing the ring

- Leave jumps and other equipment as you found them

- Do not stop in the middle of the rail if there are horses behind you. Move to the center or leave the arena to dismount

- Lunging should only be done so in designated places

- Oncoming horses should be passed left shoulder to left shoulder

- When passing horses from behind, pass on their inside, not their outside

- Know the meaning of ribbons in horses' tails and use them if your horse meets the criteria:

  a) A Red ribbon means the horse kicks

  b) A Green ribbon means just that….the horse is green

  c) A Yellow ribbon means caution, whether a stallion or aggressive

  d) A White ribbon means a horse is for sale

- Riders should not pass at a faster gait: match your speed to the traffic flow

- Announce your moves to others, whether you are passing or what line you are about to jump

- Allow proper spacing between you and the horse in front of you

- Leave gates as you find them

- Be patient

- Stay off the phone while you are riding. Stay alert and aware, and communicate your plans with other riders

Equine Releases and Waivers

Signed releases and waivers are necessary if you operate a boarding barn, not just for riders but for all visitors allowed on your property. This is essential to protect yourself and your business. An equine release form will waive all rights the signer may have against you as a barn owner, manager, or employee for death, injury, or property damage. By signing a waiver, the signer agrees to indemnify and hold harmless the equine professional from any lawsuit or action and agrees to pay any attorney fees that may arise from a filed suit. A release will state that any activity involving equines involves the risk of severe bodily injury or death. A copy of your state's liability act and a sign posted at the entrance to your property should also be included.

Your release should state that the participant releases the professional, owner, manager, and employees from liability for injury or death that may occur from a horse. Most releases include the language that there are specific risks inherent in equine activities and a statement that the participant is knowingly assuming those risks.

While most states have Equine Activity Statutes, laws will vary from state to state, so be sure to use a release that is appropriate for your state. Most states will enforce liability waivers and releases if they are correctly worded and filled out properly. While generic forms can be found online, it is best to consult with an equine attorney to draw up a release for your specific needs, or at least be sure to amend the generic form to meet the needs of your farm.

An accident is just that…an accident, such as a rider falling- where nobody is negligent, nobody is responsible, and the injured person must suffer the consequences.

However, a well-written liability release and waiver will become essential if the injury is a result of a stable owner, manager, trainer, or employee being negligent. You can still be sued for negligence or willful misconduct, but having a liability release will fill the gaps left by an Equine Activity Statute.

For a liability form to be enforceable, it needs to:

1. Inform the signer of the risks

2. Get the signer to accept those risks

The release should be very specific about the risks the signer is about to undertake, spelling out whether it is for a lesson, lease, or boarding.

A well-written release will acknowledge that a horse may suddenly and without warning spook and, as a result, buck, rear, stumble, fall, bite, kick, or behave in such a manner as to cause injury or death.

Simply stating that "horseback riding is dangerous" is not enough.

A well-written release will state that the signee agrees to release and hold harmless the *farm, employees, owners, and any independent contractors* from any injury or death resulting from a horse-related activity. It should spell out what those activities may be, including grooming, riding, trailering, or turning a horse out. It is important to list everyone who can be sued, including trainers, vets, farriers, and stable hands.

Having a good release and waiver goes hand in hand with having good insurance. Consider establishing your business as an LLC (Limited Liability Company), which will separate your business from your personal assets and protect your private funds should you be sued.

Security Deposits

A topic hotly debated on social media is whether or not to require a security deposit. It appears to be a regional issue, and higher-end barns are more likely to require a deposit. Deposits are typically equal to one month's board and can be used as the last month's board once the horse owner gives notice. Barn owners are asking for a deposit to pay for extensive damage caused by the horse and to cover themselves if the owner owes any backboard or leaves without giving notice.

If asking for a deposit, check with your state laws, because many states will require a deposit to be placed in an interest-earning account. Barn managers should understand that it is in the nature of horses to cause wear and tear and destruction, whether from kicking and breaking a board, cribbing, crushing a fed tub, or pawing a hole in the stall. Determining what a horse's owner should pay for can be a fine line, and proving that the horse in question did the damage may be challenging. Asking for a security deposit to cover unpaid bills is one thing, but to think that a barn owner can recoup money for normal wear and tear is bordering on being unreasonable and having unrealistic expectations in boarding.

> *A friend called me and was frantic. She was boarding at the same high-end barn with the hidden hay room and it was steadily going downhill not only in the quality of care but also in that no maintenance was performed on fencing, pastures, or anywhere else. One of her horses had gotten tangled in field wire fencing due to it not being maintained, and now a wall had collapsed between the stall of one of her horses and another boarder's horse. The barn owner demanded that the boarders pay for the wall repair. My friend did end up paying a handyman to come out and repair the wall, but she left immediately for a new facility. She knew if she left without paying for the repair, the owner would have sued her, which she wanted to avoid having to go through. Barn owners have a responsibility to provide safe facilities and to keep them in good repair. Horse owners should be diligent in holding their barn manager or owner responsible for maintaining the barn in good order, and if not, they should give their notice.*

Insurance

There are several types of insurance for equines and farms, and while some may need just one kind of coverage, others may require several different policies.

Several types of policies provide coverage for the horse. The most common is full mortality, a life insurance policy the owner takes out on their horse. The owner is listed as the beneficiary in case of death. Although exclusions may exist, this "All Risk" policy will cover death from any cause. This type of policy also covers for theft. The beneficiary will receive financial reimbursement for the agreed insured value of the horse in the event of death or theft. Full mortality is required to purchase Major Medical policies.

Major Medical and Surgical endorsements are an additional policy the owner can take out, providing coverage for surgery, major illnesses, and injuries. Depending on the insurance company that you go with, some will offer an Equine Surgical and/or colic-only policy. These policies have a deductible for each incident and will have a limit on the amount the policy will cover per incident per horse per year. Major medical policies are subject to review before being renewed each year and are subject to exclusions. For example, a horse that has undergone colic surgery, for which the policy paid out, may be excluded from colic surgery upon renewal.

These policies require a veterinary health certificate and may be limited by the horse's age, breed and discipline.

A Loss of Use endorsement will reimburse the owner in case the horse becomes permanently unable to continue its use as the owner has stated on the policy. Permanent lameness, injuries, or disease that prevents the horse from performing at full capacity will fall under Loss of Use. It is not uncommon for the policy to require the horse to be euthanized or turned over to the company in order to collect, and it can sometimes be challenging to prove that the horse is no longer useful for its stated purpose.

Other types of policies available include Medical Assistance and Air Transit.

Care, Custody, and Control insurance covers all horse operations involving horses that are not owned by the farm but reside on the property. This policy covers boarded horses, horses being bred or in training. This type of coverage promises to pay any sums you are legally obligated to pay for damage to these horses in your care. Personal horses are not included in this type of insurance.

There are two types of liability insurance: Personal Horse Owners Liability (PHO) coverage and Commercial General Liability (CGL). Boarding farms may require their boarders to have a PHO covering bodily injury or property damage to a third party caused by the insured's horse. A CGL is needed if you operate a commercial equine facility, whether it be for boarding, instruction, training, breeding, sales, or hosting events.

The insurance cost can be relatively affordable, but there are factors to consider, including where you live, the declared value of the horse, and the type of coverage you want to buy. There are insurance companies that only handle equine and farm insurance. They are typically owned by horse people who understand the language and can explain what type of cover will suit your needs properly.

The bottom line is that as a barn owner, having the correct farm insurance is imperative to stay in business and is a cost that needs to be factored into running your business. As a horse owner, you can have peace of mind, knowing that your horse is covered and that you will not have to make any difficult decisions based on how much money is in your bank account, or you can gamble and be willing to fork over potentially thousands of dollars for vet bills.

Employees

Operating a barn means you will need employees. It is unrealistic to expect the barn owner to do everything, even if you run a small operation of just a few horses. This is a hot topic on social media, as evidenced by barn managers discussing what is considered decent pay, whether insurance should be offered, the dilemma of hiring undocumented workers, and whether or not to file taxes. Unfortunately, running a barn has rarely been treated as a business; instead, it is treated as a side hustle or hobby, and as a result, barns may not make a profit and/or have a hard time keeping employees.

Traditionally, working in a barn environment has been a low-paying job. Many barns may trade board and/or lessons in exchange for help, and at one time, it was not uncommon for barns to utilize their "barn rats" -kids who hung out all day in the barn- to do barn chores in exchange for riding time. Times have changed, of course. Barn rats are not as common, immigration status is scrutinized, and employees don't always want to work hard manual labor for little money when they can make more money working in an air-conditioned coffee shop.

There is much debate as to what a fair rate for paying barn help is. There does appear to be a direct correlation between pay and the turnover rate, but sadly, many barns do not want to accept that fact. Barns that tend to pay lower wages have a high turnover and are advertising for new help every few months. They pay around $10- 15 an hour but then complain that they don't have reliable help or the employees don't have the necessary experience. Other barns advertise for help, and they stipulate unreasonable expectations, such as working six or even seven days a week; some barns want the same employee to work a few hours in the morning and then return for the late afternoon shift, and they expect an employee to muck 20 or 30 stalls in a few hours, with only a wheelbarrow.

Potential employees are no longer putting up with low wages and bad work conditions. When help wanted ads are placed on social media, potential employees ask questions in the comments section of the ad rather than waiting until the interview. They want to know what the pay is, how manure will be handled, and how many stalls they are expected to muck. A payment of $130- 150 per day may sound good until you realize that you are expected to work 10- 12 hour days, muck 20- 30 stalls, and work six days a week! When one does the math, they will realize they are working for almost minimum wages. Employees do not want to have to haul manure out to a pile behind the barn, through mud, with a wheelbarrow! And potential employees want insurance and time off, just like in any other industry. Just as the barn should be a suitable environment for the horse, it should also be a suitable environment for employees. Employees need living wages. They should be able to afford housing, food, and clothing. Barn staff should not be subsidizing the clientele or the barn owner's hobby and lifestyle. Employees should feel they are appreciated, respected, and well-compensated.

Good barns know that good employees come at a premium. And these employees should be compensated with living wages, health insurance, and days off. Employers should file taxes and 49 out of 50 states require businesses to purchase workers compensation insurance. Workers Compensation will protect you and your assets, so the cost is worth it. Working around horses can be dangerous at times, and accidents happen. All it takes is for one accident to happen, and your out-of-pocket expenses can be catastrophic if you have to pay for any medical expenses. Coverage will protect you from some injury lawsuits by employees as well.

Many barns let boarders work off their board, which can be a great situation for everyone; however, if your boarder is injured while working for you, such as being kicked while turning out a horse, you can still be liable for their injuries. Therefore, anyone working for you should be treated as an employee, given a paycheck, and covered by workers' compensation. It is best if your boarder pays the full board fee and you write them a check for their hours worked.

Background checks should be performed on potential employees, especially when children are around. No boarder should have to worry about a convicted sex offender working in their barn, and no barn owner wants to be liable for any wrongdoing on the part of their employee. Boarders and all employees should always be made to feel safe in the barn. Since the adoption of Safe Sport by the United States Equestrian Federation (USEF), any participant in a USEF competition is bound by and must comply with the Protecting Young Victims from Sexual Abuse and Safe Sport Authorization Act of 2017. Safe Sport not only protects against sexual misconduct, but bullying, stalking, hazing, and harassment are also under the jurisdiction of the USEF.

Barn owners need to figure out how to incorporate the expense of good employees into their finances. Will they be able to rely on the cheap labor of barn rats or exchange work for board? Will they be filing W2s and providing workers compensation and health insurance? All lengths should be taken when hiring staff that are knowledgeable in the equine industry. While many people can be taught how to muck stalls and dump feed, anyone unfamiliar with horses should be overseen by someone with more experience. Boarders don't like to see new faces every time they come to the barn and don't need to worry about whether or not the employee can recognize a colicing horse or know how to give the right feed. They want to know that employees know how to handle their horses, won't lose their temper, and will know what to do when a horse is injured. Bad employees can ruin a good barn's reputation overnight, so more thought and consideration should be given to the hiring practices.

As a horse owner, seeing how a barn treats its employees will indicate how your horse may or may not be treated. A horse owner should be concerned about a barn that hires anybody, especially without performing a background check. There are too many stories of employees being abusive to the horse, not giving supplements or giving the wrong feed, of employees stealing, and even of sexual predators working in the barn. When inquiring about boarding, take note of the employees. Are they happy? Do they seem knowledgeable? Ask how long they have been employed at the barn. Poor attitudes can be a red flag.

I boarded at a barn that had one employee for approximately ten horses. The owner sometimes helped, but most of the work was left to this one employee. She lived in an apartment above the barn, and we all marveled at how well she did her job. We would joke that she would hear a horse going to the bathroom from her apartment and run downstairs to pick the stall! After about nine months of boarding, the truth came out about why she was always energetic and kept the barn organized and well-run. She had a cocaine habit, which was why she was like the Energizer bunny. It was also discovered that the owner was an alcoholic, and suddenly, their two addictive personalities had a major head-on collision, and it was BAD. They were fighting all of the time, and it was highly toxic. Boarders, the owner's husband, and their kids were dragged into this. But it was the horses who suffered, with stalls not being cleaned properly. While most of us began looking for a new barn, the employee was fired. This was after two weeks of fighting. It was like a lover's quarrel that would not end. We all breathed a sigh of relief, but things did not improve, as the owner was now always hung over and barely functioning. She hired a homeless guy, stuck him in the barn apartment, and expected him to know how to muck and feed. Even though he seemed friendly and nice, the women in the barn were uncomfortable being alone with him. Within a week, most of us had left.

Running a stable should be treated like any other business, with attention given to employees, wages, contracts, rules, taxes, insurance, and waivers. Having all these in place before you hang that OPEN sign will ensure your boarding stable gets off to a smooth start.

Chapter 15
How to Be a Good Barn Owner/Manager

A random sampling that Common Sense Horse Keeping asked on social media revealed the following suggestions for being a good barn owner or manager:

- The horse should always come first

- You are being paid to care for someone's horse, which may mean more to them than anything else in the world. You are being paid to feed, stable and keep a watchful eye on their horse

- You are being paid to meet each horse's needs. If you are overwhelmed by providing quality care, then you need to make changes

- There will be delicate/pain-in-the-butt horses, and there will be rugged/easy horses to care for. In the end, it averages out

- This is not a get-rich career; it is a labor of love

- Common sense is to provide clean shelter, clean water, adequate turnout, and good quality hay and feed

- Horses have needs, including requiring blankets, fly masks, clean water and medicine. You cannot expect to run a barn and not have to perform any of these duties. It is all a part of horse keeping

- You are probably in the wrong business if you constantly bash your boarders, their horses, or your business online

- Communicate!

- Hold meetings monthly to communicate updates and introduce new boarders

- Everyone should work together for the well-being of the horses and others

- Respect and kindness!

- Talk to your boarder privately regarding any issues

- Remember that the client's horse is considered a family member and that clients worry about their horses!

- Be patient and answer questions, especially if the horse owner is new to horse ownership

- Communicate any changes impacting the schedule of boarder's horses, such as changes in turnout or feed

- Respect the owner's right to self-determination of their horses

- Stay out of barn drama unless it is a safety or horse issue. Let boarders work it out for themselves

- It is not your responsibility to make horse ownership affordable to others. You should never be operating at a loss

- You are not a door mat

- Just as boarders set the tone for the barn environment, so do barn owners. If you are unhappy, participate in gossip, and are resentful, you will attract the same in boarders

- Everything needs to be figured out, and everything averages out in the end!

- Keep an open mind. You may learn something from a boarder!

- Love, love, love horses

- Hire only knowledgeable staff

- The barn should be clean and safe

- Don't stop learning. Learn the latest about feed and nutrition, first aid, and anything else related to horses!

Chapter 16
How to Be a Good Boarder

And social media also responded to suggestions for being a good boarder:

- Be kind and respectful

- Communicate clearly

- Shadow your barn owner for a few days and experience the hard work and stress of running a barn

- Offer to help out, whether watering, sweeping, cleaning the tack or feed room, dumping feed, or hosing off sweaty horses!

- Offer to watch the barn so the owner can run errands

- Everyone should work together for the well-being of the horses and others

- Clean up after yourself

- Be courteous to other boarders

- Understand things aren't perfect

- Respect and kindness!

- Pay your board on time

- If you have a problem, don't discuss it with other boarders. Talk to the owner or manager

- Understand that time is money and that very little money is made from boarding

- Make sure your horse is trained and well mannered

- Respect the experience of your barn owner or manager

- Remember that your owner lives on the property. Respect their personal space and boundaries

- Your horse is ultimately your responsibility

- What seems like quick and simple requests are actually a non-stop deluge when multiplied across all boarders

- The barn owner has his reasons for doing things. If you disagree with them, don't move there or move if you are already a boarder

- Special requests should only be requested when it has an impact on the horse's well-being, not because of a whim

- The kind of hay bag you use matters because if it takes too much time to fill (along with everyone else's,) that is time and money it is costing the barn owner

- Appreciate everyone who is caring for your horse

- Understand just how much it costs to run a barn. Insurance, wages, taxes, maintenance, utilities, and more exist. Barn owners should not be subsidizing your hobby

- Barn owners are not at your disposal 24/7 unless there is an absolute emergency

- Understand that the barn is not a social place for the owner, manager, or employees. It is their work space and should be treated as such

- Treat the property better than your own

- Boarders are responsible for creating the culture of the barn's environment. If you are respectful, peaceful, and happy, the space will follow suit, whereas if you are grumpy, entitled, and petty, the space will not be enjoyable to anyone

- Be upfront. If you have financial difficulties, let your barn owner know rather than dodging them when the board is due

- If you see something that needs to be done, just do it!

- Follow the rules

- Your board bill covers hay and feed, taxes, insurance, maintenance, equipment, riding space, experienced horse care, and labor

- Be educated! Learn about horse care

- If you are going to come to the barn on holidays, plan to help with chores

- Owners need to visit their horses, groom them and make sure they have manners

- Be available for emergencies

- You are paying the barn owner for the ability for you to have a horse. If there were no boarding stables, what would you do?

Acknowledgements

This book is dedicated to my husband Peter, and our children, Andrew, Jen, and Amanda, who have had to put up with this addiction of mine to horses! It has been an amazing journey and I am so glad that they were along for the ride, whether they wanted to or not!

I also dedicate this book to the memory of all the horses I have been privileged to know and love, who have all taught me in one way or another about caring for horses and that IT IS ALL ABOUT THE HORSE! It has been an honor to have been their Kahu: their guardian, protector, steward and honored attendant of their soul.

I would like to express my appreciation to Dr. Rebecca Giminez Husted of Technical Large Animal Emergency Rescue for sharing with me her vast knowledge on fire safety and prevention and on disaster planning. I will always remember her kindness and generosity.

A special thank you to Jennifer M. Toegel for supplying some of the photos for the cover and in the manuscript from her portfolio at Max and Maxwell Equestrian Photography/Jennifer Juniper Photography LLC. She was beyond generous for finding such beautiful photos for me to use with not much notice!

Sadly, most of my mentors are no longer with us, but I hope they knew the impact that they had on this horse-crazy kid, and for those who continue to inspire me, I thank you from the bottom of my heart.

And many, many thanks to my dear friend, Diane Hartman Postrech, my partner in crime on my riding excursions as a child in Western Pennsylvania. There are not many people who can boast of being friends with someone for almost 60 years! Without Diane's editing skills, this book would have stalled out when others had no faith in my book....Diane never lost faith in me!

The author on Cricket, with Diane and Smokey. 1970's era, McMurray, Pa.

Recommended Reading and Authors

A Horse By Nature, by Mary Ann Simonds

Begin and Begin Again by Denny Emerson

Complete Equine Veterinary Manual by Tony & Marcy Pavord

Guide to First Aid For Horses by Dr. Kellon

Horse Brain, Human Brain, by Janet Jones, PhD

Horse Nutrition Handbook by Melyni Worth

Horse Owners Guide to Toxic Plants by Sandra McQuinn

Know Better to Do Better by Denny Emerson

Linda Tellington-Jones books

Mark Rashid books

No Bored Horses, by Amanda Goble

The Compassionate Equestrian by Allen M. Schoen, DVM and Susan Gordon

The Essential Hoof Book by Susan Kauffmann and Christina Cline

The United States Pony Manual of Horsemanship, Books 1-3 by Susan E. Harris and Pony Club

Index

Printed in the USA
CPSIA information can be obtained
at www.ICGtesting.com
CBHW082015190824
13414CB00031B/199

9 798985 810172